EFFECTIVE DECISION SUPPORT SYSTEMS

**THE TECHNICAL PRESS — UNICOM
APPLIED INFORMATION TECHNOLOGY REPORTS SERIES**

Editor: Gautam Mitra, Brunel University

Fourth Generation Languages and Application Generators
   Edited by David Martland, Simon Holloway, I. Bhabuta

Information Technology in Physical Distribution Management
   Edited by Robert L. Lewis

Expert Systems and Optimisation in Process Control
   Edited by Abe Mamdani and Janet Efstathiou

Computer Controlled Interactive Video
   multi media authoring systems
   Edited by Tony Droar

Geometric Modelling and Computer Graphics: Techniques
   and Applications
   Edited by R. A. Earnshaw, R. D. Parslow, J. R. Woodwark

Effective Decision Support Systems
   Edited by John Hawgood and Patrick Humphreys

Software Quality Assurance, Reliability and Testing
   Edited by Chris Summers

Major Advances in Parallel Processing
   Edited by Chris Jesshope

Interactions in Artificial Intelligence and Statistical Methods
   Edited by Bob Phelps

Effective Decision Support Systems

Edited by
John Hawgood
PA Computers and Telecommunications, London
Patrick Humphreys
London School of Economics and Political Science

The Technical Press
in association with Unicom Seminars Ltd

© Unicom Seminars Ltd 1987

All rights reserved. No part of this publication may be reproduced, stored in a retrieval system, or transmitted in any form or by any means, electronic, mechanical, photocopying, recording, or otherwise without the prior permission of Gower Technical Press Limited.

Published by Gower Technical Press Ltd, Gower House, Croft Road, Aldershot, Hants GU11 3HR, England.

Gower Publishing Company, Old Post Road, Brookfield, Vermont 05036, U.S.A.

ISBN 0-291-397441

Printed by Antony Rowe Ltd, Chippenham, Wiltshire

Contents

Summaries — vi

Notes on Contributors — ix

1 Introduction — 1
   Patrick Humphreys

2 When Goals Conflict — 13
   John Hawgood and Patrick Humphreys

3 SLIM-MAUD: The Assessment of Human Error Probabilities Using an Interactive Computer Based Approach — 20
   Dr D. E. Embrey

4 Negotiating Environmental Issues: A Role for the Analyst? — 33
   Joanne Linnerooth

5 Ranking Multiple Options with DECMAK — 49
   V. Rajkovic, M. Bohanec and J. Efstathiou

6 Effective Decision-Making — 61
   Jimmy Algie and William Foster

7 Relationships between Reliability and Management — 88
   I. A. Watson

8 Early Experience in the Application of Decision Analysis to Selected CEGB Problems — 129
   K. G. Begg

9 Competitor Marketing Analysis and Planning — 137
   R. S. Stainton

10 Methodology for Decision Support in Conflict Analysis — 143
   William L. Cats-Baril

11 Conferencing to Consensus — 176
   Lawrence D. Phillips

Summaries

1. Introduction by Patrick Humphreys

2. When goals conflict by John Hawgood and Patrick Humphreys

Managers must continually cope with conflicting goals. Either their own organization's motives are mixed, or other stakeholders involved have different objectives. Conventional decision support systems take no account of this, as they assume a simple financial objective. Managers generally cope well in their day to day business in making tradeoffs between different goals, or different groups' interests without help from technology. But when there are particularly complex and significant choices to make, possibly affecting many people for many years, some help with analysis and assessment of possible policies may not come amiss. Preference technology (incorporating ideas from artificial intelligence and expert systems technology) plays an increasingly important part in this field, by bringing to bear the expertise of the decision analyst in problem solving and the expertise of the manager in the problem to be solved. This chapter intoduces the practical use of preference technology when goals conflict through a discussion of four case studies in different organizational settings.

3. SLIM-MAUD: The assessment of human error probabilities using an interactive computer based approach by Dr D E Embrey

SLIM-MAUD (Success Likelihood Index using Multiattribute Utility Theory) is a computer based technique which uses expert knowledge to quantify the probability of human errors in critical tasks. It can be applied in both commercial and engineering risk assessment. The technique identifies the causal factors influencing the likelihood of errors, and allows cost benefit analysis to be carried out to determine the most effective strategies for error reduction.

4. *Negotiating Environmental Issues by Joanne Linnerooth*

With the emergence of more complex environmental problems, there is a growing interest in more cooperative forms of policy making that enlist the support of industry and the public. An important question arises how traditional forms of expertise and decision support can be adapted to support the participants of environmental negotiations. This paper explores this question in the context of three separate policy settings: an adversarial, multi-stakeholder process for determining the bounds of a regulatory program for hazardous wastes; and an international negotiation for the resolution of the economic and distributive issues for sharing the resources of the ocean floor. It is shown that there are several ways that the analyst can contribute to the process of negotiation: by providing empirical and strategic support to a participant; by promoting "mutual learning" among the participants; or, by helping a third party in his or her role as mediator.

5. *Ranking multiple options with Decmak by V Rajkovic, M Bohanec and J Efstathiou*

The role of computer-based organizational approach to multiple-options decision-making is discussed in this paper. A sequence of organizational phases for multiattribute decision making is described. On the basis of a practical example, two computer-based decision models are explained. They are based on spreadsheet and expert systems approach, respectively. For the expert system approach, the DECMAK expert system generator is used. By these models it is shown that the computer can play a more active role in supporting our cognitive processes in decision making rather than just helping us by documentation and calculations.

6. *Effective decision-making, planning and evaluation by Jimmy Algie and William Foster*

This article illustrates how managers may make faster yet more reliable individual and team decisions on issues, allocate scarce resources, and evaluate results and performance. A case study illustrates how a corporate user applied the method to develop, implement and evaluate company strategy.

7. *Relationships between reliability and management by I A Watson*

The connections between plant safety and reliability and organization and management are examined firstly by describing how human error is included in plant failure assessment. From the possibility of common influences on the significant tasks and the way human action is affected through the associated network of human intentionality the connecting links are described. Methods of analysing organization and management are outlined which should help to control these influences. Evidence from two major accidents are examined.

8. <u>Early experience in the application of decision analysis to selected CEGB problems by K G Begg</u>

In recent years international issues such as Acid Rain have been approached using Decision Analysis. The Environmental Studies Section of the CEGB has therefore become increasingly interested in the use of Decision Analysis for a wide range of environmental questions. Some of the problem areas in introducing the technique within the organization are discussed and early in-house model developments are described. Some aspects of choosing and assembling appropriate decision aids and gaining acceptance for their use are considered.

9. <u>Competitor Marketing Analysis and Planning by R S Stainton</u>

Predicting market share and profitability is difficult. Trying to determine what competitors will do in the future and assessing their strengths is even more so. COMAP provides a tool for examining projected competitor behaviour in relation to one's own behaviour and a way of analysing the results so that better product strategies can be devised and contingency plans established.

10. <u>Decision Support in conflict analysis by William L Cats-Baril</u>

This article describes a methodolgy to analyse conflict. The methodolgy consists of: identifying the stakeholders and their assumptions and goals, identifying the issues underlying the conflict and their feasible levels of resolution, developing and analyzing treaties (a set of specific levels of resolution for all issues), and following a structured process of negotiation and consensus building to agree on a given treaty. An application of the methodology is discussed in the context of providing family planning services to adolescents.

11. <u>Conferencing to consensus by Lawrence D Phillips</u>

Teams of people working on issues of major importance to their organization are finding that group decision systems can help them to make better decisions in less time. The paper discusses three systems, all of which help groups to reach a shared understanding of a problem and a commitment to action. In each of these systems, the group is helped by a facilitator who guides the process of problem solving and uses a computer on-the-spot to explore participants' judgment and preferences. Experience with these systems shows that they help groups to build a sense of common purpose, and enable difficult decisions to be taken without compromises.

Notes on Contributors

<u>Jimmy Algie</u> is Director of Management Decision Programme at the Brunel University, where he undertakes research and consultancy on decision-making in industry and public services; and Co-Director of two firms - one which develops decision support software, another which applies decision software in the course of managing a manufacturing and retail operation.

<u>Katherine G Begg</u> is a Senior Engineer in the Environmental Studies Section of the CEGB and is involved in both the technical and political aspects of environmental issues. She was the UK expert on the UNECE Group of Experts on effects of pollutants on Materials for a number of years and is now the UK delegate to the UNECE Group of Experts on Electricity and the Environment.

<u>Marko Bohanec</u> received the BSc degree in computer sciences from University of Ljubljana. Since 1981 he has been employed at the Jozef Stefan Institute, working on research and applications of decision-making methods. He implemented the DECMAK expert system generator and used it in decision-making consulting.

<u>William L Cats-Baril</u> Since joining the Faculty of the School of Business Administration at the University of Vermont, he has been teaching courses in Decision Theory, Design of Decision Support Systems, and Information Systems Policies. His major areas of research are the development of decision aids to support ill-structured problems and expert systems. He is a Principal Investigator at the Vermont Rehabilitation Engineering Center and a Research Fellow at the London School of Economics.

<u>Janet Efstathiou</u> received the BA degree in physics from Oxford University and the PhD from Durham University. She is a lecturer in the Department of Electrical and Electronic Engineering, Queen Mary College, University of London. Her research interests are in the application of artificial intelligence techniques to complex decision problems and the control of industrial processes.

David Embrey is Managing Director Human Reliability Associates, a consulting company specializing in reducing human error in the power, process and service industries. He has worked in the nuclear power generation, chemical processing and service industries on the problem of human error. He chairs the Human Reliability Assessment Group sponsored by the United Kingdom Atomic Engergy Authority, and has lectured and consulted in the USA, Far East and many European countries.

William Foster is a lecturer in the Mathematics Department of Brunel University, Senior Associate Research Fellow in the Brunel Institute of Organization and Social Studies, and Co-Director of a commercial software house specialising in decision insight and advice programs.

John Hawgood is a senior consultant in the Development Division of PA Computers and Telecommunications, where he is mainly concerned with knowledge based decision support. He was Director of Computing at the University of Durham from 1964 to 1980; during this time his main research was into methods for assessing the benefits of computer systems through participative system design projects. He has been the Secretary of the International Federation for Information Processing's Working Group on Decision Support since its foundation in 1982. For seven months in 1984 he was a member of the European Commission's Information Technology Task Force, helping to co-ordinate the ESPRIT programme, in which he remains involved as researcher, adviser, project administrator and reviewer.

Patrick Humphreys is a lecturer in the Department of Social Psychology at the London School of Economics and Political Sciences and Deputy Director of the Decision Analysis Unit. He has directed projects on group and individual decision making with multiple objectives and developed and implemented decision aiding systems for medical and vocational counselling. He has developed MAUD, an interactive micro computer-based system that helps the user to clarify and model objectives in a decision problem. Author and co-author of a number of articles and books on decision making.

Joanne Linnerooth attended Carnegie-Mellon University and the University of Maryland, where she studied industrial engineering and economics. In 1974, she joined the International Institute of Applied Systems Analysis where she has worked with inter-disciplinary teams on such problems as the risks and public acceptance of nuclear energy, the siting of LNG terminals, the transportation of dangerous goods, the disposal goods, the disposal of hazardous wastes, and, most recently, the process of international negotiations. She has published extensively on topics related to the economics of safety and the risks and social/political questions of modern technological systems.

Lawrence D Phillips is the Director of the Decision Analysis Unit, a self-funding research group that he founded in 1974. He lectures and carries out action research for various commercial, industrial and governmental organisations in Great Britian and abroad. His research includes work on how people assess risk, form preferences and take decisions, how groups of people solve complex problems facing organisations, and how group decision support systems can help groups to be more effective.

Vladislav Rajkovic received the BSc and MSc degrees in electrical engineering from the University of Ljubljana. In 1970 he joined the Department of Computer Science and Informatics at Jozef Stefan Institute in Ljubljana. Now he is also a lecturer in computing at University of Maribor, School of Organizational Sciences Kranj. He does research and development in the field of decision making using intelligent computer support and consulting in decision-making for industry and government institutions.

Roy Stainton is Director of Management Science at the Henley Management College, which is associated with Brunel University. He is also Principal of his own Management Consultancy operation, with contracts to several large companies. He has spent many years in industry in senior management positions before joining Henley. He is immediate Past President of the Operational Research Society.

Ian Watson is a Chartered Electrical Engineer. He began his career in electronics and then moved to avionics. He was leader and manager of many projects from the VC-10 automatic landing systems to the development of the first generation of digital auto-pilots. In 1975 he joined the UKAEA National Centre of Systems Reliability where he worked on projects concerned with systems reliability relating both to safety and plant availability of a variety of power and process plants. He has also been concerned with research and development into common mode failures and human reliability. He became Head of Systems Reliability Service in 1982.

1 Introduction

Patrick Humphreys
London School of Economics and Political Science

Many organisations have experienced difficulties in attempting to solve decision problems through the use of traditional 'in-house' decision making processes and methods, due to:

(a) The complexity of the problems, i.e., it seems that too many conditions, constraints, and consequences must be simultaneously considered.

(b) the uncertainty related to the objectives and preferences of those concerned. Managers must continually cope with conflicting goals: their own oganization's motives may be mixed or other people involved (such as shareholders, employees, customers or taxpayers) have different objectives.

(c) the lack of available information connected with the complexity of the problems, the uncertainty, and the problem-solving methods themselves.

Quite a number of decision support models and software packages attempt to provide assistance for the solution of such decision problems, but many of them are not really used very much by the actual decision makers, for a number of reasons: (i) some of them are too artificial, using models and language that are too abstract, and are difficult for the actual decision makers to understand; (ii) some of the models and methods do not consider the decision makers' own preferences and judgements; and (iii) a number of them are not interactive or cooperative, so that the decision maker and those concerned do not interact during the decision-making process, either with each other or with the decision support system chosen.

The chapters in this book describe decision support methods which avoid these pitfalls. They concentrate on building conceptual models, that is, models which reflect the way decisions makers actually think about the problems they face, and which can be described in the language they want to use. They describe techniques which are founded on the use of decision makers' and experts' own subjective judgments. They explore decision support processes which are always interactive, although sometimes the interaction is between stakeholders in the decision making, sometimes between decision maker and analyst, and sometimes between decision maker and a computer-based support system.

A major difficulty with respect to the use of such methods in practice, is knowing how to select a particular method, when to use it, on what material, and how to embed the use of the method within the general problem handling and decision process.

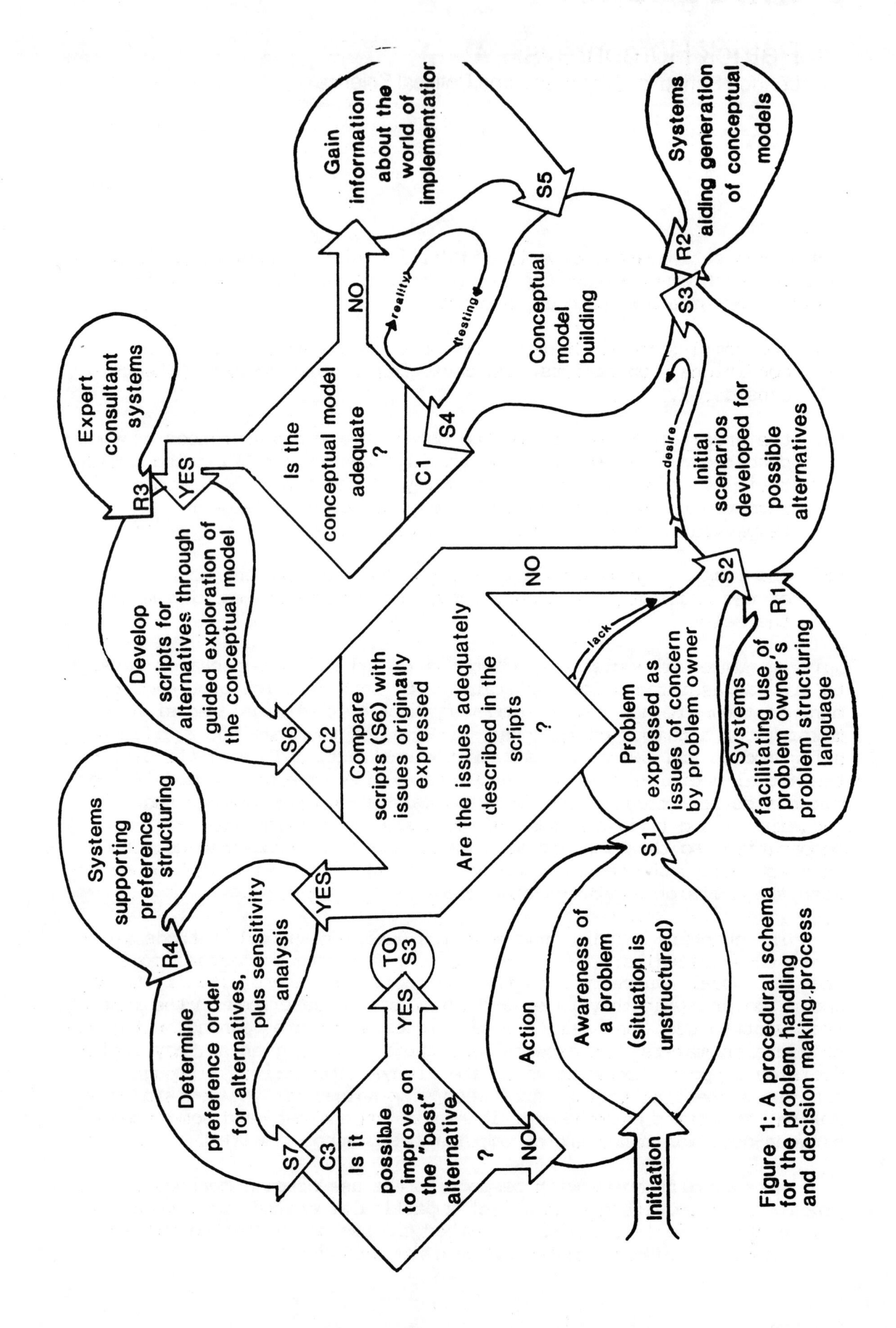

Figure 1: A procedural schema for the problem handling and decision making process

Many specific examples of how this qustion was successfully tackled in practice are given in the following chapters. Here, by way of introduction we present a <u>general procedural schema</u> (i.e., framework for handling the problem) for the problem handling and decision making process, and then indicate how the topics and cases presented in each chapter illustrate the operation of this schema in practice.

A general procedural schema

This schema, whose outline is given in Figure 1, has been developed within the framework of Checkland's (1981) soft systems methodology. We describe below the seven principal stages (S1 through S7) in the schema. We will also indicate how progress through the schema may be facilitated in practical applications by systems and tools located in four categories (R1 through R4 in figure 1), each providing a qualitatively different kind of support to the decision maker.

Starting from the initial entry at stage S1, following the procedural schema is rather like playing a board game. The procedural schema is the board, the player are the stakeholders in the problem handling and decision making process. Vari and Vecsenyi (1984) identify the pricipal stakeholder roles here as: <u>Decision makers</u> who have the executive power to define the use of outputs of the decision making process, <u>proposers</u> who have the power to make recommendations to the decision makers, <u>experts</u> whose function is to supply inputs to the currently modelled problem structure, and <u>those concerned with the implementation</u> who play an active role in the realization of an accepted solution. Vari and Vecsenyi define two further stakeholder roles in situations where a decision support system or decision aiding technique is used: those of the <u>client</u> who initiates the decision support, and of the <u>consultants</u> or <u>decision analysts</u> who advise on methods of problem representation and decision making procedures.

The process moves sequentially through the stages indicated in the procedural schema, but with considerable discretion being accorded to the players concerning (i) the way they develop the process within each stage, (ii) when they move from one stage to the next, and (iii) how they decide whether or not to traverse the cycle in the overall process (comparisons C1, C2, and C3). In the case where all stakeholder groups share a common goal for the decision, then the board need be traversed with just one playing piece. This is because a consensus should be achievable between the various stakeholder groups on what to represent at each stage. However, when stakeholder groups may be in conflict or have diverse motivations, pursuing separate goals, then the sequence of stages from S2 onwards has to be traversed separately in developing and refining the concerns of each group.

One should note that there is no finish point in this board game. In real world organizational decision making, problems are not solved in an absolute sense. Taking action marks a discontinuity or the end of a round in the process (Kunreuther, 1983), but this does not mean that new problems, requiring different knowledge representations, will not arise subsequently. Hence, the playing piece simply pauses after the point in the procedural schema where action is taken until awareness of a new problem crystallizes.

Stage S1: Initiation

At stage S1, there is merely the awareness of a problem: as the situation is unstructured, only the manifestations rather than the structure of the problem are known (something is not expected, something has to be done, etc.).

Stage S2: Expression of desire for improvement

At stage 2, the small world (Savage, 1954, Toda, 1976) or decision space within which the problem is believed to be located starts to be explored as the problem is expressed. This does not mean that one has to explore the whole world within which the decision is to be made, The small world is that which is sufficient to bound the exploration of the issues which are going to be expressed in articulating the decision maker's and other stakeholders desire to make improvements.

The decision support methods discussed in this book generally presume that any decision problem representation which may be developed is always owned by somebody (i.e., the problem owner as described by Checkland, 1981 and Vari and Vecsenyi, 1983). In cases where the overall problem is owned by more than one individual, then it is important to ensure a consensus between the various problem owners concerning the boundary of the decision space. When such a consensus is not achieved, stages S2 to S7 have to be traversed separately for each problem owners's concerns.

Note that the way the decision space is explored is shaped and constrained by the goals of the problem owners. When the exploration is predicated on some reasonably clear goal it becomes less diffuse and therefore easier to analyse.

Stage S3: Development of scenarios for options implementing objectives

The transition from stage S2 to S3 in Figure 1 usually involves either a formal or informal goal analysis: identifying problem owners' ideas about possible options for doing something about the deficiencies they have identified in describing issues. The aim here is to decompose their global goals into specific objectives, which in turn need to be operationalized (Jungermann, 1984). This involves constructing scenarios for options which appear a priori to have the possibility of meeting some - or all - of the objectives.

However, these initial scenarios may not be very realistic and so they may need to be shaped up and tested against the reality of the organization or social context in which the decision is taken. Thus, the goal analysis feeds into stage S4 where the conceptual model for representing the decision problem and exploring the effects of possible options is generated. This transition marks the end of inductive pre-analysis and the beginning of logical analysis: that is, starting to think of how to generate the appropriate structure to simulate those options which are currently identified, through developing and 'reality testing' the scenarios associated with their representation.

Stage S4: Formulation of the conceptual model for the investigation

The first step in stage S4 is to assemble the statements of objectives and the scenarios which were generated in stage S3. These collectively represent what Checkland called the 'rich picture' for the investigation. Subsequent steps are designed to convert this picture into a conceptual model through discovering whether the elements of the rich picture can be assembled into a coherent structure. This requires a primarily logical analysis while at the same time checking whether the 'descriptive signs' (Carnap, 1939) identified within the structure being built map appropriately onto the actual, identifiable states and conditions within the organization. This, in turn, involves reality testing of the conceptual model by, for example, checking then with the personnel actually carrying out functions identified within the model (by interview, or observation, or, less accurately, by relying on the opinion of persons with managerial or expert knowledge of how a particular function is or could be actually performed).

Stage S5: Gaining information about the world of implementation.

The reality testing circuit shown in figure 1 thus comprises two stages: conceptual model development (S4) and information gathering (S5). Traversing this circuit enables one to test out the extent to which a decision maker's desire to gain control over the implementation of a particular course of action is likely to be realized in practice. Activating stage S5 means incurring the cost (in time, effort and perhaps money) of information gathering, and thus branching to this step is usally based on the decision that the value of this information (Raiffa, 1968) is greater than the cost of obtaining it. This value will depend on how the current status of the conceptual model is perceived. In cases where the conceptual model is considered to be free of contradictions, and of intolerable areas of fuzziness, and no one is uneasy about its fit with reality, then the model is likely to be judged adequate in its current form, and further reality testing will be suspended in favour of moving to stage S6.

Stage S6: Representation of options developed within the conceptual model

Once the conceptual model has been judged adequately verified, stage S7 in the procedural schema, it is desirable for the original problem owners and other stakeholders to be able to compare the various options developed within the conceptual model with their originally expressed objectives and issues of concern. This involves guided exploration of the conceptual model in language similar to that originally used by the problem owner which may be compared directly with the issues raised initially in stage S2.

This comparison (C2 in Figure 1) may indicate that between S2 and S6 certain issues which were expressed 'got lost' through focussing on other issues when operationalizing problem owners' objectives within the conceptual model. If these issues still need to be expressed, then option generation is not complete and further work is required in stages S3 and S4. If extensive reality testing procedures were used, the final structure of the conceptual model may be rather different from that of the problem owner's initial objectives. In this case, the scripts have a didactic role, helping problem owners to understand how their overall goals can best be translated into implementations of objectives which conform more closely to organizational or social realities.

7. Stage S7: Choosing an option

At stage S7, the remaining task is to determine the appropriate preference structure within which the options described in S6 are to be assessed, so that their benefits and disadvantages on the criteria or attributes which comprise the structure can be traded off against each other in deciding on the 'best option overall' (Edwards and Newman, 1982).

This is the major focus of the computer-based decision support systems reviewed in this book. Systems like MAUD (described in chapters 2 and 3), DECMAK (described in chapter 4) and PDS (described in chapter 5) are systems which support preference structuring through working in direct interaction with the analyst in using his or her own language.

Whatever preference-structuring support system is employed, it is desirable to conduct a sensitivity analysis on the extent to which the choice of an option depends on the importance assigned to the various criteria within the preference structure. If a particular option is found to dominate the others on all the major criteria, its choice as a basis for action is likely to be reasonably non-controversial (Svenson, 1979; Montgomery, 1983). Taking the action to implement this alternative ends the current round of the process, and brings us within the procedural schema shown in Figure 1 to await, at stage S1, the start of the next round, when a new problem arises.

The sensitivity analysis may, on the other hand, indicate that the alternative identified as 'best' in the (level 1) preference ordering 'could be improved' (i.e., it is suboptimal on some criteria), or even that an alternative ordered second or third might be preferred if *it* could be improved on one or more criteria. It is just as important to verify this conjecture as it was to verify the options initially explored in stage S3 within the round. Hence, in this case, comparison C3 in Figure 1 indicates that one should move to stage S3, develop the scenarios operationalizing the objectives for revised option, and then proceed as before through stages S4 and S5 (revising and verifying the conceptual model). The script consequently developed for this new option in stage S6 can then be evaluated against the pre-existing scripts for other options in stage S7 to ascertain whether or not the goal of formulating an 'even better' option was in fact achieved.

Providing effective decision support

The general procedural schema shown in Figure 1 is applicable to a very wide range of situations involving organizational change in the service of the desire for improvement. It is cognitively rather than behaviourally based; that is, it is designed to support thinking about how problem owners might design and implement alternative options under the general goal of seeking ways to overcome, or alleviate problems of which they are aware. It is not prescriptive; instead, it provides a guide to ways of supporting problem owners' discretionary activities in scenario generation, deciding on whether (or to what extent) deep verification is required concerning the feasibility and realism of plans of option implementation, and, finally exploring and making trade-offs between alternative descriptions of options explored within the conceptual model in deciding on the course of action that will actually be taken.

Support is provided for problem owners, planners and analysts facing procedural uncertainty through interpreting the procedural schema as a game, comprising seven stages (S1 to S7), which should be traversed in a sequence permitted according to the layout given. That is, discretion can be expressed about when to move from one stage to the next, and, at points C1, C2, and C3, about which stage to move to next.

The procedural schema also clarifies some common pitfalls in decision making involving the implementation of management of organizational changes. For example, a common pitfall, discussed by Vari and Vecsenyi (1983), is for an analyst to take a client's problem at its face value in stage S2, or to consider only that part of the problem actually expressed as issues at this stage. The analyst will often desire to move the analysis as quickly as possible to stage S7, where he or she is likely to possess special expertise in helping the client to develop a 'requisite' preference structure for evaluating alternative options and deciding upon action (Phillips, 1984). The problem owners may concur with this desire, as it accords with their own desire to take action as soon as possible to alleviate the problem.

However, while there is a pathway from S2 to S7 (through C2), shown in Figure 1, traversing this path can be understood as a violation of the rules of the game as the pathway from S2 to C2 can only be traversed in the appropriate direction, since the starting conditions from C2 have to be the scripts developed in stage S6, not in stage S2.

Although the general rule holds that one disturbs the stage sequencing S1 to S7 shown in Figure 1 at one's peril, this does not mean that an equivalent amount of effort has always to be expended at each stage in every investigation. The rule here is that within each stage most effort should be expected and most support provided at the stage where it is most needed. The decision support case studies presented in the following chapters avoid pitfalls that would result from violation of the rules of the general procedural schema, but describe how decision support efforts may have to to be focussed at different points in the schema, according to the nature of the problem being faced.

In chapter 2 , John Hawgood and Patrick Humphreys introduce applications of computer based decision support systems which provide preference technology (class R4 in figure 1) designed to aid decision makers in cases where goals conflict. They give four examples. In the first, stakeholder groups of teenagers and students had different patterns of interests, but could agree to represent them in the same small world at stage S2 in figure 1. The preference technology employed was the Abacon chart, but as the interests were different, separate

Abacon charts were developed to show the preference structure of each stakeholder group at stage S7. Developing the best option, from the points of view of both the stakeholder groups was achieved by looping back at point C3 in figure 1 to stage S3, so that informed discussions on what would be the best improvements could be held with the stakeholder groups.

The second example also involves looping back to stage S3 in improving a "best" alternative, and here the preference technology used at stage S6 (PA point profile) supported the decision makers by helping them to concentate on the most important factors of a product to improve. The third example describes how the preference structuring ability of MAUD was used to aid in the development of a negotiating strategy by a small business consortium for use in transactions with a state authority. Here the problem was not so much how to improve on the best alternative from the point of view of the consortium, but to discover why the state authority did not prefer it. This was achieved through looping between stages S7 and S4 in developing the different conceptual models held by the parties to the negotiation, and evaluating the attractiveness of alternatives characterized within them. The fourth example is a contrasting application of MAUD, used to structure the judgment of experts (concerning nuclear power plant operations) within an already devloped conceptual model. Here MAUD helped the experts, working in groups, in exploring the conceptual model (stage S6) and in structuring the results of this exploration (stage S7).

In chapter 3, Joanne Linnerooth discusses possible roles for analysts and decision aiding techniques in supporting negotiations. She describes how these roles vary when the context is (i) a multiparty adversarial process, (ii) an organizational decision setting where a regulatory agency is expected to meet stakeholders' conflicting expectations and (iii) explicit negotiations around the table where stakeholder groups have a shared interest in reaching agreement.

In the first context, the cycle shown in figure 1 has to be traversed separately for each stakeholder group, and analysts are more likely to provide effective support in an advocacy role for a particular stakeholder group, rather than attempting to gain acceptance of a single analysis for all groups. In the second context, the circuit need be traversed for only one stakehoder group (decsion makers within the organization) but, at stage S4, care has to be taken to build the conceptual model in such a way that it will allow each of the conflicting requirements to be explored in formulating and simulating implementation strategies. In the third context, the analysts themselves may form the first stakeholder group, traversing the cycle as far as stage 5, with the goal of developing a conceptual model accptable to all parties in the face-to-face negotiation. The cycle is traversed a second time during the negotiation itself. This time the scenarios advanced by various stakeholder groups at stage S3 are simulated in the analyst-developed conceptual model, and the results evaluated by all participants at stage S6. The success of this third approach depends critically on the acceptability of the conceptual model to all stakeholder groups, and Linnerooth dicusses key factors which promote this acceptance.

In chapter 4, David Embrey describes in detail the operation of SLIM-MAUD, the special version of MAUD employed in example 4 in chapter 2. SLIM-MAUD implements Success Likelihood Index Methodology, which evaluates experts' preferences for success rather than failure when evaluating the reliability of human performance on complex tasks. The methodology translates these preferences into relative probabilities of success on alternative tasks within a given domain. In comparative trials with other methodologies, the SLIM-MAUD technique has been found to be especially good at structuring expert judgment of human performance on highly complex tasks involving small but potentially disastrous probabilities of failure. Embrey also describes SLIM-SARAH, an extension to MAUD which provides comprehensive support for discovering how to improve options at stage S7.

In chapter 5, Vladislav Rajkovic, Marko Bohanec and Janet Efstathiou describe facilitatory procedures within the early stages in the procedural schema which can improve the support potential of preference technology at stage S6. Issues covered here are formation of a decision making group (stage S2), identification of options (stage S4) and identification of attributes (stage S5). They describe also DECMAK, a system which can provide effective support at both stages S5 and S6. Like MAUD, DEcMAK is intended to provide direct interactive assistance to a decision maker facing a multi-attributed decision problem. Unlike MAUD, though, it is not based on multi-attribute utility theory (MAUT). Instead, DECMAK elicits the user's decision knowledge, expressed as rules in the decision maker's own language. Exploration of the decision space (i.e., the small world within which the problem is located) is facilitated by a programme which checks the consistency of the option generation process (stage S4) and a programme which generates reports, the latter offering a full inference trace (through stages S5 and S6), or a short executive summary.

DECMAK is less powerful, in the mathematical sense, than tools based on multiattribute utility theory. It cannot, for example investigate the tradeoffs that stakeholder groups wish to make between multiattributed alternatives when goals conflict, in the way that MAUD can. However, DECMAK deserves special consideration on account of its total commitment to the natural language and reasoning modes of the decision makers, and for its emphasis on aiding decision making through exploration rather than prescription.

In chapter 6, Jimmy Algie and Bill Foster decribe PDS (Priority decision system), which provides preference technology in a different way from MAUD and DECMAK, which explore how options may be characterized on relevant attributes (in terms of ratings or rules), as a basis for developing a preference order. PDS relies upon the decision maker's direct estimation of preferences between alternatives, either through rating each one on its own, or by considering them in pairs. This technique is called judgment analysis. Algie and Foster describe also how judgment analysis may be extended into applications beyond simply establishing priorities between options. In particular they describe WPS (work priority system) and BPS (budget priority system). These extensions are useful in applications where demands conflict and where decisions must be made (at stage S6) on the relative emphasis to be placed on each demand in establishing planning priorities.

In chapter 7, Ian Watson concentrates on the nature of conceptual models which can support decision making in relation to complex technical processes, showing how these models are quite distinct from the engineering models of the same processes. In understanding the nature of such models it is important to view decision problems and the capabilities of systems which may aid in their solution, at a number of different levels of abstraction. Watson describes how this can be done through applying the five level framework proposed by Humphreys and Berkeley (1985) for representing both decision problems and capabilities of decision support systems and tools.

The key advantage of the 'levels' framework is that it permits integration across levels: results of operations at a high level define the constraints at lower levels. Moreover, these levels of problem representation mirror Jaques' (1976) account of levels of abstraction of organizational roles, from shop and office floor (level 1) to managing director of an enterprise (level 5). The findings from this comparison are likely to be of particular importance for the future design and implementation of multilevel management and decision support systems.

In chapter 8, Katherine Begg describes some decision analytic modelling techniques currently employed by the Central Electricity Generating Board, particularly in its environmental studies section, where the sujective judments of stakeholder groups must often be taken into acount.

Early attempts to use decision analytic techniques within the CEGB were largely unsuccessful due, in the main, to the insistence of decision analysts that problem owners (decision makers, stakeholders, expert assessors) should jump from stage S2 in the schema shown in figure 1 straight to stage S6. Thus, the decision analytic model with which the analyst was familiar was usually applied, regardless of its lack of correspondence to the conceptual models actually used by the problem owners, or the reality of their experience of forming judgments within them.

The current programme of implementing decision support techniques within the CEGB environmental studies section is intended to avoid these pitfalls through embedding such techniques within a wider consideration of the whole process of handling environmental decision problems. This had led to an additional emphasis on option generation (stage S4) and investigation of risk associated with the decision (Stage S5) in practical applications. Hence, while MAUD is currently used, care is now taken to ensure that an appropriate "front end" is constructed in moving from the scenarios advanced by stakeholder groups (stage S3) to the generation of options which can be evaluated within MAUD (Stage S5).

In chapter 9, Roy Stainton discusses ways of providing decision support for managers in organization operating in competitive marketing situations. He points out that the traditional tendency of multicriterion decision making methods to focus on supporting stage S7 may well identify "the winning system", but that focus may at the same time prevent the consideration of "new ways of doing things". The latter is essential in order to ensure long term, rather than merely short term, success in competitive marketing situations and Stainton shows how support for this goal can best be achieved through focussing on stages S4 and S5: conceptual model building and simulation. This allows managers to try out various new strategies in advance, recognising that competitors may adopt different approaches in different environmental states, while incorporating established marketing expertise.

Systems which provide decision support in this way are still in their infancy but Stainton suggests that much of the knowledge to construct such "experience systems" has already been worked out in the field of simulated war gaming, and could well be applied here. Initial applications in companies in fast moving consumer goods (FMCG) and retailing are described.

In chapter 10, Willy Cats-Baril describes how the use of the general procedural schema shown in figure 1 may be extended to provide the basis fo a general conflict analysis methodology, which has ten steps. The methodology involves two complete traversals or rounds (Kunreuther, 1983) of the schema, the first round supporting the conflict analysts and the second round supporting conflict resolution among the stakeholder groups.

In the first round, steps 1 to 3 of the methodology take the analysts through stages S1 and S2, working under the assumption that as the stakeholder groups are in conflict, they will not necessarily locate the problem in the same small world. Hence an additional assumption analysis (step 3) is required so that the analysts can gain a general understanding of the problems and identify ideological versus technical sources of conflict.

In Steps 5 and 6 of the conflict analysis methodology, the analysts go through stages S3 and S4 iteratively in considering the goals and issues raised by each stakeholder group, leading to the development of a conflict model identifying possibilities for compromise built on the grounds for resolution identified in the conceptual models of the stakeholder groups. In steps 7 and 8 the analysts form and evaluate options which comprise treaties which are likely to resolve the conflict, and conduct sensitivity analyses of the treaties with spokespersons from stakeholder groups. Stage 9 ends round 1 with the development by the analysts of a strategy of negotiation. This in turn sets the scene (stage S1) for round 2.

In stage 10, all the spokespersons from the various stakeholder groups are brought together and presented by the analysts with the results of round 1. This starts stage S2 of round 2. Cats Baril indicates how the subsequent group decision making (stages S3 to S7 in round 2) may be facilited through procedures used to guide the group discussion, rather than through the provision of formal or computer based support methods.

Finally, in chapter 11, Larry Phillips extends the discussion of techniques which facilitate group decision making initiated by the previous chapter to describe Decision conferencing. In this form of group decision support, problem owner and key stakeholders (usually high level managers in the organization where the decision problem is located) meet together with decision analysts for a two-day period.

Interactive computer support is provided, so that a computer-based model incorporating the differing perspectives of the participants in the group can be developed and reviewed on-the-spot. However, Phillips describes how the facilitatory role of the analysts in taking participants through each of the stages shown in figure 1 is just as essential a component of successful decision conferencing as is high quality interactive computer support.

References

Carnap, R., 1939. Foundations of logic and mathematics. International Encyclopedia of Unified Science. Chicago and London: University of Chicago Press.

Checkland, P., 1981. Systems thinking, systems practice. Chichester: Wiley.

Edwards, W. and Newman, J.R., 1982. Multiattribute evaluation. Sage University paper series on Quantitative Applications in the Social Sciences, 07-026. Beverley Hills and London: Sage.

Humphreys, P.C. and Berkeley, D., 1985. Handling uncertainty: levels of analysis of decision problems. In G. N. Wright (ed), Behavioral Decision Making. New York: Plenum.

Jaques, E., 1976. A General Theory of Bureaucracy. London: Heinemann.

Jungermann, H., 1984. Construction and evaluation of scenarios from a psychological perspective. Paper presented at the Fourth International Symposium on Forecasting, London.

Kunreuther, H., 1983. A multi-attribute, multi-party model of choice: descriptive and prescriptive considerations. In: P.C. Humphreys, O. Svenson and A. Vari (eds), Analysing and aiding decision processes. Amsterdam: North Holland.

Montgomery, H., 1983. Decision rules and the search for a dominance structure: towards a process model of decision making. In: P.C. Humphreys, O. Svenson and A. Vari (eds), Analysing and aiding decision making processes. Amsterdam: North Holland.

Phillips, L.D., 1984. A theory of requisite decision models. Acta Psychologica, **56**, 29-48.

Raiffa, H., 1968. Decision Analysis. Reading, Mass: Addison Wesley.

Savage, L.J., 1954. The foundations of statistics. New York: Wiley.

Svenson, O., 1979. Process descriptions of decision making. Organizational Behavior and Human Performance, **23**, 86-112.

Toda, M., 1980. Emotion and decision making. Acta Psychologica, **45**, 133-155.

Vari, A. and Vecsenyi, J., 1983. Decision analysis of industrial R&D problems: pitfalls and lessons. In: P.C. Humphreys, O. Svenson and A. Vari (eds), Analysing and aiding decision processes. Amsterdam: North Holland.

Vari, A and Vecsenyi, J., 1984. Selecting decision support methods in organizations. Journal of Applied Systems Analysis, **11**, 23-36.

2 When Goals Conflict

John Hawgood
PA Computers and Telecommunications, London
Patrick Humphreys
London School of Economics and Political Science

Introduction: what is the problem?

Managers in all organizations, whether public or private, are continually faced with the need to resolve conflict between goals.

This arises in two ways. First, the organization itself may have multiple goals which are not totally consistent. For example, a village inn-keeper may have the dual goal of making a living and being friendly to everyone. Most of the time the two goals can be served together, but at closing time he may have to be firmer than he would if friendship were the only criterion. Secondly, different people affected by decisions may have different interests. A bus company may have goals of making money, creating employment, providing a social service and avoiding accidents. These four goals correspond to the interests of owners, employees, passengers without alternative means of transport, and the road-using public generally (known as "stakeholders").

What is preference technology?

The trade-offs between conflicting goals are the normal day-to-day business of all managers, and they cope remarkably well without help. But when there are particularly significant decisions, affecting the whole future of the business, managers may find they can be aided by some programs that have been developed over the last few years for personal computers. These programs, together with the presentation media, are known as "preference technology". The idea behind them is "multi-attribute utility theory", which is not really so much a theory as a careful step-by-step description of how people can make the best trade-offs between their conflicting objectives, when making choices in complicated situations. Usually people don't analyse their own decision processes, but when they do try to do so, they often find themselves making lists of all the important factors contributing to their goals, and the likely impact of proposed changes on each. Preference technology is, in essence, just a way of using the PC to help in making and revising these lists in complex situations, and presenting them to managers and other people involved in a decision, in a way that clarifies the basis for their choice to be made. These are expert systems in which the expert is the ordinary stakeholder.

In some situations, where goals conflict, the problem can lie at a higher level than that which can be helped by any preference technology directly. Sometimes different stakeholders may locate the problem within quite different worlds and be unable to understand how other stakekeholders even think about the problem. Or different stakeholders may use quite different language to express the problem, making incompatible claims about how the problem should be approached. Methods for exploring and resolving these types of conflicts are beyond the scope of this paper, but are discussed by Humphreys and Berkeley elsewhere. [1]

If conflicts between the stakeholders at these higher levels do not exist, or have been resolved, then they are usually able to agree on evaluating the options under consideration in terms of how well they meet their various goals. In the following, we give four examples covering multi-goal and multi-stakeholder problems in the private and public sectors.

Case 1: Public library service for young people

When preparing to refurbish a branch library, a team of librarians investigated the needs and preferences of users and potential users in the age range 13-19. There turned out to be two clearly identifiable stakeholder interests, which we will name "teenagers" and "students". The same person might belong to both groups but usually each visit to the library could be classified as clearly representing one or the other types of interest.

Teenagers were using the library as a leisure facility. To them the most important attributes of the service were the stocks of 'pop' cassettes for loan and the provision of magazines for their age-group. Other factors such as a pleasant coffee bar, etc. were rated lower.

Students were using the library in connection with their school or college work. The most important factors to them were quite different - study space, multiple copies of recommended books, good stock of reference books, and convenient opening hours.

The two "Abacon" charts reproduced overleaf were prepared to illustrate for these two groups and for other stakeholders (adult users, librarians, the management board) the likely consequences of two alternative policies to improve the library service for young people.

The two polices were deliberately chosen to benefit the two groups differentially:

A) Provide more study tables and some duplicate text books and close later in the evenings.

B) Provide more 'pop' cassettes and a coffee bar with sitting place.

There was not enough money or space to adopt both policies.

---

[1] P. C. Humphreys and D. Berkeley, "How to avoid misjudging judgment", Social Behaviour, volume 2 (in press).

Figure 1: Impact of proposals A and B for Teenagers

Importance

```
-   - A -   -   -   -   -   - B -   - Pop cassettes
-   -   - A -   -   -   - B -   -   - Magazines
-   - A -   -   -   -   -   - B - Coffee Bar
-   - B -   -   -   -   - A -   -   - Late opening
-   -   - B -   -   - A -   -   -   - Reference
-   - B -   -   -   -   -   - A - Study space
-   -   - B -   -   - A -   -   -   - Textbooks
```

Performance

Figure 2: Impact of proposals A and B for Students

Importance

```
-   - B -   -   -   -   -   - A - Study space
-   -   - B -   -   -   - A -   -   - Textbooks
-   -   - B -   -   - A -   -   -   - Reference
-   - B -   -   -   -   - A -   -   - Late opening
-   - A -   -   -   -   -   - B -   - Coffee Bar
-   -   - A -   -   - B -   -   -   - Magazines
-   - A -   -   -   -   - B -   -   - Pop Casettes
```

Performance

The diagrams (Figs 1 and 2) show the impact of the two proposals as seen by each group separately, by plotting goal importance vertically and the performance of the policies, against each criterion, horizontally. On such a diagram, it is the top right-hand corner which is most desirable: of course, option A appears there for students, and option B for teenagers.

After a discussion involving all the stakeholder groups, a consensus was achieved on a compromise policy, which was the following:

   C) Provide more study tables, more pop cassettes and a coffee
      machine (without sitting space), and close later in the evening.

Case 2: Improvement of a product

Manufacturer X called in consultants to advise about the lack of success of an improvement programme that they had been carrying out for one of their established products. First, a large number of users of this class of product were asked for their opinion about the relative importance of 20 characteristics of such products. Then a smaller number of users of Manufacturer X's old product "X1" and the improved product "X2" were asked to rate the performance of the two products in respect of the 20 characteristics. The performance/importance relation for X1 is shown in Figure 3, and that for X2 in Figure 4 overleaf. It can be seen that X2 was rated much better than X1 on a group of characteristics which were of low-to-middling importance, but not on the most important characteristics. For the next product improvement programme, Mnufacturer X was able to concentrate on the most important features to improve - with better results.

The preference structuring tool used to produce the graphical presentations shown in figures 3 and 4 was a PA Point Profile (a front-end for the software package Lotus 1-2-3). In each figure, the crucial region of high importance and high performance is indicated by the converging diagonal guide-lines.

Case 3: Developing a negotiating strategy for a business consortium

A consortium of small businesses within the leisure industry experienced an urgent need to develop a negotiating position with a state authority. This was a direct result of a meeting between representatives of the consortium and the state authority charged with providing members of the consortium with essential facilities in return for collecting licence fees on the hire services they offered.

Much dissatisfaction was expressed at the meeting at new proposals put forward by the state authority concerning the manner in which hire licence fees should be calculated. While a number of modifications or alternative strategies had been suggested at the meeting, none seemed to lead to a clear negotiating strategy.

Figure 3: <u>PA Point Profile: assessment of product X1.</u>

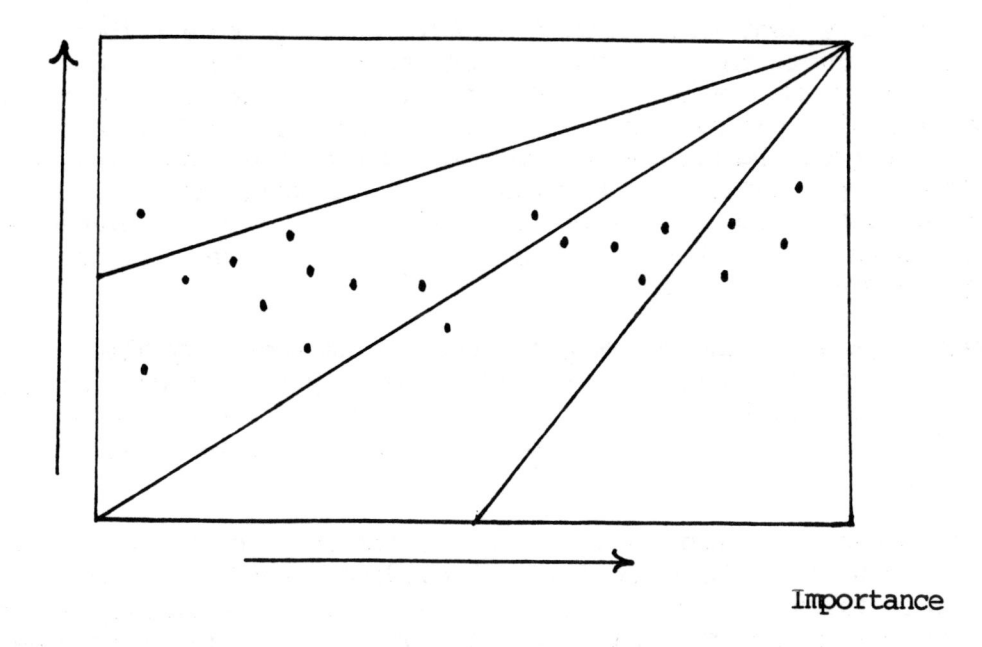

Performance

Importance

Figure 4: <u>PA Point Profile: Assessment of product X2.</u>

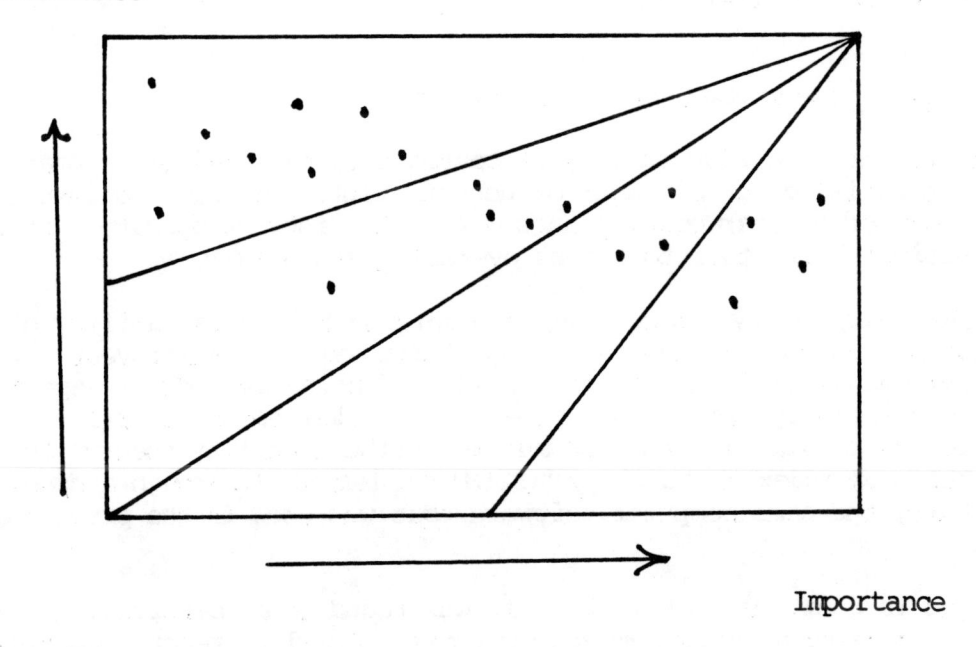

Performance

Importance

A few days after the meeting, the secretary of the consortium used MAUD, an interactive computer programme based in multi-attribute utility theory, to clarify both the consortium's own preferences, and those which fitted the perspective of the state authority.

First, the secretary used MAUD himself to help identify the attributes which were important to the consortium in characterising the various proposals. Then, with the help of MAUD, he evaluated the various options proposed by each side for raising the necessary licence revenue. He did this twice, once from the perspective of the goals of the consortium, and then from the perspective of the goals of the state authority.
This revealed that, from both sides' points of view, it was desirable to choose a different option for charging hire licences than that currently proposed by the state authority.

In using MAUD to analyse the options, the consortium secretary also discovered that the state authority should be equally indifferent, from its own perspective, to raising additional licence revenue either from hire operators, like the members of the consortium, or from private users of its facilities.

This insight opened a new negotiating position for the consortium: they could now approach the state authority with evidence that the authority should not be in favour of even its own proposal. They could propose that any new, more desirable proposal should raise additional licence revenues from private users, rather than from themselves, without running any risk of being accused of special pleading.

Faced with arguments that the consortium had been able to develop through interacting with MAUD, the state authority completely abandoned the proposal it had made at the meeting, coming up with a new set of proposals for negotiation, all of which were agreed by both sides to be more attractive than the original one.

Case 4: Discovering what expertise for what tasks

A recurring problem in a wide variety of contexts is the need to estimate risks where actuarial data is meager or non-existent. One such context is the control room of nuclear power plants where the risks of operator errors need to be estimated in order to assess overall plant safety.

The U.S. Nuclear Regulatory Commission, recognising the unavailability of actuarial data on operator errors, recently embarked on a multi-year research programme to evaluate the feasibility of using methods of expert judgement to estimate operator error rates. Included among several methods investigated was one based on multi-attribute utility theory, the "success likelihood index methodology "(SLIM) implemented through a special version of MAUD, the same computer software that was used in the previous case study.

This technique is known as SLIM-MAUD. It was found to be particularly effective in assessing a variety of complex tasks found in reactor control rooms where operators actions can only be described at the system level (choosing appropriate courses of action in handling transient situations).

Other techniques involving experts giving direct estimates of error rates, or making paired comparisons, were as effective as the multi-attribute utility-based technique for assessing low level sample tasks examining the human-machine interfaces with components, instruments, displays and controls. However, none of these other techniques were as effective as SLIM-MAUD in assessing the complex, system-based tasks.

Using SLIM-MAUD had the additional benefit that it provided a clear picture of the _types_ of expertise most appropriate for the assessment of tasks at each level and of _how_ to best structure the knowledge provided by the experts. This led to the recommendation that, in any group making human reliability assessments for system-level tasks, experts with operational expertise should be well represented, as there was much higher consistency in their SLIM-MAUD assessments than was the case with experts with other sources of expertise.

For assessing low level tasks, however, the SLIM-MAUD analysis indicated the the first priority should be to have one or two experts with human factors experience, but that they should be supported by one or two group members with other sources of expertise, in order to achieve optimal structuring of expert judgement at this level. [2]

Conclusion: Solving the Problem

In this paper, we have outlined a range of situations where preference technology, in the form of personal computer-based decision support systems, enabled the solution of multi-stakeholder, multi-goal decision problems. It is important to remember that the success depended on two preconditions which were met in each of the cases we described:

(i) That the various stakeholders located their views of the problem within the same world (in other words, they were not worlds apart from each other).

(ii) That they agreed that the fundamental issues could be addressed in terms of how well the particular options being considered (or which could be thought up) met their multiple goals, even though the order of importance of these goals might be different for different stakeholders.

Finally, the success of this approach in practical applications stems from the fact that preferences technology, unlike other techniques which _prescribe_ solutions, enables the stakeholders themselves to solve their problem as they see it.

---

[2]. This study was carried out under contract to the Department of Nuclear Energy, Brookhaven National Laboratory, Upton, Long Island, New York 11973. A full report is given in NUREG/CR-4016 (available from the U.S. National Technical Information Service, Springfield, VA.22161, U.S.A.)

3 SLIM-MAUD: The Assessment of Human Error Probabilities Using an Interactive Computer Based Approach

Dr D. E. Embrey
Human Reliability Associates Ltd

1. **INTRODUCTION.**

The assessment of human reliability has become a topic of increasing interest in recent years. This is because human errors have been implicated as important causal factors in major disasters such as Three Mile Island, Bhopal and Chernobyl. In this context, major hazard industries have attempted to incorporate human reliability considerations into the standard reliability assessment techniques used to evaluate risk.

The approach taken by these techniques is to decompose the system being assessed into hardware components, e.g. pumps, valves, pipes. A 'failure model' is then constructed which postulates various ways in which the system can fail. Probabilistic data on the failure of the components (derived from operational experience when available) are then assigned to the individual components in the model, which are then combined together to give the overall probability of failure. In Probabilistic Risk Analysis (PRA) this result is then compared with a risk criterion to evaluate whether or not the risk is acceptable. If not, design or other changes may be recommended and the analysis repeated until an acceptable failure probability is obtained.

In real technological systems, human errors in performing critical tasks need to be considered as part of safety assessments. Such analyses are usually referred to as human reliability assessments. Concern for assessing and optimising human reliability is not confined to large scale technical systems such as nuclear power or process plants. The manager of a finance house or a hospital, for example, will also be very interested in identifying and estimating the likelihood of human errors in critical tasks within the organisation.

Although the derivation of a numerical estimate of error probabilities is an important aspect of human reliability assessment, it is equally important to identify the factors that influence this probability. This enables cost benefit analyses to be conducted to investigate the effects of changing these factors on the error probability. Such analyses can be viewed as a means of supporting decision making with regard to where expenditure can most effectively be applied to provide the maximum degree of error reduction. Subsequent sections of this paper describe the Success Likelihood Index Methodology (SLIM). This is capable of providing both numerical estimates of human error probabilities, and also a context specific error prediction model which enables cost benefit evaluations to be performed.

2. THE SUCCESS LIKELIHOOD INDEX METHODOLOGY

The Success Likelihood Index Methodology (SLIM) is a widely applicable technique which can be used to assess human error probabilities in both proceduralised and cognitive tasks (i.e. those involving decision making, problem solving, etc.). It assumes that expert assessors are able to evaluate the relative importance (or weights) of different factors called Performance Shaping Factors (PSFs), in determining the likelihood of error for the situations being assessed. Typical PSFs are the extent to which good procedures are available, individuals are adequately trained, the amount of time available to perform the tasks is adequate etc. If numerical ratings are made on these PSFs for the specific tasks being evaluated, these ratings can be combined with the weights to give a numerical index, called the Success Likelihood Index (SLI). The SLI represents, in numerical form, the overall assessment of the experts of the likelihood of task success. The SLI can be subsequently transformed to a corresponding human error probability (HEP) estimate.

The SLIM technique is implemented using a microcomputer based system called MAUD (Multi-Attribute Utility Decomposition), the resulting technique being called SLIM-MAUD. A detailed description of the SLIM-MAUD technique and case studies of applications are available in reference (1).

SLIM-MAUD is essentially a system for capturing the domain specific expertise of knowledgable individuals with regard to the relative impact of various factors on human performance. For this reason, it is usual to use the technique in a consensus mode, employing a small group of individuals with experience of the situations being evaluated, together with a 'facilitator' who assists in the knowledge elicitation process. Detailed descriptions of this process are given in reference (5), which describes an evaluation study which investigated the effectiveness of the technique.

3. APPLICATION OF SLIM-MAUD - AN ILLUSTRATIVE EXAMPLE

3.1 Definition of Situations and Subsets

The first phase of applying SLIM-MAUD involves carefully defining the situations to be evaluated by providing the judges with as much information as possible regarding the characteristics of the tasks, the individuals who will perform them, and any factors that will influence the likelihood of success. The tasks are then divided into subsets for which the task success probabilities are influenced by common sets of PSFs. Each subset is then assessed in a separate SLIM-MAUD session, as illustrated in this example.

The following descriptions define the general characteristics of the tasks considered in the example analyses and the conditions under which they are performed. These descriptions are hypothetical, but could be applied to a number of tasks encountered in both the process industries and commercial situations. All of these tasks are classified as being in the same subset, as their success probabilities are influenced by similar PSFs. They are thus evaluated in the same SLIM-MAUD session.

Task A

Task A is proceduralised and both stress and time pressure are high compared with the other tasks under consideration. The consequences of failure are moderately low, and the task is the least complex of all the tasks. However, it requires the most teamwork for effective performance.

Task B

This task involves slightly more diagnosis and is much more complex than task A. The stress level is the lowest of all the tasks considered, as is the time pressure. There is considerable teamwork involved in performing the task and the consequences of failure are more severe than in task A.

Task C

Task C is primarily diagnostic in nature. The stress level is the second lowest and time pressure and consequences of failure are the lowest of all the tasks considered. Complexity is moderate and there is little teamwork required.

Task D

Task D requires a moderate degree of diagnosis. Stress level is somewhat high, but there is no time pressure. Consequences of failure are moderately high and complexity is the highest of any of the tasks. Teamwork is not required.

Task E

Task E is proceduralised and involves a moderate level of stress. Time pressure and consequences of failure are both low. Complexity is high and there are moderate teamwork requirements.

Task F

This task is the least complex of all the tasks and the most highly proceduralised. There is very little stress involved but a moderately high degree of time pressure. However, it involves more teamwork than any other task, and the consequences of failure are severe.

3.2 Elicitation of PSFs

The computer initially presents a random set of three tasks from those to be assessed, and then asks the judges to think about how one of the tasks differs from the other two in a way which is significant in affecting the likelihood of success. This wording is used to 'break the ice' and encourage the team to think of ways in which tasks differ along various PSF dimensions. The computer then asks the judges to name the end points of the PSF that has been elicited. A typical PSF might be 'Time Presssure', and the corresponding end points would be 'High Time Pressure' to 'Low Time Pressure'. The other PSFs relevant to these tasks are the degree to which tasks are proceduralised rather than requiring diagnosis, the stress level, time pressure, consequences, complexity and degree of teamwork required.

3.3 Rating the Tasks on the PSFs

The computer generates a linear scale from 1 to 9 using as endpoints the designations provided by the user, e.g. 'Low Time Pressure' and 'High Time Pressure'. Each task is then presented in turn and the assessor assigns a rating between 1.00 to 9.00 on the scale for each task, to reflect the actual conditions that occur in each of the tasks being assessed. Examples of the form of these ratings are given in figure 2, table (b). Comparison between the description of the tasks given in Section (3.1) and the corresponding ratings in table (b) indicates how the task characteristics are transformed into ratings by the judges. It is important to note that the ratings on a particular PSF are intended to be relative to the ratings for all other tasks on that PSF. Thus, the ratings are not in any sense absolute.

3.4 Ideal Point Elicitation and Scaling Calculations

MAUD next asks the judges to identify the _ideal_ point on the particular scale being used. With certain scales, e.g. in the current example: 'Low Time Pressure' to 'High Time Pressure', the optimal rating, in terms of promoting human reliability, may be at some intermediate value between 1 and 9, e.g. 4. This is because both extreme time pressure and also too much time being available to perform the task might both be expected to degrade the likelihood of success (the latter because the individual performing the task may be insufficiently motivated).

After the ideal rating for a particular PSF has been elicited, MAUD then rescales all the other ratings for this PSF in terms of their distance from the ideal point, the rating which is closest being given a value of 1, and that which is furthest, zero. Intermediate values are scaled accordingly.

Having completed the ideal point rating, MAUD then elicits another PSF from the judges. The tasks are then rated on this PSF and the ideal point determined as before. This process continues, with the judges being asked directly about possible PSFs that can influence the likelihood of success, until they indicate that the set of PSFs is complete.

3.5 Independence Checks

The rescaled ratings for each task on the various PSF scales are subsequently multiplied by their respective relative importance weights and these products summed to give an overall SLI for each task (see section 3.7). In order for this procedure to be valid, it is important that the scales are independent. If two scales, e.g. Low stress to High stress, and Low time pressure to High time pressure, effectively mean the same thing, then erroneous results will be produced because the contributions from effectively the same PSF will be entered twice in the calculation of the SLI.

In order to avoid this problem, MAUD monitors the correlations between the ratings produced on the different PSF scales. If the scale ratings exceed a certain level of correlation, MAUD asks the judges if they mean the same thing by the two correlated scales. If this is the case, MAUD asks them to define a new scale which combines the meaning of the two correlated scales. The tasks are then re-rated on the new scale. If, on the other hand, the correlation between the ratings on the original pair of scales is coincidental, the judges tell MAUD that the scales actually have a different meaning, and they are subsequently treated as independent.

3.6 Weighting Procedure

This part of MAUD is entered after all the tasks have been rated on all the PSFs. The weighting procedure is concerned with evaluating how much emphasis is to be given to each of the PSFs in terms of its effect on the likelihood of success. In order to do this, the computer presents a pair of hypothetical tasks to the judges. These tasks are characterised by two of the PSFs that have been selected earlier. Figure 1 shows the format of the computer frame. It is important to note that tasks 1 and 2 are generated by the computer in order to elicit the relative importance the judges place on the various PSFs. Tasks 1 and 2 do not correspond to any of the tasks A to F that are being assessed.

The **X** on the diagnosis scale for task 1 is set at the worst rating of all the tasks assessed on this PSF. The **X** on the Time Pressure Scale is set at the ideal value for this scale. For Task 2 these conditions are reversed, i.e. X on the diagnosis scale is set at the ideal value and the time pressure **X** is set at the worst value that had been assigned to any of the tasks.

Imagine you had to choose between Task 1 which scores as follows:

Task 1

Requires Diagnosis   Explicit Procedures Available

    I.....I.....I.....X.....I......I.....I.....I

High Time Pressure   Low Time Pressure

    I.....I.....I.....I.....I.....X.....I.....I.....I

and Task 2 which scores as follows:

Task 2

Requires Diagnosis   Explicit Procedures Available

    I.....I.....I.....I.....I.....I.....I.....I.....X

High Time Pressure   Low Time Pressure

    I.....X.....I.....I.....I.....I.....I.....I.....I

which task has the highest likelihood of success, 1 or 2?

      Figure 1: Computer Frame Showing Use of Trade-Off Procedure
              to Obtain Relative Importance Weights.

If the judges choose task 1 as having the highest success likelihood, the computer will then move the cross half a unit to the left on the time pressure scale so that overall, task 1 will become slightly less likely to succeed (because time pressure will have increased). If the judges still prefer task 1 after this change, the cross will again move to the left to make task 1 less attractive. This process will then continue until the judges' preferences switch over and they prefer task 2. (If 2 had been chosen initially, the cross on the first (diagnosis) scale of 2 would have moved to the left to make 2 a less attractive option. Note that the cross only changes position on one of the four scales). From the point at which the judges' preference changes over, the computer can calculate the relative importance assigned to one PSF as compared with another. Similar trade-offs are made with all the other PSFs that have been elicited, until their relative importance is evaluated. (N-1) trade-offs are required, when N is the number of PSFs.

3.7 Calculating the Success Likelihood Index

The SLIs for each of the tasks which have been evaluated using SLIM are calculated from the following formula:

$$SLI_j = \sum W_i \cdot R_{ij}$$

where

SLI_j = the Success Likelihood Index for task j (j = no. of tasks)

W_i = normalized importance weight for the ith PSF (the weights for all the PSFs sum to 1)

R_{ij} = Scaled Rating of Task j on the ith PSF (the rating is scaled in terms of its distance from the ideal point as discussed earlier).

3.8 Outputs from the MAUD Session

Figure 2 shows the outputs from a typical SLIM-MAUD session. Table (a) gives the tasks, together with their associated SLIs, ranked in order of descending likelihood of success. Table (b) provides the actual ratings of each task on each PSF, together with the ideal ratings. Table (c) gives the rescaled ratings (in terms of their relative distance from the ideal point) and the relative importance weights of the PSFs as inferred from the trade-off phase in the MAUD procedure. The SLI values in table (a) are calculated from table (c) by multiplying the relative importance weights for each PSF by the rescaled ratings for a particular task.

Thus, for Task D the SLI is calculated as follows:

rescaled rating x weight   PSF

    0.80 x 0.25 = 0.20   Proceduralized v. diagnostic
    0.43 x 0.16 = 0.07   Stress level
    0.67 x 0.21 = 0.14   Time pressure
    0.67 x 0.10 = 0.07   Consequences
    0.14 x 0.24 = 0.03   Complexity
    0.50 x 0.04 = 0.02   Teamwork

$$SLI = \sum W_i \cdot R_{ij} = 0.53$$

Table (a): Success Likelihood Indices

		SLI	
1.	Task F	0.61	Highest Success Likelihood
2.	Task B	0.59	
3.	Task C	0.57	
4.	Task E	0.53	
5.	Task A	0.50	
6.	Task D	0.46	
			Lowest Success Likelihood

Table (b): Ratings of Task on PSFs

PERFORMANCE SHAPING FACTORS	TASKS F B C E A D	IDEAL RATING
Explicit Procedures Available (1) to Requires Diagnosis (9)	1 3 6 2 2 4	(1)
Low Stress Level (1) to High Stress Level (9)	3 1 3 5 8 5	(4)
Low Time Pressure (1) to High Time Pressure (9)	8 2 2 7 9 6	(4)
Minor Consequences (1) to Severe Consequences (9)	4 5 7 6 6 5	(8)
Simple (1) to Complex (9)	3 7 5 7 1 8	(1)
No Teamwork Required (1) to Requires Teamwork (9)	1 5 3 2 1 3	(3)

TABLE (c): Rescaled Task Ratings on PSFs and Relative Importance Weights

RESCALED RATINGS ON TASKS

F	B	C	E	A	D
1.00	0.60	0.00	0.80	0.80	0.40
0.71	1.00	0.71	0.43	0.00	0.43
0.33	1.00	1.00	0.67	0.00	1.00
0.00	0.33	1.00	0.67	0.67	0.33
0.71	0.14	0.43	0.14	1.00	0.00
0.00	0.00	1.00	0.50	0.00	1.00

PSF SCALES AND RELATIVE IMPORTANCE WEIGHTS

PROC./DIAG.	-	0.25
STRESS LEVEL	-	0.16
TIME PRESSURE	-	0.21
CONSEQUENCES	-	0.10
COMPLEXITY	-	0.24
TEAMWORK	-	0.04

1 = Best, 0 = Worst task on a particular PSF.

Figure 2: SLIM-MAUD Outputs

The products of the rescaled rating and the importance weight for a particular PSF indicate the contribution of that PSF to the overall likelihood of success for the task under consideration. Thus, for the current example, the dominant PSF is the extent to which the situation is proceduralized as opposed to requiring diagnosis (this accounts for about 38% of the SLI), followed by the presence or absence of time pressure (26%). This information can be useful for cost benefit analyses, as will be discussed subsequently.

4. CONVERSION OF THE SLIs TO PROBABILITIES

The SLIs generated in a SLIM-MAUD session are relative measures of the likelihood of success of each of the tasks considered in the session. In order to transform these to human error probabilities (HEPs), it is necessary to calibrate the SLI scale for each set of tasks considered. There are several routes via which calibration can be achieved, all of which rely on the following assumed relationship between SLIs and HEPs:

$$\log \text{HEP} = a\, \text{SLI} + b \quad (1)$$

where a and b are constants.

Support for this relationship comes partly from the related Paired Comparisons technique, which also scales tasks in terms of the judged likelihood of success, and for which work discussed in references (3), (4) and (2) confirms a logarithmic relationship. Reference (1) gives experimental support for the validity of this relationship in the context of SLIM, and also provides a theoretical justification.

Determination of the constants in the equation requires that at least two tasks for which the HEPs are known are included in the SLIM session, and that the SLIs for these tasks are assessed. This produces two simultaneous equations from which the constants a and b can be calculated. These constants can then be substituted in equation (1) to produce a general calibration equation for converting SLI values to HEPs for the remaining tasks in the set being assessed.

Several possible sources for calibration data exist. One possibility in the power and process industries is to use data from training simulators. Once the needs for calibration data have been established, training simulator sessions can be directed towards acquiring this data. Some data also exists from direct observations carried out on plants. Absolute probability judgement, employing techniques such as those described in reference (2) can also be used. In a commercial context, similar techniques can be applied. More sophisticated approaches to calibration are described in section (6).

In this example, we will assume that one of the above techniques has been used to obtain HEPs for the two tasks with the lowest and highest SLIs, i.e. 10^{-2} corresponding to an SLI of 0.46 (task D), and 10^{-3}, for an SLI of 0.61 (task F) as shown in table (a), figure 1. The resulting calibration equation allows the following HEPs to be calculated for the remaining tasks:

	SLI	HEP
Task F (calibration)	0.61	1.0×10^{-3}
Task B	0.59	1.4×10^{-3}
Task C	0.57	1.9×10^{-3}
Task E	0.53	3.4×10^{-3}
Task A	0.50	5.4×10^{-3}
Task D (calibration)	0.46	1.0×10^{-2}

These results indicate that task A is four times as likely to fail as task B.

5. USE OF SLIM-MAUD FOR SIMULATIONS AND COST-EFFECTIVENESS ANALYSES

Because SLIM-MAUD evaluates HEPs as a function of the PSFs judged to be the major determinants of human reliability, it is possible to perform simulation or 'what if' analyses by varying the ratings on PSFs. The results summarized in tables (b) and (c) of figure 2 provide information useful for deciding on the most effective changes that might be made to the tasks to minimise the likelihood of error. The first consideration is to determine which of the PSFs is amenable to change. Thus, the 'consequences' PSF is probably an intrinsic characteristic of the tasks under consideration and cannot be modified, whereas 'time pressure', for example, could probably be reduced by suitable planning or restructuring of the situation, at least for some of the tasks.

The next question is the degree of change which is possible. This is given by the distance of the judges' rating from the ideal point for the task and the PSF being considered. Thus, as shown in table (b), figure 2, the potential for improvement of task 5 on the 'time pressure' PSF is greater (5 points), than tasks 3 and 2 (2 points). This table also gives the direction of change required to achieve the optimum rating. The third factor which needs to be taken into account is the relative importance of the various PSFs. Obviously, modifying a PSF in the direction of the optimum will have the greatest effect on the SLI for those PSFs which have greatest associated weights.

In summary, SLIM-MAUD provides explicit guidelines for the analyst and designer in terms of which aspects of the tasks are amenable to change, the magnitude and direction of the possible changes, and which of the modifications will be most effective. When used in conjunction with external information, such as the cost of possible modifications and the criticality of the situation being assessed, SLIM-MAUD constitutes a useful tool for cost-effectiveness evaluations, in addition to its quantification capability.

6. THE SLIM-SARAH APPROACH

As described in earlier sections, the SLIM-MAUD approach is a systematic methodology for eliciting PSFs from expert judges, and for deriving the relative importance of these factors in terms of their influence on the likelihood of a task being successfully accomplished. The technique enables tasks to be rated on the PSFs and provides checks to ensure that these are independent. MAUD was originally developed as a general purpose program to assess individual decision making or preference problems in great detail. From the perspective of the human reliability analyst, who may need to analyse a large number of different types of task, the use of the full MAUD methodology may not always be practicable.

The major disadvantages of MAUD from this perspective are that it takes some time to exercise, and its facilities for performing rapid 'what if' analyses are less comprehensive than is desirable for human reliability applications. In addition, MAUD does not contain any specific facilities for carrying out the conversion of SLIs to probabilities. The need to convene a team of judges for each evaluation is also a major practical problem. In order to overcome these problems, Human Reliability Associates have developed a comprehensive software package called SARAH (Systematic Approach to the Reliability Assessment of Humans). SARAH is designed to generalise the results of an initial MAUD session to other tasks for which the error probability is determined by the same PSFs with the same relative importance weights. SARAH contains comprehensive facilities for transforming SLIs to error probabilities and for performing sensitivity analyses. The way in which SARAH is used to evaluate tasks using a series of reference databases is described below.

6.1 Development of Reference PSFs and Data Base

SARAH is designed to utilise pre-defined reference databases which have been set up by prior MAUD sessions for specific types of tasks. Thus, it is assumed that the probabilities of success of all tasks of a particular type in a specific domain are determined by the same set of PSFs with a fixed profile of relative importance weights. Given this assumption, it is possible to take a representative set of tasks from the domain of interest (ideally with associated empirically determined HEPs) and to perform a MAUD evaluation on these tasks. The result of this evaluation is the identification and weighting of the PSFs perceived to influence the likelihood of success together with the derivation of SLIs for each of these reference tasks. These data constitute the reference database which is used by SARAH.

6.2 Calibration of the Reference Data Base by SARAH

The next stage of the procedure involves establishing a calibration relationship between the SLI values developed for each of the reference tasks and the corresponding HEPs. Two alternative procedures are used, depending on whether the HEPs are derived from reliable empirical data (i.e. frequencies of errors divided by the number of opportunities for the error to occur) or whether they are generated by absolute probability judgements or other subjective methods.

The first stage in both procedures is to input to SARAH the MAUD data shown in figure 2 (this is written as a disk file during the MAUD session as an option in the program). The error probabilities corresponding to the SLIs for the reference tasks are then input to SARAH as part of its calibration module. The best fitting regression line between the log HEPs and the SLIs is then generated by the program and shown on the microcomputer screen as a scatterplot. The function of this display is to provide feedback regarding the consistency of the judges SLI values with the corresponding HEPs. If there are gross irregularities in the fit because of one or more "outliers", two strategies are possible.

In the case where reliable empirical data are used for the HEPs, it is assumed that the outliers are due to a rating strategy being used which is discrepant from that employed for the other reference tasks. The judges are then asked to reconsider these ratings until the discrepancy is resolved, and a consistent fit is obtained.

Where subjectively derived HEP data have been used, the situation is more difficult because it cannot be assumed that any inconsistencies are due solely to problems with the rating of tasks on the PSFs. In this case, the judges are asked to reconsider both the HEPs and the PSF ratings for any discrepant tasks, together with the overall pattern of the data for the other tasks in the reference data base.

Experience has shown that in most cases it is possible to obtain a reasonably satisfactory calibration relationship by these procedures. It should be emphasised however, that this calibration relationship is, strictly speaking, only valid for the judges who originally set up the reference database. This is because there may be differences in the way that different judges rate tasks on the PSF dimensions. This could lead to different SLIs being generated for the reference tasks and therefore a different calibration relationship being required. This problem can be overcome by ensuring that any new users of a database first carry out the calibration procedure described earlier. This involves re-rating the reference tasks, and obtaining the scatterplot of the relationship between the SLIs calculated from these ratings and the log HEPs for the tasks. This "customisation" procedure ensures that a valid calibration relationship is developed.

6.3 Quantifying New Tasks Using the Reference Database

Once the calibration relationship has been established using the technique described in the last section, evaluation of new tasks is straightforward.

The first step is to decide whether or not the task or tasks to be evaluated belong to any of the reference databases available. This is decided on the basis of whether or not the success likelihood of the tasks is determined by the same PSFs with the same relative importance weights as those in one of the reference databases. Once the task is assigned to an available database, this is called up from disk using SARAH.

The description of the new tasks to be evaluated is input to SARAH. All the tasks in the database (both reference tasks and tasks to be evaluated) are then displayed in the form of a matrix. This allows easy comparisons between the PSF ratings for the reference tasks and those to be evaluated. The new tasks are then rated on each of the PSFs in turn, using the matrix display. SARAH then automatically calculates the SLIs for these tasks, using the PSF weights developed for the reference tasks. The calibration equation derived for the reference tasks is then used to calculate the HEPs for the new tasks from these SLIs.

6.4 Data Manipulation and Display Facilities within SARAH

SARAH offers a wide variety of facilities for performing "what-if", sensitivity and cost-benefit analyses. For example, any task rating or PSF weight can be changed and the corresponding effects on the error probability can be determined. The results of up to sixteen different sensitivity analyses can be stored and compared if required. A variety of output formats are available, which show either subsets or all the data analyses that have been carried out.

7. CONCLUSIONS

The SLIM-MAUD/SARAH methodology is a logical, systematic approach to determining human error probabilities based on the knowledge possessed by expert judges. Obviously, its internal validity rests on the availability of appropriate expertise in the domain of interest. Evaluations of the approach have been carried out in the area of human error evaluation in nuclear power, as described in reference 5. The results of these evaluations indicated that the methodology was superior to other judgement based approaches, especially for the evaluation of complex tasks involving judgement and decision making. With regard to external validity, this can obviously only be determined empirically when adequate data becomes available from real world tasks. In the absence of such data, the external validity of the numerical probability estimates produced by the approach depends on the quality of the calibration data used.

Possibly the most powerful feature of the approach is the fact that it provides a means of making prescriptive statements with regard to how human reliability can be improved in specific situations. When combined with cost data, this facility enables the most cost effective changes to be made to improve human reliability within given budgetary constraints.

The SLIM-MAUD/SARAH approach is the product of several years of research and development which has produced an effective and versatile technique for use in a wide variety of applications.

ACKNOWLEDGEMENTS

The development of SLIM-MAUD was supported by the Office of Nuclear Regulatory Research of the US Nuclear Regulatory Commission, contract monitor Dr. T.G. Ryan, through Brookhaven National Laboratory. The MAUD software was developed by Dr. P.C. Humphreys and Ms. A. Wishuda of the Social Psychology Department, London School of Economics.

REFERENCES

1. Embrey, D.E., Humphreys, P.C., Rosa, E.A., Kirwan, B., and Rea, K. (1984). "SLIM-MAUD: An Approach to Assessing Human Error Probabilities Using Structured Expert Judgement". NUREG/CR-3518, (BNL-NUREG-51716). Department of Nuclear Energy, Brookhaven National Laboratory, Upton, New York 11973, for Office of Nuclear Regulatory Research, US Nuclear Regulatory Commission, Washington, D.C. 20555.

2. Comer, M.K., Seaver, D.A., Stillwell, W.G. and Gaddy, C.D. (1984) "Generating Human Reliability Estimates Using Expert Judgement". Vols. 1 and 2. NUREG/CR-3688 (SAND 84-7115). Sandia National Laboratory, Albuquerque, New Mexico, 87185 for Office of Nuclear Regulatory Research, U.S. Nuclear Regulatory Commission, Washington, D.C. 20555.

3. Hunns, D.M., (1982) "The Method of Paired Comparisons". In: Green, A.E. (Ed). High Risk Safety Technology. Wiley: Chichester, England.

4. Pontecorvo, A.B., (1962) "A Method of Predicting Reliability." <u>Annals of Reliability and Maintainability.</u> Volume 4.

5. Rosa, E.A., Humphreys, P.C., Spettell, C.M. and Embrey, D.E. (1985) "Application of SLIM-MAUD: A Test of an Interactive Computer-Based Method for Organising Expert Assessment of Human Performance and Reliability." NUREG/CR-4016 Brookhaven National Laboratory, Upton, New York, USA, for Office of Nuclear Regulatory Research, U.S. Nuclear Regulatory Commission, Washington, DC 20555.

4 Negotiating Environmental Issues: A Role for the Analyst?

Joanne Linnerooth
International Institute for Applied Systems Analysis, Austria

I. INTRODUCTION

A fundamental element of environmental policy making is negotiation. Even in the adversarial system of the United States, regulatory agencies and other governmental decision makers implicitly negotiate problem definitions and solutions with public stakeholders to avoid costly court battles. These interactions are developing into more explicit negotiation forums with the growing awareness that all participants can reduce procedural costs through direct cooperation rather than confrontation. In the U.S., new institutions to accommodate negotiated policy making are therefore evolving; these institutions are kin to the pluralistic committee structures found in much of Europe. More cooperative forms of environmental policy making present a challenge and an opportunity to analysts. How can traditional forms of expertise, including the fact-finding and strategic decision aids, be adapted to support the participants of a negotiation or even to improve the outcome of a negotiated settlement? A challenge to designers of systems for "decision support" is to find the relevant links for adapting these systems to provide "negotiation support".

In linking these concepts, it is important to understand the interrelationship between decision making and negotiation, and particularly the institutional contexts in which they occur. This paper will examine three separate contexts selected to illustrate the diversity of both concepts and ultimately the diversity of the tools that can potentially provide support. The first context is a multi-party, adversarial process where the stakeholders interact only through indirect negotiation and where decisions are taken in more formal court proceedings; the second context is an organizational decision setting where positions are again implicitly negotiated, but internal to the organization; the third context is an explicit, around-the-table negotiation where the parties have a shared interest in reaching an agreement. This latter context shows the successful use of a computer model in providing support for a negotiation. This success, however, is tempered by the rather novel conditions surrounding the case, and cannot be easily transferred to other negotiation contexts. It is shown that political traditions and institutions can severely constrain, as well as present opportunities, to the use of many types of decision and negotiation aids.

---
[*] The author takes full responsibility for all views expressed in this paper.

II. DECISION SUPPORT AND NEGOTIATION SUPPORT

Early "expert" and "decision support" systems have, for the most part, not been distinguishable from more conventional notions of expertise and policy analysis except for the introduction of the computer and its capacity for processing and displaying large quantities of information. By capturing the knowledge of the decision maker or expert with regards to the structure of the problem and analysing this in search of a solution, computerized decision support has been in the form of "facts", "analyses", and "prescriptions".

This view of a support system has been described by Humphreys (1986, p.3) as proceeding in three phases:

i) Modelling declarative knowledge in terms of facts and rules,

ii) making prescriptions for action, and

iii) formalizing this into a decision support system to be applied by the decision maker.

These deterministic applications of expert systems have proven effective only for limited types of problems, specifically for single decision makers addressing well-structured issues.

A recent and promising development distinguishing expert and information systems from decision aiding and support systems (DSS) is the emergence of software to support individual and organizational decision makers who do not enjoy unitary goal hierarchies and who are facing ill-structured problems. This new perspective sees decision aiding systems as addressing the realities of many individual and organizational decision settings, where problems do not come neatly packaged and where the decision makers are better served by creative help in structuring the problems at hand and generating alternatives for their resolution. An important focus, therefore, of recent research has been on developing interactive systems that help the user in problem structuring and exploring lines of analysis, but not in providing solutions.

As attention moves from providing information to the decision maker to providing more strategic help, it is natural to address the context of the decision. One important context is a negotiation. Thus, analytical tools are being developed to aid the *process* of negotiation, where negotiation can be characterized as an interactive process by which two or more people or parties seek cooperatively to do better than they would have otherwise (Lax and Sebenius, 1985). Clearly, many decision settings are negotiations; however, much of the work on aiding decision makers has not taken into account the negotiation setting. Besides providing analytical or strategic support to the participants of a negotiation, recent experience has shown that the analyst can improve the negotiating process and outcome by providing a forum for mutual learning and understanding and/or by supporting a third "neutral" party.

At this point, there may be some confusion about the analyst's role in aiding decision makers, in aiding decision makers as negotiators, and in aiding the process of negotiation. Table 1 shown below might be useful. It distinguishes between empirical, "fact-finding" analyses and more strategic analyses, both of which may be useful for decision makers, negotiators, and for aiding the negotiating process.

Most policy analytical work falls into the empirical, fact-finding category and includes the usual types of expertise in structuring the problem at hand and in providing the scientific evidence (Table 1, (1)). Information and expertise is traditionally considered to be the property of the individual participants, but a new concept of consensual information or "neutral" expertise as providing an agreed basis to a negotiation is emerging (Table 1, (3)). This concept of knowledge as common property is, however, problematic since it assumes a problem consensus on the part of the principles. Besides "fact-finding" analyses, strategic analytical help (Table 1, (2) and (4)) can also be useful to decision makers, e.g., decision analytical support and strategic planning, to negotiators as well as to third parties who are responsible for aiding a negotiation process.

Consider, first, "fact-finding" analyses. With the many different ways to structure problems and to choose assumptions and data, as well as the often conflicting scientific opinions, it is generally difficult to label empirical analyses as fully factual, and they often take on a more

Table 1. Types of analytical support for decision makers/negotiators and the negotiating process.

	Decision Makers/ Negotiators	Negotiating Process
Fact-finding	(1) e.g., Information and expert systems	(3) e.g., Common knowledge base
Strategic	(2) e.g., Decision analysis; Strategic planning	(4) e.g., Game-theoretic aids for third parties

subjective character. This becomes problematic when analysts turn from supporting the single decision actor to supporting a negotiation. Since there may be no "hard facts", negotiating parties will naturally turn to scientific opinions which bolster their particular positions. It will be difficult to reconcile these "factual" differences since they are entangled with party interests.

Even recognizing the social and political construction of science and knowledge, many view the negotiation process as foremost an exercise in joint learning to reach common understandings and eventual solutions. An hypothesis underlying much of the literature on the use of computers to facilitate or aid negotiations is that information forms a neutral ground for agreement which can free the path for trading off legitimate differences in interests. Raiffa (1985), in noting the enormous scientific complexity in international environmental disputes, notes also the important question of the interrelation between facts and interests:

> Negotiators must argue the merits of their cases, but they don't know the physical facts. There is a need for some mutual learning. How do they learn together and still protect their own interests? (p. 45)

The second type of analyses shown on Table 1 is strategic analyses for decision makers or negotiators. They can take many different forms. The most common include decision analytical tools, game-theoretic models, and other broader applications of policy analysis. A key element of such analyses is an accounting of the decision maker's values and realizing his or her goals within the decision context, e.g., the possible responses of "opponents" to a decision or negotiation stance.

These same concepts are being usefully adapted to aiding the participants of a negotiation by providing strategic advice to the individual negotiators (see, e.g., Ury and Fisher, 1985). An important recent development in this type of strategic advice is the departure from the concept of negotiation as positional bargaining to a concept of negotiation as an exercise in joint or cooperative problem solving. The analyst can also provide tools to help a third party intervenor in his or her role as facilitator ((4), Table 1). An underlying theme of this type of analytical support is that negotiated outcomes are too often inferior in the sense that there may exist alternatives which would be preferred by all the parties in the negotiation. The question is how the analyst can structure and aid the negotiation process so that better or more "efficient" outcomes are reached. This question is fundamental to the development of strategic negotiation support tools. By understanding the preferences of the negotiating principles, a third party can help the negotiating process by expanding the options and exposing inferior bargaining outcomes.

There are essentially three different ways that the computer can play a role in aiding the *process* of negotiation (as opposed to aiding one of the bargaining partners). As discussed above, it can provide a common knowledge base, even a model showing causal relationships on the substantive content of the negotiations ((3), Table 1). Alternatively, the computer can provide strategic help ((4), Table 1). In a game-theoretical vein, the computer can actually simulate negotiated alternatives, showing the distributive results among the bargaining partners and discovering "joint gains". The computer might also act as a kind of "group therapist" facilitating communication among the participants of a negotiation.

In the following section, I will explore three different policy settings where decision support as well as negotiation support tools proved, or might have proven, helpful. Some inherent limitations to their use will also be discussed.

III. ADVERSARIAL POLICY PROCEDURES: The Siting of an LNG Terminal

In the early seventies, Western LNG Terminal Company applied to the US Federal Power Commission for approval of three sites on the California coast to locate an LNG receiving terminal:[1] Point Conception, Oxnard, and Los Angeles. These applications generated considerable controversy on the federal, state, and local levels concerning the need for natural gas, the safety of locating a terminal at the populated Los Angeles and Oxnard sites, and the environmental damage of locating a terminal at the pristine Point Conception site. The most frightening possibility was that the storage tanks would fail catastrophically, releasing a large quantity of natural gas which would vaporize into a cloud that might travel over a neighbouring population centre and then ignite. The conflicts and negotiations among the many groups involved were exacerbated by the disparate results of the risk analyses commissioned by different groups.

The political battle over siting the LNG terminal in California raged for over ten years and is a classic example of a multi-stakeholder process involving indeterminate issues, like the future needs of energy and the safety of a poorly-understood technology. The details of the case are described elsewhere (see Kunreuther, Linnerooth, et.al, 1983). The concern in this paper is the potential for providing expert and decision support to individual or organizational stakeholders, or even in facilitating a negotiated agreement among the stakeholders.

"Macro" Support Systems

Consider first the most ambitious type of support system which would weigh and compare the welfare costs and benefits of the decision to import LNG to California and for selecting a site. In theory, the calculus of welfare economics can be applied to siting decisions, where the social costs and benefits of the alternative sites (including no site) can be weighed and the "best" site chosen. This exercise will require interpersonal and intergroup utility comparisons, but, again in theory, the choices can be laid out in a kind of macro-welfare support system. Such analyses could be used by a regulatory agency or a facilitator in negotiating an agreement among the different stakeholders. It is no surprise, however, that this type of analysis was not carried out in the California siting case. At no point in the ten-year process did analysts in the LNG siting case have the opportunity to frame the problem as a social choice among all the possible sites, including no site.

The use of this type of support system was precluded by the incremental dynamics of the decision process. The problem whether and where to site the facility in California was approached in a series of subproblems, and these subissues were generally decided upon in an adversarial hearing process. The question whether California needed an LNG terminal was settled in hearings involving the Federal government, the California state government and

---

[1] Liquified natural gas (LNG) is a potential source of energy which requires a fairly complicated technological process that has the potential, albeit with very low probability, of creating severe losses. For purposes of transporting, natural gas can be converted to liquid form at about 1/600 its gaseous volume. It is shipped in especially constructed tankers and received at a terminal where it undergoes regasification and is then distributed. The entire system (i.e., the liquification facility, the LNG tankers, the receiving terminal, and the regasification facility) can cost more than $1 billion to construct.

the industry. The positive conclusion then locked California into finding a site. State hearings were, then, conducted for each of industry's proposed sites, resulting in a stalemate. This stalemate was broken by a legislated change in the California siting process, whereby the California Coastal Commission (CCC) was handed the task of screening and ranking sites (with considerable input from the public) and the Public Utility Commission had the job of choosing from the ranked sites. This process also required that the top ranked sites be again subjected to a hearing process, where issues such as earthquake risk and the feasibility of a safe design were at issue.

The *process* as opposed to the siting decision shows that at only one point, the ranking of all potential sites by the CCC, was the choice framed in a comprehensive way. As will be explained below, the CCC chose *not* to have an explicit decision support system laying out the pros and cons of the different alternatives. Throughout the remainder of the process, the decisions were framed as a choice between two or maybe three sites. If, as in this case, the problem at hand is formulated as a choice between site X and site Y, the content of the debate, including the analyses, are more narrowly focused than if the problem is framed in more general terms of whether to have a facility at all and where it should be located. The latter formulation is more appropriate for "systems thinking" and for support systems that allow the stakeholders to explore various problem formulations and to generate imaginative alternatives (e.g., an alternative not considered was spreading the risks by locating several storage facilities along the coast). The choice between two sites substantially narrows the dimensions to be considered.

Approaching problems through a series of subproblems suggests that there may be significant constraints of a political, institutional nature in finding applications for a "macro" support system, or even for what Humphreys describes as fifth or maybe sixth-generation concerns in information technology development: going beyond the formalized, essentially deterministic systems to address more fundamental issues of how to support problem structuring, policy formulation and decision making. Fifth and sixth generation support is useful for situations where decision makers, who are not the "problem owners", have discretion in how to structure the problem and determine the important criteria. But as shown here, even "non-problem owners" may lack this discretion. For example, the citizen groups who participated in hearings over the choice between the CCC's ranked sites had little choice but to accept the problem as structured by the formal agenda of the hearing process.

The Strategic Importance of "Facts"

What types of analyses and expertise, then, surfaced during this decade of conflict in California? The answer is primarily "fact-finding" analyses concerning (1) the need for LNG in California and (2) the safety risks of a terminal. At least five risk analyses were produced, each of which attempted to quantify the very low probability event of a catastrophic failure of an LNG storage facility. The results of these analyses differed remarkably, for example, the risk of a citizen living at one site, Oxnard, was estimated to be between 10^{-6} and 10^{-7} by one study and between 10^{-7} and 10^{-10} by another – a difference of three orders of magnitude. These discrepancies were, in part, due to the differences in the choices made by the analysts in defining the boundaries of the risk problem they were addressing. One study of the Oxnard site focused on a geographical area that put 15,000 people at risk; another study considered a broader area that put 90,000 people at risk. Two of the three risk assessments prepared for another site, Point Conception, considered risks involving transport ships, the transfer of LNG to shore, and the storage tanks on shore; the third study considered only risks involving the transport ships. One major risk to an LNG facility is sabotage and another is war; none of the various California risk assessments, however, included either possibility (Kunreuther, et.al., 1982)

The large discrepancies in the results of these studies, the shaping of the problem frames, the assumptions chosen, and the presentation of the results illustrates a crucial, and often overlooked, aspect of multi-stakeholder processes. There is an essential need for participants *to argue and justify* their policy positions. Whereas the emphasis in decision making and decision support systems is to generate alternatives, analyse the uncertainties, and show the pros and cons of the choices, the emphasis in the (adversarial) policy arena may be more on taking stances which are easily defensible even if this means covering over or ignoring uncertainties. Deterministic, factual evidence has been traditionally accepted as a legitimate and credible defense of a policy argument.

The opponents and proponents to the LNG facility recognized that "risk" was the weak link in making a case for or against the facility (for whatever reasons) and thus both seized upon this issue, molding it to support and justify their case. Thus, the assumptions were hidden, the uncertainties not calculated, the data carefully chosen, and presentation formats constructed to direct attention to one aspect or another of the safety of the operation. The risk analyses in this multi-party process were not an *ex ante* input into party decisions, but were mainly an *ex post* exercise aimed at supporting party arguments. As Majone (1979) has observed, there is a role for the analyst as a producer of policy arguments - more similar to a lawyer - than to a problem solver.

A Role for Strategic Decision Support?

In this adversarial process, the analysts/lawyers recognized the power of scientific arguments, and the decision context called for deterministic, empirical analyses of issues which were inherently uncertain. How, then, would have more strategic support systems for aiding the stakeholders, or even for supporting a negotiated settlement, have fared?

Consider, first, analyses for aiding the individual stakeholders. In the sequential or incremental procedures, the individual or organizational actors, who clearly confront problems in the sense of subjective representations rather than any objective realities, nonetheless may lack full discretion to structure the problem at hand. There is thus a "public" DSS agenda, where the key features are argumentation and justification, as well as a "private" agenda, where the client can explore alternatives, problem structures, and strategies. While the actors from industry, government, and citizen groups could have each benefited from a wide ranging analysis of alternatives taking into account their preferences or the preferences of those they were representing, such analyses would have exposed the weak links in their public arguments and rendered them more vulnerable in the policy arena. Clearly, confidentiality is a key consideration.

A strategic decision support system for aiding individual or organizational actors may be useful, then, only if confidentiality is possible. It must still confront the well-documented problems of diffuse organizational goals, ill-defined issues, and so forth. A DSS will not, however, replace the need for more deterministic, knowledge-based analyses that have traditionally been employed for lending credibility to and justification for an actor's public position.

A Role for Negotiation Support?

Finally, consider the potential of settling the siting issues raised in this LNG case by means of a direct negotiation, and the possibilities for analytical support. Two characteristics of the LNG siting process would have fundamentally affected the potential for a more open negotiated settlement: the complexity of the issues involved and the indeterminancy of the scientific questions. An unbounded negotiation addressing the full gamut of questions - whether and where to site a terminal - would have been confounded by the intricacies and interrelations of the numerous and complex subissues. For this reason, incremental processes have evolved in order to frame the issues in well-defined and clear-cut terms. Negotiation can be useful in settling these subissues, but cannot replace the usual, and maybe inefficient, incremental procedures.

The greatest potential for more explicit, out-of-court negotiations in procedures such as illustrated by the LNG siting case would appear to lie in the selection of the ranked sites. The state of Massachusetts, e.g., has legislated a siting procedure where the site selection is not negotiated, but where potential communities submit bids for the amount of compensation the community would require to accept voluntarily a noxious facility. This imaginative legislation has not been fully successful since communities have not come forth with bids. One reason for this lack of cooperation has been the failure of industry to become more directly involved in its role as advocate. This problem might be overcome with a more direct, around-the-table negotiation between industry and the perspective communities (in California, for example, the top-ranked sites set out by the CCC), where compensation is an important bargaining chip.

A crucial advantage of this type of negotiated procedure would be in legitimizing the analyst's role as advocate. Rather than the court deciding on, for example, the most correct or most plausible value for the risk of the facility (which it is generally ill prepared to do) the negotiations could proceed with full acceptance of different risk values and perceptions on the part of the negotiating principles. If, for instance, the risk was viewed by the perspective community to be high relative to that shown by industry, then this *argument* for increased compensation could be challenged and debated with an ultimate compromise settlement as the goal. Clearly, if the community felt the risks were unacceptably high and not reasonably compensated, then industry would have to approach other communities, e.g., in the California case as ranked by the CCC.

There is, then, an important potential for direct negotiation in more adversarial policy procedures for environmental decision making, such as the siting of large technological facilities with their accompanying environmental risks. The analyst can contribute to this process by preparing the scientific evidence and argumentation for those participating. The analyst might also be able to aid the process by providing guidance to a third party to the negotiation, e.g., with regards to the alternatives considered and the "efficiency" of the bargaining outcomes. Is there an alternative site (and accompanying compensation) which would be preferred by all the stakeholders? This type of negotiation support may prove to be an important policy tool.

IV. AGENCY DECISION MAKING: The Classification of Hazardous Wastes

With passage of the US Resource Conservation and Recovery Act (1976), the US Environmental Protection Agency (EPA) was given the task of designing and implementing a comprehensive regulatory system for managing hazardous wastes within the broad directive of a single overriding statutory goal - the protection of human health and the environment. This task would be fulfilled by, among other things, developing a federal classification system to determine what wastes would enter the regulatory system. The difficulties the EPA would face in shaping this classification system can be appreciated by considering that most chemicals in use eventually become wastes. There are approximately 80,000 chemicals in commercial circulation, and approximately 1000 new chemicals enter commercial use each year. Using the total of world laboratory resources, about 500 chemicals per year can be tested for toxicity (at colossal expense). One test, for carcinogenicity alone, can involve 800 test animals and 40 different tissue specimens per animal for pathology examinations; that is, 32,000 specimens. This needs approximately $500,000 and 3.5 years to perform. (Wynne, 1987)

The potential breadth of the problem and the underdeveloped science accompanying the issue presented an acute dilemma to the EPA. Its regulatory attention would inevitably be selective. One possible strategy was to prepare a list of all potentially hazardous chemicals, erring on the conservative side, and to select a small set of these wastes for regulation. In this way, the Agency could limit the scope of its regulatory program to manageable and affordable proportions. With the public visibility of the issue, however, this strategy would certainly have evoked a public outcry demanding more comprehensive regulation. An alternative strategy was to be selective during the earlier, less visible, work of preparing the hazardous waste lists; only wastes whose management rendered them hazardous would be included. But this strategy violated the US regulatory principle of keeping the scientific issues (which wastes are hazardous to public health?) separate from the economic/value issues (which wastes should be regulated?). It blurred thus the distinction between risk assessment and risk management and was flatly rejected by the EPA which emphasized that:

> The fact that a waste is properly managed by particular generators or particular classes of generators, does not make a waste non-hazardous. It is only necessary that the hazard *could* result *when* wastes are mismanaged (Federal Register, May 19, 1980, p. 33113)

In sum, the EPA was under intense pressure (1) to use only scientific, health data for listing wastes, and (2) to set a comprehensive regulatory control program. Violation of either would have severely tarnished the agency's reputation and authority, but meeting both would prove impossible. Throughout EPA's two-year period of rule-making, the intended scope of the regulatory program was therefore a subject of continual internal controversy. In the words of the EPA's former Deputy Administrator:

> Certain categories of waste and certain industrial activities clearly present far more serious environmental hazards than do others. By focusing on selected priority problems to impose initial controls, EPA probably could have put a program into effect in half the time it took to establish such a broad and elaborate framework. It could then have expanded coverage to other wastes and other operations with the benefit of practical experience. By attempting to be so ambitious, the Agency delayed the whole program... Driven by the forces of environmental politics, we have repeatedly committed ourselves to goals and programs that are utterly unrealistic. (Quarles, p.xvi)

While publicly committed to comprehension, nonetheless the EPA *did* substantially reduce the scope of its program and did mix values with scientific issues - but in a way which was always *defensible* to its critics. This requires a slight digression in explaining the complex procedure by which the EPA decided on what actually is a hazardous waste.

The waste lists; The EPA developed two hazardous waste lists: (1) the wastes from standard manufacturing or industrial processing operations known to contain toxic constituents, and (2) hazardous commercial products which became wastes when discarded. The industrial waste lists were developed by examining some 200 studies of industrial wastes that had been compiled at the EPA prior to the RCRA legislation, from which 125 wastes were identified as hazardous. The EPA estimated, however, that there were over 10,000 major industrial waste processes, so the identified wastes did not begin to encompass the full gamut. This gap would be filled by requiring generators to test their wastes.

The question of concern here is the scientific information that allowed the EPA to choose these 125 wastes. The compilation of the lists began with the identification of hazardous constituents (carcinogenic, mutagenic, toxic to aquatic species, etc.). However, chemical testing, especially for carcinogens, is a complicated, costly procedure, and for this reason the EPA relied almost exclusively on other environmental regulation to identify 380 hazardous constituents, most of which came from the Clean Water Program (Dietrich, 1984). How then were these hazardous constituents compiled?

In implementing the Clean Water Act, the EPA found itself under pressure from environmental groups, at which time it hastily compiled a list of constituents hazardous to drinking water. Dietrich (1984) described this as a "hasty midnight session where a larger list was whittled down by crude analysis". A waste containing one or more of these 380 hazardous constituents was not necessarily listed. Eleven factors were identified which could justify not listing a waste.

There was, of course, detailed justification for each listed waste, including:

(1) A summary of the Administrator's basis for listing each waste;
(2) A description of the manufacturing process;
(3) An identification of waste composition, constituent concentration, and annual quantity generated;
(4) A discussion of the basis for listing each waste stream; and
(5) A summary of the diverse health effects of each of the constituents of concern (Federal Register, p. 33113).

Despite this elaborate justification, the EPA admitted that decisions to list a waste were often based on qualitative judgements, generally involving expert assumptions rather than precise field measurement (Federal Register, p.33114).[2] (Federal Register, p. 33114)

Testing Procedures: The EPA recognized that its listing procedure would not comprehensively cover the range of hazardous wastes since at least 9,800 major industrial processes had not been examined. To fill this gap, the EPA required generators to test those wastes that did not appear on the lists. The draft regulations originally proposed eight characteristics requiring testing, but these were reduced to four in the final regulation: ignitability, corrosivity, reactivity, and toxicity. By requiring the generators to test their wastes (unique to the US), the scope of the regulatory program was significantly broadened - according to one estimate by as much as 90%.

In comparison with other countries, the EPA took extreme care to keep the scientific issues separate from the political by its exclusion of management possibilities and costs in defining hazard and listing wastes (in contrast, the costs of managing wastes was an explicit consideration in listing wastes in the Netherlands). Yet, even with such strong intentions on the part of the EPA to keep science separate from policy, we find that it was not entirely a one-way process. As fears mounted within the EPA that the scope of the regulatory program was becoming unmanageable, pressure intensified to draw in the boundaries. These pressures subtly entered those areas where the EPA staff had allowed themselves sufficient discretion, such as:

– In deciding whether the concentration of one or more of the 380 hazardous constituents was sufficient to list a waste; or, if the waste was generated in sufficient quantities; or the other nine possible factors that justified not listing a waste.

– By drawing back from the 8 characteristics for testing to determine if a waste is hazardous to 4 characteristics (including toxicity).

– By choosing only 14 hazardous drinking water constituents to substantiate the toxicity characteristic.

As might be expected, artificial boundaries developed for what is and is not hazardous, such as concentration levels and volume cutoffs, which had more to do with pragmatic, administrative necessities than objective, natural science dictates.

This brief case history illustrates the extreme care taken by US regulatory authorities, and typically all the stakeholders battling for credibility in the policy process, in providing a legitimate, "scientific" basis for their policies. The scientific grounds for branding wastes as hazardous could only be stretched unnoticeably at the margins to permit the EPA to meet its own internal objectives, that of defining and limiting the regulatory scope to manageable proportions.

---

[2] Quantitative risk assessments played no particular role. According to an EPA staff member, only the most hazardous wastes and the least controversial had been identified and, thus, the EPA was correct in its assessment that there would be no consequent court battles. For this reason, quantitative justification for EPA's listing decisions was not deemed necessary.

While the need to build a scientific case to support regulatory rule making is extreme in the US with its system of judicial oversight, similar appeals to analytical authority are apparent in other Western countries (for a comparative review of procedures for classifying hazardous wastes, see Dowling and Linnerooth (1987)). In the FRG, for example, a regulatory authority appeals to "registered experts" who prepare confidential *Gutachten*. The UK, with its more cooptive and hierarchial regulatory practices, relies more on industry-government negotiation than unambiguous scientific evidence to support agency decisions.

In sum, with the uncertain science accompanying the problem of choosing "hazardous wastes" from the some 60,000 chemicals which find their way into waste streams, the EPA was facing a regulatory nightmare. Its credibility and authority hinged on finding legitimate, scientific rules for excluding or including wastes in its regulatory program and its ability to limit this program to reasonable proportions. The Agency accomplished this feat by establishing elaborate, comprehensive, and above all, scientifically justifiable rules for listing wastes, but still allowing itself enough flexibility to set boundaries on its control program.

A role for decision support?

This case study illustrates the delicacy of providing information systems or decision support in terms of "fact-finding" analyses [(1), Table 1] to an internal agency decision process. Any open recognition of the thousands of potential wastes for listing and the uncertainties and scientific ambiguities surrounding the question of "hazard" would have exposed the inherent limitations of the Agency in meeting its mandate to design and implement a comprehensive regulatory system and protect public health and the environment. Even within the Agency, individuals and departments were vying for authority and were naturally reluctant to acknowledge the inevitable arbitrariness of many of their choices. Deterministic scientific data became a goal in itself. For example, the hazardous constituents from the Clean Water Program were adopted with little discussion on their source. They had already received the mark of legitimacy in prior policy debates and could be borrowed as "factual" support for the current debate.[3]

If the underlying ambiguities of the scientific bases of many decisions were acknowledged, arguably environmental decision making would bog down in endless scientific controversy. A certain "cover up" of the scientific uncertainties is inevitable and necessary. This "uncertainty cover up" limits the proliferation of more advanced forms of decision support, or the fifth and sixth generation support systems that provide a more open assessment of the problem by taking into account the scientific uncertainties and ambiguities. These more advanced forms of support risk revealing the often subjective and *ad hoc* nature of much of regulatory practice, undermining the authority of regulatory bodies and eventually the viability of political institutions. Without a fundamental change in regulatory processes, first-generation support systems will continue to have an important place in policy making. In other words, fact-finding analyses will remain essential for providing stakeholder support.

A role for negotiation support?

In the US, the high costs of adversarial rule making are becoming of serious concern. The EPA, for example, incurred enormous expences in providing the elaborate justification necessary for each of the listed wastes - in some cases several shelf feet of analyses. This expense was necessary to defend the Agency's judgement in court proceedings. The costs of this adversarial process has led many to argue for more negotiated regulatory policy making similar to regulatory practice in many European countries. Negotiated policy making may, thus, be the political change necessary to open the way for more advanced forms of computer

---

[3] Interestingly, the resulting "lists" from the EPA will also be borrowed by many other countries as legitimate, authoritative, and "factual".

support.

Before embracing European style negotiated systems, it is important to recognize some fundamental differences which may limit the feasibility of negotiated policy making in the US with its system of checks and balances. An agency such as the EPA is responsible to the Legislature. In this case, it was given an ambitious mandate of protecting public health and the environment. An explicit negotiation concerning the scope of its regulatory responsibilities would have exposed the Agency's limited regulatory capabilities. Such a process would have required a candid recognition that the EPA could not fully meet its mandate for a comprehensive regulatory program. Resorting to a more openly negotiated process would appear to require a change in this legislated mandate.

A comparison with a European country might be useful. In Austria, with its "social partnership", regulatory policy is negotiated by representatives from government, industry, and the labor unions. Environmental groups are becoming more vocal, but are meeting resistance in joining this trilogy. The hazardous waste list was the task of the Austrian Standard Setting Institute which appointed a working group consisting mostly of government and industry representatives. Most industries potentially affected by the regulations were invited to participate. With the US, German, and Swiss lists as guides, a working committee proposed an Austrian list. After some discussion, it was agreed that a vote would be taken on each of the wastes on this proposed list. A waste would be included only with the unaminous vote of the whole working group. The waste list resulting from this process closely resembles that of the US. (For a full discussion, see Dowling and Linnerooth, 1987)

Austria, of course, had the advantage of borrowing the scientific efforts of those countries originally preparing lists. Still, it was a streamlined process which required little or no justification on the part of the government regulators, which cost the government only a fraction of the U.S. expense, and which co-opted industry by requiring its approval for listing its waste. There was no pretense of comprehension or of a list based solely on scientific grounds. An argument showing the regulatory costs to be high legitimately excluded a waste from the list. This style of regulation, however, was possible only given the accepted practice of handing standard setting to committee processes, where all the actors have an interest in its resolution. Austria's "social partnership" allowed these committees to work without a threat of court challenges. In stark contrast to the U.S., the authority of the regulatory body in meeting an ambitious legislated mandate was not at stake.

V. COOPERATIVE NEGOTIATION: The Law of the Sea Conference (LOS)

The previous two case studies have focused on the use of decision support systems to aid actors in a multi-stakeholder system and on the potential for more directly negotiated settlements. Formal decision "power" rested with designated regulatory or other governmental bodies, although these bodies were not the sole problem owners since other stakeholders could challenge them in the legal system. The use of more advanced support systems for aiding the participants in these adversarial proceedings was shown to be seriously limited by the historical role of scientific evidence and the strong incentives to understate the inherent ambiguities. Since all stakeholders stand to gain from reduced litigation costs, direct negotiation of environmental, regulatory issues was highlighted.

With the growing interest in negotiated rule making, it is important to ask how computerized support systems might play a constructive role. In particular, will they meet the same sort of obstacles as their counterpart, decision support, has met in the adversarial setting? This section presents an example of the *successful* use of the computer in aiding a complex negotiation over the mining of the deep seabed. This is an application of a "fact-finding" or more deterministic analysis in aiding the *process* of negotiation ((3), Table 1). It will be shown that the computer can play a constructive role under some conditions, but this role is limited by the nature of the negotiation context.

The LOS Negotiations

The problem of deep-sea mining of "manganese modules"[4] became an important issue for reaching an international agreement on the common use of the oceans (for a full account, see Sebenius, 1981). In 1970, the U.N. General Assembly had declared these deep sea resources to be the "common heritage of mankind", and the task of the negotations was to find a system for their equitable sharing by the nations of the world.

A conflict arose between the developed countries, which expected to mine the seabed and which argued for a seabed authority that would do little but register claims, and the developing countries (the "Group of 77") which argued for an international body as the sole exploiter of the seabed. After six years of intensive negotiations, an agreement was reached by over 140 countries on the financial arrangements of a compromise "split the difference" formula.

That an agreement could be reached among so many countries with strong differences (developed vs. developing, socialist vs. market economies, land-based producers and consumers of ocean minerals, and countries with and without seabed technology) is astonishing, and seems to be partly attributable to the joint exploration and learning made possible by a computer model developed at the Massachusetts Institute of Technology (MIT). This model, which was developed independently of LOS, worked out the engineering and financial aspects of nodule recovery and processing, including cost figures on research and development, capital investment, transportation, and so forth. Uncertainty was well documented with sensitivity analyses, but the results were essentially deterministic. The "baseline", 18% profitability result from the study contradicted claims made by the developed countries that the return would be so low as not to permit any proposed payments to the international community and, at the same time, deflated the arguments of developing countries that seabed mining would be so profitable as to virtually fuel their economies.

With the conflicting interests involved, it is worth examining the question why the MIT model gained credibility with the majority of the negotiating countries. Sebenius points to a number of factors which led to the acceptance of the model: (1) the model was developed independently of the LOS Conference; (2) the presentation of the model's results by the MIT group highlighted the uncertainties (increasing further its credibility) and attacks were responded to with straightforward technical responses; (3) the model's results fully pleased no delegation, confirming in some sense its neutrality; and (4) the chairman of the financial group, who was highly respected, strongly favoured and supported the acceptance of the model. After the presentation of the model, the Norwegian delegate asked that his compromise proposal be evaluated, followed by the evaluation of a rather extreme proposal put forth by a developing country. Both proposals were shown to be inadequate on important aspects. A proposal then made by the chairman relied heavily on the MIT model.

Sebenius shows how the apparent certainty of the model that had attracted delegates to the study gave way to a realization that the uncertainty was inevitable. This realization led eventually to a two-track financing scheme depending on the profitability of the mining operations, a scheme which all the delegates saw as advantageous, even given their different expectations about the future. The model played a significant role in fashioning this accord, and in the words of Sebenius:

> Here, then, was a complex negotiation that did not proceed in ignorance. Rather, the deliberations of dozens of delegates from various foreign, mining, and finance ministries constituted a lengthy mutual education process. A great deal of information was exchanged and a powerful tool was generally available to analyze proposals, to help invent new ones, and to lay out implications for the parties' economic interests. While pure bargaining necessarily took place in tandem with analytic investigation, it is hard to imagine a more intensely rational process in a negotiation among so many nations. (p. 87)

---

[4] The nodules are composed of commercially promising quantities of copper, cobalt, nickel, and manganese.

Sebenius attributes the acceptance of the model largely to the properties of the model, itself, that established it as unbiased, competent, and credible. Since there are so few similar examples of the acceptance of a common knowledge and analytical base, and since all modelling efforts - the MIT model included - have an inherent, subjective component, it is important to look beyond the model to explore the external conditions which led to a *willingness* on the part of the delegates to find a common knowledge base. What distinguished the LOS Conference from other negotiation forums where such a willingness for mutual learning would have been unlikely?

One factor which may have been crucial was the "win-win" nature of the negotiations. Although conflict arose over the question, "which nations stand to gain the most", the setting was such that no country was likely to lose absolutely. Thus, there was a strong motivation for the delegates to settle their differences and arrive at a formula for resolving the distributive issues. This may be contrasted with, for example, the LNG siting case where certain stakeholder, such as the citizen action groups, were motivated to highlight the differences and stall any resolution of the issues.

Another contributing factor may have been the "newness" of the issue and, therefore, the absence of entrenched interests within the institutional settings of the countries involved. The immaturity of the issue was evidenced by the lack of existing analytical studies, except for the scattered documents prepared by industry and the few bureaucratic centres dealing with the problem of mining manganese modules. Without the overriding need to justify the positions of home institutions, the delegates were freer to embrace "neutral" evidence. These nonalignments also freed the path for coalitions to form within the context of the negotiations, and much of the arguments were in the spirit of legitimizing these coalitions. Sebenius, thus, notes the value of the MIT model as providing seemingly objective analysis which could be used as justification for the delegates to abandon their positions and not have to admit the merits of the "opponents'" arguments (p.84). Again noting the contrast with the LNG case, stakeholders which have invested a great deal in analytical support for their arguments and which are backed by institutions with a strong interest in maintaining positions, are not likely to embrace freely a "neutral" analytical base.

Finally, it is important to note that while the interests of nations differed dramatically, a common problem definition or frame was shared by the delegates: What would be the profitability of mining manganese modules and how should the profits be distributed? This shared economic formulation of the issue undoubtedly contributed to the common acceptance of an essentially engineering/economic model. Resolution of the issue was not muddled by different perceptions of the issue and different "rationalities" which so often characterize debates on environmental issues. Also, the delegates shared a certain homogeneity in terms of professional backgrounds (e.g., most were members of ministries such as mining, foreign affairs, and finance) which may have more than offset their heterogeneity in terms of national/cultural backgrounds, and which undoubtedly contributed to the acceptance of a common issue frame and eventually to a common analytical base. Cultural anthropologists have often noted the shared culture of like professionals from even different countries as opposed to dissimilar subcultures within a country.

In sum, the "win-win" nature of the negotiations, the newness of the issue and apparent absense of strongly entrenched institutional forces outside the negotiations, and the homogeneity of the delegates in terms of professional backgrounds most certainly played a role in creating a willingness on the part of the delegates to engage in common learning and in adopting a "neutral" information source. These conditions are glaringly absent in more adversarial policy debates such as illustrated by the case of siting an LNG terminal in California. A real challenge to negotiation analysts is to create the conditions which may lead the principles of a negotiation to embrace the concept of "mutual learning". This will only be possible with a recognition of the political role which "knowledge" has traditionally played in policy debates. Unless the political conditions or the negotiation context are changed, the power of knowledge will continue to be a crucial element of debate limiting any efforts at "mutual learning".

VI. CONCLUDING REMARKS

With the emergence of more diffuse and heterogeneous environmental problems, such as toxics control and hazardous wastes, regulatory agencies are facing mounting and sometimes intractable problems in implementing regulatory programs. The controlling organizations do not have the resources to "police" such complex systems, but must rely more and more on the voluntary compliance of industry (see Wynne, 1987). Experience in Europe shows that one important advantage of negotiated regulatory rules is that industry, having agreed to them, is more likely to comply. For the regulatory agency, the alternative to more negotiated, cooperative forms of behaviour, similar to the pluralistic committee structures in Europe, is not only serious noncompliance but also mounting costs of litigation from industry and environmental groups. If the alternatives which a party has to negotiation determine its bargaining or negotiating power (see Lax and Sebenius, 1985), then, in many respects, the power of U.S. regulatory agencies is seriously eroding with the increasing difficulties in implementing and enforcing regulatory rules. With this shift in power away from the governmental authorities, all parties may stand to gain from more cooperative, direct negotiations of environmental and regulatory policies.

The growing interest in more cooperative forms of policy making presents a challenge and opportunity to analysts. How can traditional forms of expertise, including the fact-finding reports and strategic, decision aids, be adapted to support the participants of environmental negotiations? This paper has explored this question in the context of three separate policy settings: an adversarial, multi-stakeholder process of siting an LNG terminal in California; an internal agency decision process for determining the bounds of a regulatory program for hazardous wastes; and an international negotiation for the resolution of the economic and distributive issues for sharing the resources of the ocean floor. It was shown that the potential for a negotiated settlement and the type of analytical support useful for improving the process and outcome of the negotiations are crucially dependent on the issue and the policy context.

Keeping in mind the importance of political context, there are essentially three ways in which the analyst might contribute to the process of negotiation. The analyst can provide empirical and strategic support to aid a participant of the negotiation. The analyst can attempt a consensus on the scientific and empirical input to the negotiation by promoting "mutual learning" among the participants. Finally, the analyst can aid the process by which issues are negotiated by promoting the mutual generation and exploration of scenarios, or by helping a "neutral" third party explore outcomes in terms of the preferences of the negotiating principles.

Aiding the Principles

Providing empirical evidence to the principles of a negotiation is the most usual form of analytical intervention. Evaluative and normative analyses are also useful, but generally as confidential support. Factual, empirical analyses, (contrary to the distinction made earlier between "fact-finding" and more strategic analyses), are often, themselves, an important part of the *strategy* of the stakeholder. The strategic role they play influences the form of the analyses and ultimately the types of decision support which may be appropriate for aiding decision makers and negotiators. This political role of information, and the shaping of information to meet strategic needs, was shown in both the LNG siting case and the EPA waste selection case. During the process of siting an LNG terminal in California, several highly professional risk analyses surfaced, none of which, however, attempted to broaden the bounds of the problem or to highlight the uncertainties. This "uncertainty cover-up" was seen again in the US EPA process of listing wastes as hazardous, where deterministic analyses of the hazards of chemicals (to fish) became the legitimate source for listing wastes.

This appeal to scientific determinacy is typical of adversarial policy debates and limits the use of more advanced forms of decision support for use in policy forums (they may still serve the confidential use of participants) and also colours the types of support which will be helpful to participants in adversarial negotiations. The constraints on using strategic decision support were cogently illustrated during the process of siting an LNG terminal in California. After the California Coastal Commission was assigned the task of ranking sites for a potential LNG terminal, the head of this Commission was approached by a well known and competent decision analyst to explore the possibility of ranking sites with the use of multi-objective decision analysis. The head of the CCC was known to be a strong advocate of this type of analysis; nonetheless, he turned down the consultant's offer. The reasons he cited were the exposure it would give the CCC to its internal decision logic and the resulting loss of control of the agency over its negotiating strategy (Kunreuther, Linnerooth, et.al., 1983).

Promoting "mutual learning"

The hypothesis that information can form a neutral ground for agreement, which can free the path for trading off legitimate differences in interests, is intuitive and appealing. Yet, it rests critically on the notion of an objective reality and ignores the inherent subjective component of much of what is labeled as factual evidence. Although the degree to which objective reality is coloured by the perceptions of the observers and by the social context is a matter of academic debate, there is little disagreement that many current environmental issues are characterized more by scientific disagreement than a consensus on the facts. In this atmosphere, it is natural that stakeholders, as hearing participants or negotiation principles, turn to advocacy reports and empirical evidence to bolster their causes. There will be little interest or incentive to engage in mutual learning or even to establish rules of evidence to guide the scope and content of the scientific argumentation. The strategic importance of information and empirical argumentation in policy debates and negotiations will limit the potential for mutual exploration of scenarios and joint learning.

Given the strategic importance of information and "facts" and the disincentives for seeking mutual understandings in adversarial proceedings, cases such as the LOS negotiations, where 140 nations rallied around a common problem formulation and analytical structure embedded in a computer model, stands out as truly exceptional. The circumstances surrounding the negotiations appear also to have been extraordinary in that so many factors leading to a willingness on the part of the delegates to except a common problem frame were present: the "win-win" nature of the outcomes created an incentive to reach a consensus on the scientific/economic questions; the newness of the issue precluded the influence of strongly entrenched institutional forces outside the negotiating arena; the homogeneity of the delegates in terms of professional backgrounds counterbalanced national cultural differences; and the existence of a chairman as a strong advocate of the use of a computer model opened doors for the MIT team. Rarely is the polititical context so favorable to the concept of "mutual learning". In the words of Sebenius (1981):

> Models can be the modern tools of pragmatism where a larger, perhaps political conception is shared, where an overall negotiating "formula" is maintained by the parties, or where divisive factors outside elegant, analytic frameworks are held in check. Models can skillfully mediate policy disputes, but their roles are precarious when ideologies or basic values actively clash.... The knowledge models produce and conciliatory movement they inspire are important, but are hardly the end of the story (p.93).

Supporting a third-party

A recent, and potentially fruitful, direction for the analyst is supporting the negotiation process by providing analytical aids to a third-party in his or her role as arbitrator, facilitator, or one of the many other forms of mediation (see Raiffa, 1982). The ultimate aim of the facilitator is to improve the outcome of the negotiation in the sense of improving the position of all the negotiating parties. The analyst can potentially help by uncovering inferior outcomes, or those for which alternatives can be found which would be preferred by all the parties (or at least not be considered worse). In other words, the analyst can explore outcomes in terms of the preferences and values of the negotiating partners, possibly with the use of a computer model. This type of support, although actual experience is scarce, does not require a change in adversarial traditions and is a natural extension of the historical role of the mediator. As such, it is one of the more promising directions for development and application.

References

Dietrich, G. (1984) Former Head, Office of Solid Waste, EPA, Personal interview, Wash. D.C.

Dowling M. and J. Linnerooth (1987) The Listing and Classifying of Hazardous Wastes, *Risk Management and Hazardous Waste*, Springer Verlag, Berlin.

Fisher, R. and W. Ury (1981) *Getting to Yes*, Boston: Houghton Mifflin.

Humphreys, P.C. (1986) 'Intelligence in Decision Support' in B. Brehmer, H. Jungermann, P. Lourens and G. Sevon: *New Directions in Research on Decision Making*, Amsterdam, North Holland.

Kunreuther, H., J. Linnerooth, et.al. (1983) *Risk Analysis and Decision Processes: The Siting of Liquid Energy Gas Facilities in Four Countries*, Springer Verlag, Berlin.

Kunreuther, H., et.al. (1982) Liquid Energy Gases Facility Siting: International Comparisons, Proceedings of an IIASA Workshop, 22-26 Sept., 1980, CP-82-36, IIASA, Laxenburg, Austria.

Lax, D. and J. Sebenius (1985) The Power of Alternatives or the Limits to Negotiation, *Negotiation Journal*, Apr.

Majone, G. (1979) 'Process and Outcome in Regulatory Decision Making' in C.H. Weiss and A.H. Barton (Ed.): *Making Bureaucracies Work*, London, Sage.

Quarles, J. (1982) *Federal Regulation of Hazardous Wastes: A Guide to RCRA*, Environmental Law Institute, Wash. D.C.

Raiffa, H. (1982) *The Art and Science of Negotiation*, Cambridge, Mass. Harvard University Press.

Raiffa, H. (1985) Mock Pseudo-Negotiations with Surrogate Disputants, *Negotiations Journal*, Apr.

Sebenius, J. (1981) The Computer as Mediator: Law of the Sea and Beyond, *Journal of Policy Analysis and Management*, Vol. 1, 77-95.

Wynne, B. (1987) *Risk Management and Hazardous Waste*, Springer Verlag, Berlin.

5 Ranking Multiple Options with DECMAK

V. Rajkovic
School of Organisational Sciences, and Jozef Stefan Institute, Yugoslavia

M. Bohanec
Jozef Stefan Institute, Yugoslavia

and

J. Efstathiou
Queen Mary College, London

1. INTRODUCTION

Decision-making can be treated as the selection of a particular option from a given set of options to best satisfy some given set of aims or goals. For that purpose we have to collect and organize appropriate information about options and define goals for description of options. Our cognitive processes have to be supported in the sense of knowledge elicitation. Our decision knowledge has to be represented in a way that is easily understood, updated and actively used by participants in the decision-making process.

A lot of data of different kinds and importance are involved in decison-making. These data are often incomplete or even missing. A decision-maker has to transform the data into knowledge for making, explaining and defending his decision. Therefore, decision-making can be treated as a special learning process which has to be organized in a way to reach an active knowledge for a reasonable and justifiable decision to be made in the shortest possible time.

It is known that information technology can give a new quality to decision-making. For that purpose, an active collaboration between man and machine is needed. This means not only documentation and number-crunching, but also higher levels of decision data processing, obtainable with the application of artificial-intelligence methods [4,11].

In the following sections, the organizational phases of the decision-making process are briefly described and discussed. According to these phases, a particular example of employee selection is shown. The example is treated using two decision making methods. The first is based on a type of extended spreadsheet approach [8] and can be used as an introductory step toward the second method, which is an example of an expert system generator.

The expert system approach will be shown by the aid of DECMAK software [2,3], with special emphasis on the synthesis of decision knowledge and its usage for multiple-option ranking and explanations of decisions.

2. PHASES IN MULTIATTRIBUTE DECISION-MAKING

Multiattribute decision-making methods (MADM) describe options according to a chosen set of attributes (parameters, criteria). Each option is decomposed and represented by corresponding values of attributes. Usually, attributes are evaluated separately. A final option value (overall utility) is then obtained by a kind of aggregation formula, e.g. a weighted sum of individual attribute values. The overall utility, which is usually numerical, provides a basis for ranking options and the final decision [10].

In the decision-making process, the following phases are most often applied:

(1) Forming a decision-making group
(2) Identification of options
(3) Identification of attributes
(4) Decision-knowledge acquisition
(5) Analysis and evaluation of options
(6) Explanation of results
(7) Implementation of a decision

The above order of phases is not necessarily fixed. Phases are interrelated and can be iteratively repeated, but they should not be overlooked because of their importance for systematic knowledge acquisition and processing. Following the phases helps mainly to reduce the possibility of overlooking important information.

2.1 Forming a decision-making group

Most often, decision-making is a team task. Of course, there are cases when we have to decide on our own or someone else makes the final decision. Even in these cases a team is useful because more information can be gathered and verified.

Our goal is to decide on the basis of an information picture, as completely as possible. This reduces the possibility of overlooking important facts and, consequently, of making a wrong decision. Therefore, the formation of an appropriate decision-making group is very important. In the group, representatives of all the segments influenced by the decision should participate. They should know their segments and be motivated to reach a quality decision. During the decision-making process, they should learn more about the problem and be able to coordinate their individual or segmental goals with other members of the group. Their role is invaluable in justification of decisions and in implementation of a chosen option, e.g. new technology, plant location, or assignment of a new employee.

Regarding effectiveness of the group, it is helpful to have a decision analyst who conducts the work of the group. The analyst should come from outside the environment influenced by the decision.

2.2 Identification of options

Options are possible decisions from which the best has to be chosen. How they can be identified or generated? Sometimes it is simple, because they are offered by suppliers or vendors. The problem becomes more difficult when options have to be generated by the decision-making group according to the company's development strategy and the existing possibilities. In this process, it is most important not to forget to take into account any sensible option.

Following practical experience, options should only be identified in this phase. A deeper analysis is not recommended, because it may influence attribute and decision knowledge elicitation.

2.3 Identification of attributes

In this phase, a set of criteria for describing options, e.g. technical features, security, maintenance etc., has to be defined. Attributes should be decomposed to the level of being measured or estimated for each option. Attributes have to be semantically grouped. Possible attribute values (domains) should also be defined. For example, security can be "unacceptable", "acceptable", "good" or "excellent", or can be represented using a numerical scale from 1 to 5 [10,14].

Identification of attributes is usually very demanding and creative work. It requires a good knowledge of the problem and its environment.

2.4 Decision knowledge acquisition

Elicitation of so-called preferences is taking place in this phase. Preferences define which attributes or their values are more desirable than others. The influence of separate attribute values on the overall utility also has to be acquired. This is a so-called aggregation of partial to final utilities, which is usually expressed in terms of arithmetical or logical functions [3,5,7,10].

There is an important question to be asked about the appropriateness of an aggregation function. Does it really express our preference knowledge or is it a prescribed fact, which is valid only on certain intervals of attribute values?

2.5 Analysis and evaluation of options

Every alternative is described with values of attributes. For this description, options have to be carefully studied. Later on, the overall utility of each option is obtained on the basis of decision knowledge gathered in the previous phase.

The options can be ranked according to the overall utility value.

It usually happens that overall utility is a single number. In this case, such a value can be doubtful, especially when two options have similar values. To compare two options, more information is needed. Comparison should take place along partial values where differences are the most significant.

2.6 Explanation of results

Individual overall utility values or differences between two values is only a relative measure which should not be sufficient for a decision. If, for example, an option got 72 points on the scale between 0 to 100, and the next worse option got 68, then the difference of 4 points is not enough to justify the decision. Reasons for such a difference should be found and verified.

This is not only important for an appropriate decision, but also indicates possible weak points of the chosen option, which may convert into negative arguments if the conditions of the decision problem and its environment somehow change.

2.7 Implementation of the decision

Usually, this phase is not considered part of the decision-making process. But the real quality of the decision also depends on connections between this and previous phases of decision-making. This is the phase of realisation of the chosen option, which has to be monitored along with the goals and decision-knowledge. Changes always occur. If they influence our decision, it is helpful to repeat some of the previous phases and maybe reduce the possibility of implementing the decision incorrectly.

3. AN EXTENDED SPREADSHEET METHOD

The method will be explained on a practical example of employee selection. The first and the second phases mentioned above are decision-situation dependent and we will therefore start with the third phase, identification of decision attributes.

We wish to employ the best possible people. In this sense, the appropriate parameters are defined, such as: formal education, knowledge of foreign languages, working experience, management abilities, etc. To the attributes, possible values are assigned and put into a spreadsheet form (Tab. 1).

Tab. 1. A spreadsheet with some attributes and their values for the employee selection problem; shaded region represents acceptable attribute values.

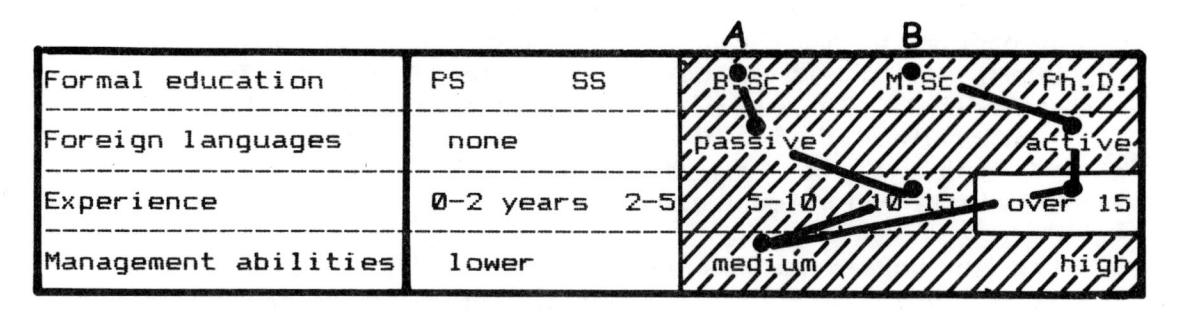

Formal education	PS	SS	B.Sc.	M.Sc.	Ph.D.
Foreign languages	none		passive		active
Experience	0-2 years	2-5	5-10	10-15	over 15
Management abilities	lower		medium		high

Next, the fourth phase deals with knowledge acquisition. In the frame of the spreadsheet method, the first step is to define attributes' weights. The more important attributes get higher weights and therefore become more influential. The next step in knowledge acquisition is to define a region of acceptable values, i.e. shadowed region in Tab. 1. This knowledge is usually reached by discussions in a decision group.

Analysis and evaluation of options (phase 5) begins with assigning attribute values for every employee candidate separately, e.g., candidate A: formal education = B.Sc., foreign language = passive, experience = 10-15 years and management abilities = medium; candidate B: formal education = M.Sc., foreign language = active, experience = over 15 years and management abilities = medium. Each candidate can be plotted in the spreadsheet, as indicated on Tab. 1.

Some values of the attributes are easily determined, e.g. on the basis of application documents, others have to be estimated by lower or higher knowledge of the candidates (interviewing, testing, etc.).

And what is the role of the computer in this process? An appropriate computer program can be helpful. Instead of writing the table on paper, it can be created and updated on a screen. The program can also help in documentation of all actions and facts, which were taken into account. Candidates are plotted on the screen. On the basis of attributes' values and the acceptable region of values, the computer calculates their overall utilities and suggests their ranked list. Once the number of options (candidates) is greater than can fit reasonably on the screen, they can be plotted sequentially or mutually compared, but there is no significant limitation regarding the number of options for obtaining the ranked list.

The advantage of information technology is especially evident in phase 6, which involves explanation of evaluation results. Values of attributes can be easily changed, which gives an opportunity to experiment and observe influences of these changes on the changes of the overall utility. This experimenting is especially encouraged by the computer and it helps in thinking creatively about values, their validity and interconnection among attributes. This is very significant in reaching higher quality decision-making.

Let us illustrate this with the above example. The first
evaluation result for our candidate A is "acceptable", while
for B is "unacceptable". But the problem is not so
"mechanically" simple. Candidate B was given higher values
according to the first two attributes, but his experience
(age?) do not fit to our minimal requirements. From the
spreadsheet (Tab. 1) it is obvious that candidate B has to be
additionally studied to find out whether his "Experience" can
or can not be compensated by his formal education and
knowledge of foreign languages.

The last phase, implementation of the decision, is also very
much context dependent. Generally, the employed person can be
carefully observed regarding his critical points. For example,
candidate A can be sent to a course for improving his foreign
language or can be employed in a position where certain lower
values of attributes (e.g. management abilities) are not too
important.

The extended spreadsheet method can also be used without a
computer. But if we have available at least a personal
computer, some of the burdens of the method can be transferred
to it. We would like to emphasize that this is not a simple
transfer of the work, but that it allows some activities, like
experimenting, which we are certainly not going to be able to
do without. In particular experimenting with options and their
values means a new quality in supporting our cognitive process
in decision-making.

4. DECMAK: AN EXPERT SYSTEM GENERATOR APPROACH

The extended spreadsheet approach may be adequate for
situations where the number of attributes is relatively
limited, e.g. up to ten. If there exist more parameters,
further structure is desired and the spreadsheet can become an
inappropriate representation. In these cases, identified
attributes are usually organized in a tree-like structure,
e.g. Fig. 1. Such a tree is subjective regarding a decision
problem and decision group. Therefore, it can be taken only as
a tool to support our thinking in a given decision situation.
If a decision problem or its environment changes, the tree of
attributes, in general, also changes.

In the tree in Fig. 1, the overall employee's utility consists
of the three subtrees, describing "education", "personal
characteristics", and "others". "Education" is in turn
described in terms of "formal education", "foreign language",
and "experience". "Formal education" is further divided into
obtained educational "degree" and "speciality". "Foreign
language" and "experience" can also be decomposed into
different languages, and experiences in different domains,
respectively.

The remaining two subtrees, "personal characteristics" and
"other characteristics", are even more open for further
structuring. A subtree can be abandoned or extended. Some
practical advice for these cases is to introduce such leaves

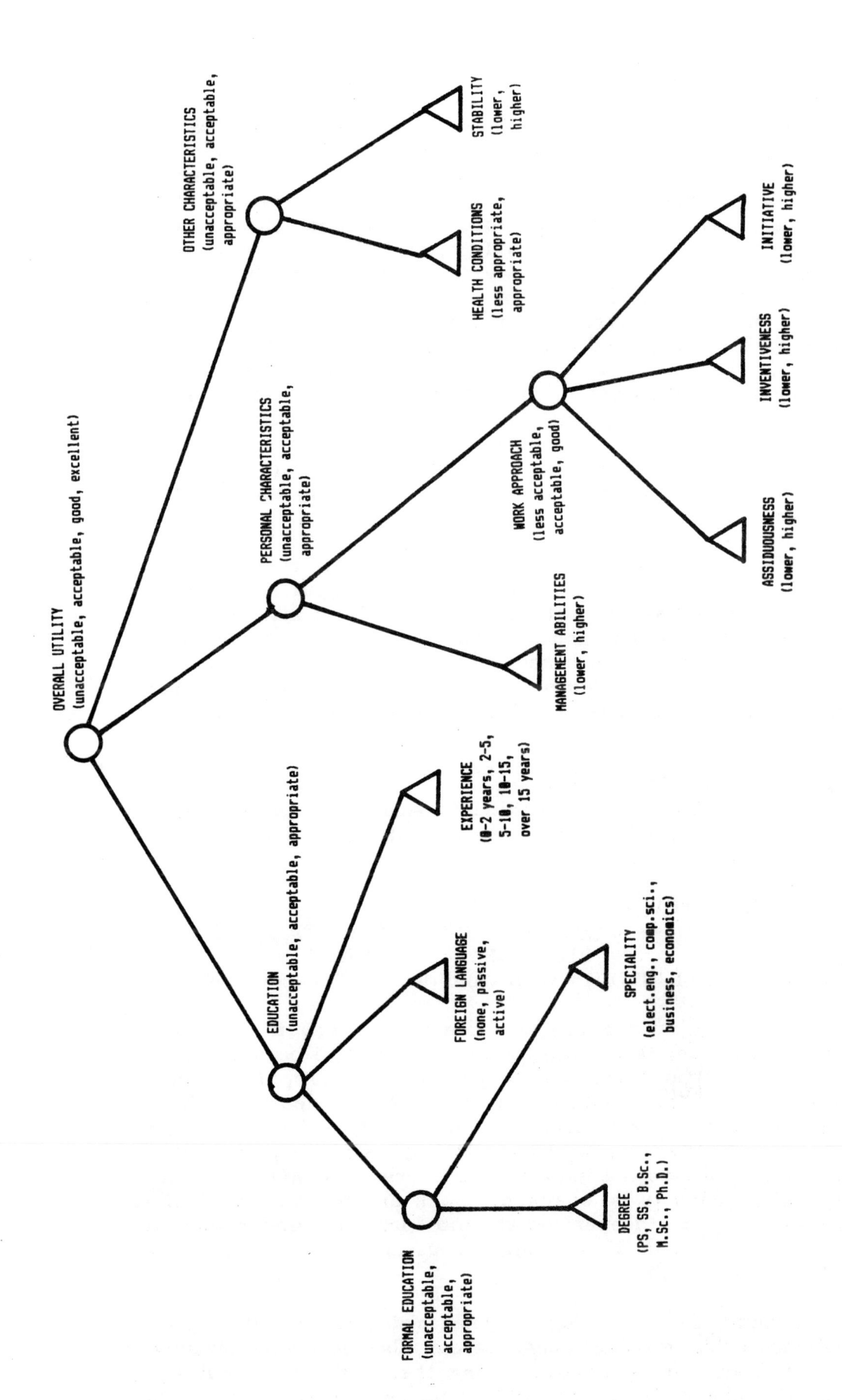

Fig. 1: An example of tree of attributes for employee selection. Attributes' domains are in parenthesis.

in the tree which can be measurable or at least estimable using available data about options. For example, if there is no data about "management abilities" of the candidate, such a leaf is not of real practical value and may be discarded.

Treating tree-structured attributes manually can be rather difficult. The DECMAK computer program, which was developed in collaboration between J. Stefan Institute, Ljubljana, and School of Organisational Sciences, Kranj, Yugoslavia, and Queen Mary College, London, supports such work [2]. According to this program, a corresponding organizational method was developed. It is based on an expert system approach, where a decision expert, on the base of his knowledge and an active dialogue with the system, builds a knowledge base for evaluation of options and explanation of decisions [3,6,8].

In the phase of attribute identification, where a tree, as in Fig. 1 is constructed, the decison-maker or decision-making group mainly work on the base of their own experiences and creativity. A decision analyst can significantly help in this work. The help of the computer is only in editing the tree and in documentation.

During decision-knowledge elicitation (phase 4), the role of DECMAK computer support becomes more significant. Decision knowledge describes the influence of lower-level attributes on the attributes of higher nodes of the tree, up to the overall utility. The description consists of logical rules, which specify higher-level values on the basis of some chosen combination of lower-level attribute values. The following are examples of two logical rules, concerning the tree in Fig. 1:

(1) If   EDUCATION is "adequate",
          PERSONAL CHARACTERISTICS are "appropriate", and
          OTHER CHARACTERISTICS are "acceptable",
   then OVERALL UTILITY of a candidate is "acceptable".

(2) If   EDUCATION is "unacceptable",
        regardless of PERSONAL CHARACTERISTICS and
                    OTHER CHARACTERISTICS,
  then OVERALL UTILITY of a candidate is "unacceptable".

Such rules are defined in a decision-making group. For each node of the tree, a set of chosen rules has to be specified. This decision knowledge is entered into the computer, which then adds the missing rules in a dialogue with decison-makers. For example, Tab. 2 is constructed. The users have to verify computer-generated rules. Why? It is possible that computer-generated rules do not express the users' opinion. In this case, they have to be changed. Such an overview of logical rules may give a deeper insight into problem understanding, which can result in discovering errors or even changing the decision-makers' minds.

The computer facilitates logical-rule maintenance. It asks questions about missing rules. It can also generate missing rules and ask for approval. During the elicitation of rules, it can also check consistency of the users' preferences.

EDUCATION	PERSONAL CHAR.	OTHER CHAR.	OVERALL UTILITY
50%	30%	20%	
<=acceptable — unacceptable —	<=acceptable — — unacceptable	— unacceptable — —	unacceptable unacceptable unacceptable unacceptable
acceptable appropriate	appropriate acceptable	>=acceptable >=acceptable	acceptable acceptable
appropriate	appropriate	acceptable	good
appropriate	appropriate	appropriate	excellent

Tab. 2: Table of logical rules for aggregation of partial utilities about EDUCATION, PERSONAL and OTHER CHARACTERISTICS into OVERALL UTILITY of a candidate.

How can Tab. 2 be read? Percentages below the attributes' names denote their relative importance regarding the final value. Their role is in initialisation of human thinking in the beginning of elicitation of rules. The percentages can also be used in the process of generating new rules. At the end, new percentages can be calculated out of rules and for verification purposes compared with initially stated percentages.

Rules in Tab. 2 are sorted according to ascending values of the overall utility. In the first part, there are rules specifying the "unacceptable" final value. The rule in the first line can be read as follows:

If   EDUCATION is lower than or equal to "acceptable", and
      PERSONAL CHARACTERISTICS are
             lower than or equal to "acceptable", and
   regardless of OTHER CHARACTERISTICS,
then OVERALL UTILITY of the candidate is "unacceptable".

The sign "_" in the table means "any value".

For the tree in Fig. 1, there are six similar tables, each for one node in the tree. With these tables an aggregation function is specified. They represent decision knowledge of a decision group in a given situation. The knowledge base can be easily edited, if necessary.

Evaluation of options (phase 5), in our case evaluation of employee applicants, proceeds as follows. Each candidate is described by values of attributes on the leaves of the tree (Fig. 1). The descriptions are entered into the computer, which on the basis of the tree-structure and the tables evaluates them in a bottom-up manner. The final value obtained is of course the most important base for a final decision. But a more elaborate analysis is also possible by inspecting partial values in the nodes of the tree (e.g. EDUCATION, FORMAL EDUCATION, WORK APPROACH, and others). By the aid of the DECMAK program, comparison of candidates regarding their relative advantages and an aggregated explanation of results can also be provided. This already belongs to phase 6, the explanation of results.

In multiple option cases, with, for example, several hundred options, the same approach can be used. At the end, options can be ranked according to the final value they obtained. But equally detailed analysis of each option can be very time consuming and unnecessary. A two or more step approach can give significantly better results. It consists of first evaluation options on the basis of only a few, but significant attributes. This provides a kind of "sieve", which gives a set of options for further, more detailed treatment, using an extended set of attributes. In each step, a separate knowledge base is used. Some steps can even be replaced by traditional methods, based on aggregation formulas [13].

The advantages of the computer support are the following. All candidates are treated equally according to the same criteria. The main feature is explanation of results which consists of the following actions:

1. explanation of the process of evaluation on the basis of rules used,
2. comparison of options,
3. identification of good and bad points of options.

It can be said that a decision-making group builds its own expert system with a decision (preference) knowledge-base. The process of knowledge-base construction encourages learning and data acquisition in the decision-making group. When it is constructed, it gives a systematic overview on the decision process and therefore reduces the possibility of making a wrong decision.

5. CONCLUSION

How can one decide on the most appropriate decision-making method? What are the goals of this selection? Which are the attributes to evaluate decision-methods and their computer support? At a first glance, answers seem to be clear. We want decision-making that leads to the best decision. Unfortunately, the quality of the decision can usually be measured when the decision process is already over. If the decision was right or wrong, only its implementation and "life" could tell. It is difficult to know what would have happened if we had decided differently. Unaccepted options are usually "dead" and they can not be compared with the exisiting, realised one.

These facts lead us to the goals, which have to be stated during the decision making process itself. For example, one of these goals is to reach the justifiable decision. Justification in discussion reduces the possibility of a wrong decision. An argued decision can be reached with a critical comparative analysis of all options, based on an appropriate information picture. Such a picture can be achieved with more or less tedious work. Therefore, one of the goals is also the quality of work during the decision-making. It can be expressed by the time needed for a decision, engagement of the people involved and their motivation. Of course, the price of the decision-making process also has to be known, in spite of the fact that the price of the process is usually comparatively low with regard to the investment we are deciding on.

As we can see, the point is to organise a process which is mainly information-driven. This leads to the critical evaluation of the use of information technology. The advantages of the computer itself, which are complementary to the advantages of a human being, have to be properly used. The role of the computer is not only in reducing a total amount of human work, but also in supporting humans' creative work. How? With an appropriate representation of information, e.g. graphics, rules, tree-structure and others, which best fit to a real situation. The representation should also encourage creative thinking and generate new ideas. Different views on the same information are desired.

The DECMAK method, which is an expert system method, leads to explicit expert knowledge about a decision-making process [3,4,6]. This knowledge can be displayed in different ways. In the phase of knowledge acquisition, it is usually realised that there are many more rules and conclusions than expected. So, our decision knowledge is richer, the supporting argument is better founded and therefore there is the higher possibility of a better decision. But at the end we have to know that the computer may be very helpful in this process, but it does not make a decision - it is the human being, who makes it.

REFERENCES

[1] Alter, S., Decision Support Systems: Current Practice and Continuing Challenges (Addision Wesley, 1980).

[2] Bohanec, M., Efstathiou, J., Rajkovic, V., Rule-based Decision Support Software: User's Manual V 1.0 (J. Stefan Institute, Ljubljan, Internal Report DP-3192, 1983).

[3] Bohanec, M., Bratko, I., Rajkovic, V., An Expert System for Decision Making, in Processes and Tools for Decision Support, ed. H.G. Sol (North Holland, 1983).

[4] Coombs, M., Alty, J., Expert Systems: An Alternative Paradigm, Int. J. Man-Machine Studies 20 (1984), 21-43.

[5] Dujmovic, J.J., The Preference Scoring Method for Decision Making, Informatica, vol. 1, no. 2 (1977), 26-34.

[6] Efstathiou, J., Rajkovic, V., Multiattribute Decision Making Using a Fuzzy Heuristic Approach, IEEE Transactions on Systems, Man and Cybernetics, SMC-9 (1979), 326-333.

[7] Fox, J., Formal and Knowledge-based Methods in Decision Technology, in Proceedings of the 9th Conf. on Subjective Probability, Utility and Decision Making, Groningen, 1983.

[8] Hawgood, J., The ABACON Chart - A Visual Aid to Benefit Assesment, Automation Benefit Appraisal Consultant Limited report, Durham (1977).

[9] Holroyd, P., Mallory, G., Price, D.H.R., Sharp, J.A., Developing Expert Systems for Management Applications, Int. J. of Mgm. Sc. 13 (1985), 1-11.

[10] Keeney, L.R., Raiffa, H., Decisions with Multiple Objectives: Preferences and Value Tradeoffs, (John Wiley & Sons, 1976).

[11] Michie, D., (ed.) Expert Systems in the Microelectronic Age (Edinburgh University Press, 1979).

[12] Rajkovic, V., Bohanec, M., A Cybernetic Model for Computer-Aided Decision Making, Proc. 9th Int. Congress on Cybernetics, Namur (1980).

[13] Rajkovic, V., Bohanec, M., Multiple Options Ranking: A Nursery School Example in Strategic Decision Support: (Eds.: Humphries, P., Larichev, O., Vari, A., Vacesenyi, J.), IIASA publication (in preparation).

[14] Zadeh, L.A., The Concept of a Linguistic Variable and its Application to Approximate Reasoning- I, II, III, Information Sciences, 8 and 9 (1975), 199-251, 301-357, 43-80.

6 Effective Decision-Making

Jimmy Algie and William Foster
Brunel University, London

INTRODUCTION: DECISION TECHNOLOGY

Managers have mainly used micro-computer programs to handle and communicate known data and information more efficiently. However, information is only valuable if it actually helps people make more effective decisions within the time they have available to them and no managers ever have enough time.

So managers are now moving beyond information technology to decision technology - to programs which help managers make more effective decisions, plans and evaluations faster, no matter what their kind of work [1], [2], [3].

How managers are using decision technology is here illustrated in an application of three - Priorities, the Budget Priority System (BPS), and the Work Priority System (WPS). These are at once decision insight systems, which enhance managers' skills and understanding, and decision advice systems, which produce reliable individual and team decisions from managers' initally rough views and data [4], [5].

Essentially, Priorities produces from managers' views on any issue - reliable individual or team decisions, priorities, and objectives, with reliability checks and decision standards on individual and team thinking. It is referred to hereafter as the decision program. BPS and WPS produce plans, budgets, and resource allocations, and evaluate performance and results from managers' initial views, estimates and data [6], [7], [8]. These are hereafter referred to as the resource program, since they are identical except that BPS deals in money, while WPS deals in time. Managers' systematic use of these programs in a multi-national corporation is here described.

A CORPORATE APPLICATION

A multi-national corporation required one of its major Divisions, which develops manufactures and sells industrial products, to move back into profit and also expand into new markets with new products.

The organisation development (OD) manager, charged with coordinating a 2-day Divisional strategy workshop for senior managers, discovered Priorities when reviewing new management techniques.

INDIVIDUAL DECISIONS BY PRIORITIES

The OD manager first tried the decision program himself as a self-management tool, using it for half an hour to prioritise his own work (Table 1). From his initial views, the program produced his valid priorities and objectives, together with his decision standard, and pinpointed his inconsistencies.

He listed on program the main activities on his current agenda (under Activities, Table 1A). He went quickly through a judgement exercise on program, judging how much more important was one option versus another, pair by pair. The decision program calculated his priority weight from each exercise, but also informed him he had not achieved an acceptable decision standard overall.

Inconsistencies

The program pinpointed several significant illogicalities in his judgement. For example, he had judged his current work on management recruitment more important than his work on industrial relations, which in turn he judged more important than his work on industrial management relations, which in turn he judged more important than his work on management services. Yet in the same exercise, he also judged management services to warrant higher priority than industrial relations.

He revised his judgements exercise on program to remove his main inconsistencies. He found he had revised his priorities (under Priorities, Table 1A), and also achieved an acceptable decision standard (under Decision Standard, Table 1A)

Specific Projects

Taking his top priority activities, "organisation development", the OD manager repeated the exercise, this time focussing on the five main organisational development projects which comprised his organisational development work (under Table 1B). Though he achieved an acceptable decision standard on this second exercise, he needed to clarify the objectives underlying his project priorities. He repeated the exercise, focussing now on his objectives (Table 1C). He re-assessed his development projects in terms of the program produced by his organisational development priorities in the light of his objectives and their weighting (Table 1B).

This led him to prioritise longer-term Divisional training needs and ways of meeting them. He used the program to obtain the views of a sample of managers on their training needs, and piece together a participatively-agreed training plan schedule. He also tried the method out on one of the regular in-house training courses for middle managers.

MANAGEMENT PLANNING BY PRIORITIES

Having successfully piloted the method this way, the OD manager felt confident enough to use the decision program with senior managers on the Divisional strategy workshop.

The OD manager opened the Divisional strategy workshop with a 30-minute computer-assisted decision exercise, in which each senior manager tackled and resolved his most pressing individual problem (though some had never touched a computer before). The exercise was designed to clear their minds of pressing immediate issues to address a longer-term Divisional strategy. (An exercise on one of the manager's problems is illustrated in Table 2).

The senior managers established seven project groups to produce and agree key aspects of Divisional strategy - Market Potential, New Products, R & D emphasis, Services Expansion, Organisation Re-design, Accommodation, and Information Technology (IT) Development.

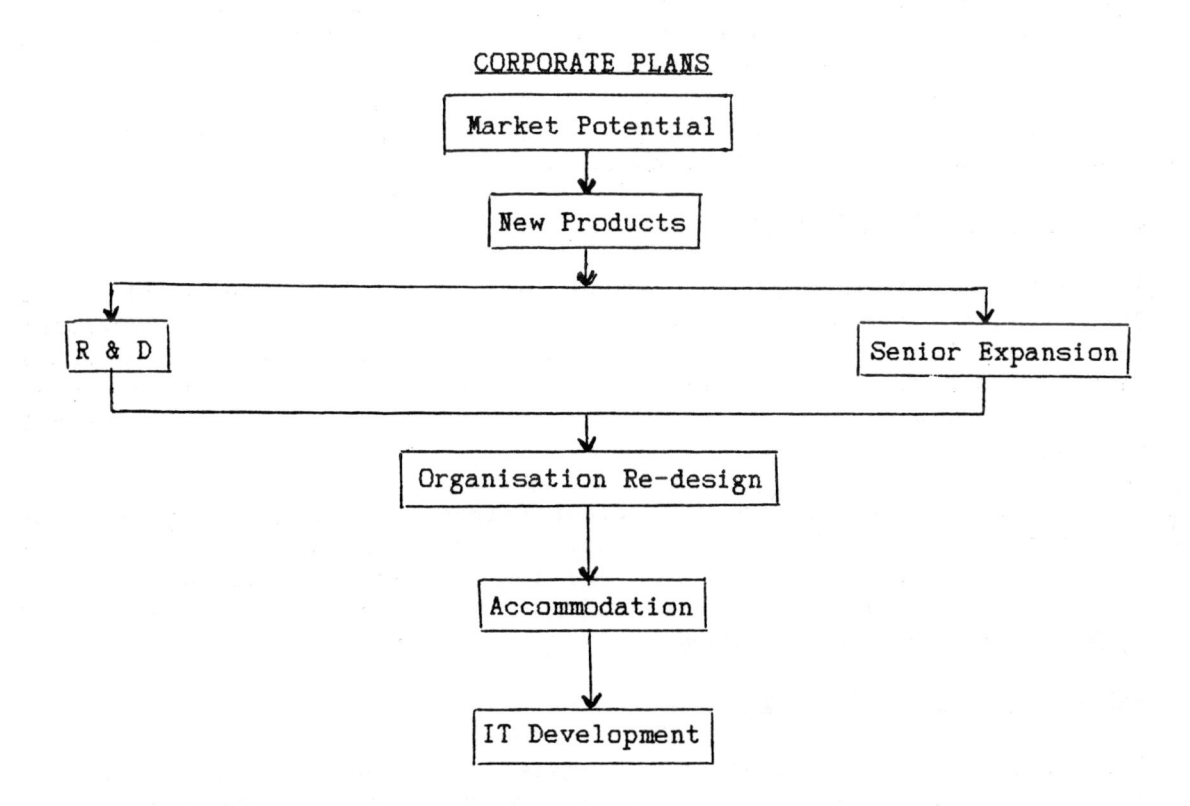

CORPORATE PLANS

```
         Market Potential
                ↓
          New Products
                ↓
     ┌──────────┼──────────┐
     ↓                     ↓
   R & D              Senior Expansion
     │                     │
     └──────────┬──────────┘
                ↓
       Organisation Re-design
                ↓
          Accommodation
                ↓
         IT Development
```

The managers had in the past been sceptical about comprehensive rational planning. They had found it "too time-consuming", and "frankly it left us with less room for opportunistic manoeuvre". But they found rational planning became a more practical option with decision technology because "it facilitates fast decisions on complex issues without loss of quality". Towards the end of the workshop, they used the program to agree "provisional guidelines" (i.e. their objectives and criteria) for Divisional strategy plans.

As part of the follow-up work, the OD and Training section made themselves available to demonstrate the decision program and to give managers on the project groups personal tuition in its use. In the event, most managers found themselves able to run the program on their own with the occasional phone call mainly for reassurance.

NEW PRODUCT DECISIONS

The New Products project group immediately shut themselves away with the decision program for a day to hammer out and agree their proposed new product strategy (Table 3). They were able to resolve and move beyond some quite fundamental conflicts between Divisional marketeers, financiers, and scientists of different disciplines. "We felt we'd done a year's work in a day" the New Products group chairman commented. Their recommendations on new product development priorities were afterwards accepted as they stood by the Divisional senior management, and became the centrepiece of the new Divisional strategy. Their planning project provided the Division with a paradigm example for subsequent use and take-up of the decision program by the other project groups (and indeed by individual managers and scientists throughout the Division on everyday issues arising).

Encouraged by the New Products plan, the other project groups used the decision program to carry through their tasks.

SERVICE EXPANSION DECISIONS

The Service Expansion project group were particularly relieved to be able to present an agreed plan, which resolved long-simmering sectional conflicts after two half-hour group sessions with the decision program spread over a month (Table 4). Their plan was also accepted by senior management with minimal amendments as a core feature of the Divisional strategy.

Whereas the New Products project group primarily used the program as a decision insight tool to help resolve some fundamental problems, the Service Expansion project group used the program as a decision advice tool to work through internal conflicts to converge towards a set of agreed decisions and priorities.

MARKET POTENTIAL DECISIONS

The Market Potential project group agreed market strategies for the two new products the New Product group recommended for immediate launch, and in doing so found they had to specify a more coherent overall market strategy for existing and new company products. They used the program in a series of group sessions over several months, revising their priorities and objectives between times in the light of information and senior management discussions. (They also used the decision program in conjunction with various quantitative forecasting techniques to produce market scenarios for the next decade).

R & D DECISIONS

The R & D project group produced an R & D orientation plan in an hour with the program, then delegated various specific R & D issues to appropriate specialist sections (in which some used decision programs, others did not need to). The R & D project group summarised their findings for the divisional strategy report, but this work continued intermittently within sections thereafter with a particular focus on evaluation of R & D projects.

ORGANISATION RE-DESIGN DECISIONS

The Organisation Re-design project group used the program to open up the range of structural options they were willing to consider and to clarify their objectives for the new structure (Table 5). They administered the method as an attitude survey to about 50 managers and scientists (again over a month's period). The Organisation project group were able to produce their recommendations on structure, secure in the knowledge of what staff would support, though these recommendations were further developed and revised by senior management in the light of wider company considerations.

ACCOMMODATION DECISIONS

The Accommodation project group reacted against their senior managers' enthusiasm for decision programs. It turned out that a caucus of managers had previously completed a revised accommodation plan for site expansion, for which they had already canvassed wide support and won the backing of a relevant senior manager. They used the decision program to present their pre-decided plan in an analogous form to the other project group reports, making one significant change to their plan in so doing (Table 6). But accommodation planning was never really uncoupled from international organisational politics in the Division. (This contrasts with experience in other companies where decision programs have been successfully used for relocation planning for example).

INFORMATION TECHNOLOGY DECISIONS

The work of the Information Technology (IT) project group was not immediately critical to the Divisional development strategy. However, the group used the program to develop the first Divisional IT strategy (Table 7), produced some immediate decisions on some long-deferred hardware and software decisions, modified Divisional IT training, and evolved a plan and procedure for managing and developing IT throughout the Division.

EXPERIENCE OF DECISION TECHNOLOGY

The managers involved in the various projects groups often worked through several rounds of the decision program, both individually to achieve consistent decisions, and as a group to achieve agreed decisions.

Some treated the program rather mechanically, as a device for simply and quickly recording and double-checking their views. Others used it to provide a self-imposed discipline for rational decision-making. Others used it to question their prejudices, explore and develop their thinking, and attain new insights and a wider vision.

In some groups, the decision program had the effect of streamlining their meetings, with most of the work completed on program in advance of or sometimes instead of face-to-face encounters. Knowing that if time ran out they could fall back on a trial group decision evolved with the program, in which everyone's views on every aspect were incorporated, managers were more willing to discuss matters more openly in more depth. They found themselves willing to raise significant points which might otherwise delay everything, without endlessly repeating the same arguments in different words. They also found the decision program enabled highly sensitive points to be confronted head-on and dealt with more rationally. Managers emerged more committed to agreed specific action, with a clearer understanding of the reasons for decisions (and of others' viewpoints).

The senior management group modified the individual project group plans to align them more coherently, using the program rather unsystematically to help them do this. They then compiled a comprehensive Divisional strategy report and agreement.

The benefits managers and scientists in the Division gained from using this decision technology varied depending on their role and style.

Senior managers pointed to its use for canvassing people's views, coordination and control, and for resolving conflicts. Middle managers by contrast tended to say of the decision program that it - "makes the complex simple", "demonstrates your points", "double-checks decisions", "gets commitment". They stressed the use of the decision program as an easy, convenient, and above all fast way of tackling immediate issues. Off-line advisors (management services, trainers, etc.) placed more emphasis on the use of the decision program as a means of achieving more rational decision-making, opening up thinking, and developing managers' skills.

The point most commonly made was that a decision program can help managers achieve a _quick_ initial decision which encapsulates their thinking and experience, using the decision standards and reliability checks as a check on illogicalities and conflicts. After a 20-minute run through, the inconsistencies and conflicts pinpointed by the program provided the focus for any further more detailed analysis and re-modelling necessary.

This contrasted with the procedure used by two or three managers, using various other data-driven methods. They undertook elaborate analysis and modelling of the issues before embarking on the main decision process. This tended to distort their fundamental experience, understanding, and sense of the whole context of the issue on hand, causing their judgements to be registered as unacceptably inconsistent on the decision standard when they came to the point of decision. They then had to use the decision program to regain a reliable coherent approach to the issue. Whereas those who had "jumped in", using the program to reach "an initial base-line decision" first, were then able to evolve and refine their decisions in any subsequent round of computer-assisted decision-making. This is not to down-play the use of the decision program for analytic and conceptual modelling, but to report what has been observed as an effective approach to such analysis in practice, which also squares with many managers' predilictions.

Overall, managers in the Division gained agreement and commitment on a coherent set of explicit guidelines. (Several emphasised that understanding had also been achieved in the process on less tangible motivations and concerns which were hitherto implicit, even semi-conscious).

ALLOCATING RESOURCES

However, many of the managers thought there was something missing:

"We've agreed the direction, but are we acting and spending accordingly?"

"How do the priorities and objectives we've agreed translate into staffing, time and money?"

"Are we mobilising our resources appropriately?"

Such questions led naturally to the company's use of the a resource program to plan and monitor their allocation of time and money to achieve their priorities. They used the program to allocate available resources appropriately across the various parts of their Divisional strategy - market potential, new products, R & D, service expansion, organisation re-design, accommodation, IT development.

Each key manager translated into resource allocations that part of the strategy for which they are accountable, calling upon colleagues to help them where they thought fit. The assistant to the senior management group then integrated the proposed allocations into a coherent company plan.

The process can be illustrated in terms of one part of the overall strategy - the OD Manager's allocation of financial resources and staff time across his five development projects. He had agreed priorities between the projects earlier (Table 1B).

RESOURCE PLANNING AND BUDGETING

The OD manager used the resource program to plan (and subsequently evaluate) the financial allocation for his five development projects over a six month period. From his and his team's views, estimates and data (Table 8A), the program produced their resource plan (Table 8B), and subsequently their resource evaluation (Tables 9A-B).

Plan Data

The OD manager's secretary collected and typed in his and his team's basic views, estimates and data on their organisation development plan (under Projects in Table 8A). His secretary typed in the previously agreed project priorities (from Table 1B), entering these in the appropriate column of the resource allocation program (under Planned Priorities, Table 8A).

The OD manager and his team estimated the *costings* and *demand* for each project (under Planned Unit Times & Demands, Table 8A). They made their estimates in terms of schemes required within each project. They decided they would give 34.7% *emphasis* to their own priorities, and 65.3% emphasis to external demands on them for completed projects (under Emphasis, Table 8A). They noted the absolute *constraints* on them (under Minimum and Maximum, Table 8A). These constraints indicated the maximum they *had* to achieve on each project no matter what, and the most they could possibly achieve on each project, within the £840,000 *total available money* for the organisation development plan over the period October, 1985 to April, 1986.

Plan

From the managers' rough views and data, the program produced their resource plan (Table 8B). This showed that they could handle some of the projects in whole or part within the available budget of £840,000 (under Handle, Table 8B). They could complete the highest priority projects B and D for example, which they had to do anyway. But they could not complete all the projects required (shown under Postpone, Table 8B). They would have to postpone parts of projects C, A and E - one whole scheme and nearly half of another (1.4) related to project C, for example, would have to be postponed unless more cash for organisation development was forthcoming.

Their plan also gave them expenditure targets (under Allocation, Table 8B), and the budget/s that would be required to complete all the projects fully (under Required Money, Table 8B). They were not at this point given any increase in budget, but were sanctioned to proceed according to their planned project targets within the existing budget in the full recognition of what could not be achieved within the period.

Evaluation Data

Half way through the plan, in January 1986, the OD Manager evaluated progress on the development projects. He recorded the resource evaluation data (Table 9A).

He had monitored what work had actually been achieved (under Handled, Table 9A) within the total budget thus far spent of £380,000. He also noted that senior management was demanding an additional scheme under project D (which was reflected in Demand, Table 9A). To the best of his knowledge, they were keeping to their planned priorities and unit costs, though he was not sure.

Evaluation

From this data, the program produced an evaluation of the section's work on organisation development (Table 9B). This showed the implications of what the section had achieved thus far (as of January, 1986).

The program indicated the <u>implied priorities and costings</u> implicit in what the section had actually achieved (under Priorities, and Unit Costs, Table 9B). The implied priorities diverged quite significantly from the priorities they had originally planned, though the unit costs did not dramatically diverge (Table 9C).

The evaluation showed the implied financial expenditures for the period so far (under Implied Allocation, Table 9B). This could be used for re-planning the projects and expenditure on them for the next period. The money required to complete all the projects fully was recorded in the light of the revised costs (under Required Costs, Table 9B). The implied <u>emphasis</u> remained as planned.

WORK ALLOCATION

The OD Manager then used the resource program to allocate (and subsequently evaluate) the work on his five development projects in terms of time (Tables 10 and 11). The process was identical, except that the resource allocated (and subsequently evaluated) was staff <u>time</u> (rather than money).

AN INTEGRATED STRATEGY PLAN

Each manager carried out similar resource exercises on the part of the strategy for which they were accountable. This ensured that allocations of financial and staff resources aligned and reflected the agreed priorities - which is a rare achievement it turns out for any manager making any complex plan without using computer-assisted resource programs.

An assistant to the senior management team used the resource priorities to incorporate all the resource allocation plans into one coherent overall strategy. The senior management group made no significant changes to this strategy plan until the results of the evaluations came through in January, 1986. The evaluations led them to significantly modify their priorities and other aspects of the plan in the light of what was and was not achievable in practice.

This is by no means unusual. Even after managers have used a resource program to ensure their planned allocations align with their priorities, their subsequent practice tends to deviate from plan if their plans are too ambitious or take insufficient account of reality. They typically use the evaluation feature of resource programs to keep their work on course through the hurly-burly of everyday working life, or to adapt their plans to the realities of working life.

The company used the computer-assisted decision and resource programs to agree a Divisional strategy (in terms of weighted objectives and priorities) to translate the strategy into appropriate allocations of finance and time, and subsequently to evaluate the implementation of the strategy. In respect of the Divisional strategy, they had coherently and consistently aligned their decisions, priorities, objectives, financial allocations, time allocations, and their practice.

Brunel research shows that on most complex issues managers' decisions tend to contradict their priorities, which in turn contradict their objectives, which contradict their allocations of resource (whether finance or staff time), which in turn contradict what they actually do in practice. (Moreover, individual managers' decisions are often unacceptably inconsistent on validated decision standards, and team decisions often contradict everyone's views). Managers can test these findings for themselves with a brief trial of the decision programs, using the programs thereafter to achieve consistency, coherence, and the best achievable agreement among themselves. Most managers' spend the working days correcting hick-ups downstream which could have been avoided by using decision programs to resolve their inconsistencies, contradictions, conflicts and disagreements at the outset.

Although the programs were seen as particularly helpful in "making the project group tick", the project structure is by no means a necessary condition for using decision programs effectively, nor do they only apply to strategic decision-making. After the Divisional strategy, the programs began to be used by many of the Division's line managers, scientists, and their teams on other matters. They typically use them for critical or fundamental decisions, for multi-disciplinary planning, for cross-sectional coordination, and often for more routine daily problem-solving and conflict-resolution. The OD manager, for example, now uses the program to prioritise and allocate his and his team's work quarterly (and sometimes even daily - "when the going gets rough"). He uses the programs on in-house training courses for middle managers, applying them to the specific topic on hand, and provides any support required by line managers as individuals or teams.

The experience of achieving and implementing a coherent strategy led the senior management group to establish a more systematic accountability system based on these decision and resource programs, in which the quality of management decision-making is evaluated. The narrative of this phase is still unfolding.

CONCLUSION: MANAGEMENT BY DECISION PROGRAMS

This company's use of decision technology illustrates how managers can readily and effectively use decision and resource programs to tackle significant major issues on hand. As was the case here, managers naturally progress to beyond one-off issues in their use of decision technology. They may begin to use decision programs more systematically as tools to agree and evaluate coherent plans on various aspects of company work, and they may come to use such programs to support an integrated planning system, or to facilitate an accountability system in which people are called to account for the quality of their decisions and plans.

This case example is just one particular way one company took up and used this kind of decision technology. It is not unusual in corporates to find the technology used in similar areas of work - company strategy, product evaluation, project planning, investment and allocation decisions, workload management, forecasting and targetting, budgeting, and performance assessment. But organisations take on and use decision programs like *Priorities*, BPS and WPS in many different ways, which reflects the versatility of some of the applications. The *content* of the work may vary, but effective *methods* of decision-making, planning and evaluation are similar across most kinds of work. This allows decision technology to be quite generally applicable in management. The diverse management issues which first made these programs nationally known illustrate the point - the resolution of the miners' strike (by NCB and NUM representatives) [9], improved diagnosis and treatment of child abuse (by the NSPCC) [10], improved team selection (by Test-cricket selectors), and handling government cutbacks by various Local Authorities [11], [12]. What most users agree is that decision programs feel significantly different from one application to the next, depending on the specific issue and the favoured style of the managers involved.

TABLES

The tangible outputs of any one application of a decision program like <u>Priorities</u> are
- option priorities (or probabilities of certain events happening),
- weighted objectives and/or criteria which justify these priorities,
- decision and agreement standards indicating what confidence can be placed in the decisions, and how far they are commonly agreed.

The tables are no mere statistical analysis, but embody worked-through judgements, values and preferences which are meaningful and illuminating to those involved. They are often only achieved after managers have revised their judgements several times in the light of their inconsistencies and conflicts.

The results which follow are <u>samples</u> of what managers produced and agreed using <u>Priorities</u> (together with WPS and BPS in the last tables). Note that some columns do not quite add up to 100.0, owing to rounding to 1 decimal place.

TABLE 1. A MANAGER'S WORK PRIORITIES
1A THE OD ROLE

	ACTIVITIES	PRIORITES (%)
1	Organisation Development	11.8
2	Management Relations	10.4
3	Management Recruitment	9.0
4	Staff Relations	8.7
5=	Management Development	7.6
5=	Management Services	7.6
7=	Staff Development	7.4
7=	Staff Recruitment	7.4
9	Management Deployment	6.2
10	Staff Deployment	5.8
11=	Communications	4.9
11=	Industrial Relations	4.9
11=	Salary Administration	4.9
14	Service Conditions	3.5
	ALL ACTIVITIES	100.0
	DECISION STANDARD	Consistent

1B OD PROJECTS

DEVELOPMENT PROJECTS	PRIORITIES (%)
1 Project B	29.4
2 Project D	26.5
3 Project C	26.5
4 Project A	11.8
5 Project E	5.9
ALL DEVELOPMENT PROJECTS	100.0
DECISION STANDARD	Consistent

1C OD OBJECTIVES

OBJECTIVES	PRIORITIY %
Organisational Effectiveness	50
Organisational Capability	25
Organisational Culture	25
ALL OBJECTIVES	100
DECISION STANDARD	Consistent

TABLE 2. A MANAGER RESOLVES A PROBLEM WITH PRIORITIES

HOW TO HANDLE LOW PERFORMANCE STAFF

OPTIONS	PRIORITIES (%)
1 Counselling Out	15.8
2 Dismissal	13.8
3 Staff Exchange	13.7
4 More Training	12.3
5 Demotion	12.0
6 Tight Supervision	11.7
7 By-passing	11.2
8 Pay Cut	8.5
9 Do Nothing	1.0
ALL OPTIONS	100.0
DECISION STANDARD	Consistent

TABLE 3. NEW PRODUCT STRATEGY

3A POLICY FOR NEW PRODUCT DEVELOPMENT

CRITERIA	PRIORITIES (%)	SUB-CRITERIA
Discoverability	45.0	Precedent, Directness, Speed, Expertise
Testability	31.0	Ease, Resources, Proof, Other Opportunities
Marketability	16.0	Profit, demand, Need, Competition, Saleability
Suitability	8.0	Market Fit, Company Fit, Substitutability
ALL CRITERIA	100.0	
DECISION STANDARD	Consistent	
AGREEMENT	Much	

3B PRODUCT PORTFOLIO

PRODUCTS	1986 PRIORITIES (%)	1994 PRIORITIES (%)
Product A	45.4	21.8
Product B	25.9	11.2
Product C	10.9	11.7
Product D	7.9	11.8
Product E	4.1	1.0
Product F	1.7	14.1
Product G	1.5	0.6
Product H	1.3	5.9
Product I	1.1	9.6
Product J	0.1	0.9
Product K	0.0	8.5
Product L	0.08	2.7
Product M	0.02	0.2
ALL PRODUCTS	100.0	100.0
DECISION STANDARD	Consistent	Consistent
AGREEMENT	Much	Much

TABLE 4. SERVICE EXPANSION STRATEGY

4A. SERVICE EXPANSION PRIORITIES
(IN THE LIGHT OF COMPANY CRITERIA)

CRITERIA (% weight) / SERVICE SECIONS	IDEALLY (10.1)	PRACTICALLY (34.2)	OPTIMISTIC (32.5)	PESSIMISTIC (23.2)	OVERALL PRIORITIES (100.0%)
R & D	30.2	28.0	40.7	14.4	29.2
Admin.	16.1	10.2	10.3	63.8	23.3
Personnel	21.8	31.8	15.6	17.2	22.1
M.S.	27.7	25.7	22.8	3.9	19.1
Accounts	4.2	4.3	10.6	0.8	5.5
ALL SECTIONS	100.0	100.0	100.0	100.0	100.0
DECISION STANDARDS					Consistent
AGREEMENT					Much

4B. SERVICE EXPANSION PRIORITIES
(INITIAL TEAM VIEWS)

MANAGERS (% influence) / SERVICE SECTIONS	M1 (33)	M2 (29)	M3 (24)	M4 (14)	TEAM PRIORITIES (100.0%)
M.S.	52.6	23.7	27.4	9.7	32.2
Accounts	13.5	24.2	19.5	52.7	23.6
Personnel	22.7	30.3	21.1	15.1	23.4
R & D	8.2	9.4	30.6	11.9	14.4
Admin.	3.0	12.4	1.4	10.6	6.4
ALL SECTIONS	100.0	100.0	100.0	100.0	100.0
DECISION STANDARDS					Consistent
AGREEMENT					Much

TABLE 5. SUBDIVISIONAL REORGANISATION
(An attitude survey)

5A ORGANISATIONAL OPTIONS

MAIN ORGANISATION OPTIONS	OVERALL PRIORITY (%)	SENIOR MANAGEMENT PRIORITY (%)	MIDDLE MANAGEMENT PRIORITY (%)	SECTION I PRIORITY (%)	SECTION II PRIORITY (%)	SECTION III PRIORITY (%)	SECTION IV PRIORITY (%)
1 Group Leader Level	13.3	16.9	21.8	12.4	8.8	12.1	7.7
2 Subdivide by Subsection	12.8	6.4	8.5	11.4	16.8	22.3	11.5
3 Subdivide by Discipline	9.7	25.3	3.0	3.6	8.7	8.0	9.6
4 Staff Officer Roles	8.0	5.8	7.1	14.9	10.8	4.1	5.5
5 Cabinet System	7.0	2.5	8.9	7.1	3.2	12.3	7.7
6 Existing Strcuture	6.8	5.3	4.3	9.6	12.2	4.6	4.9
7 Deputy Section Heads	6.7	3.8	6.6	10.3	9.7	4.1	6.1
8 2-Way Partition	6.6	12.2	10.2	3.7	4.7	2.7	6.1
9 Matrix	6.0	6.3	6.2	3.3	3.2	8.8	7.9
10 Subdivide by Function	5.2	6.1	3.1	9.0	1.3	4.9	7.0
11 Project Organisation	5.1	3.0	5.5	3.6	3.7	9.3	5.7
12 Subdivide by Numbers	4.9	2.9	3.8	1.9	9.2	0.8	10.7
13 Pool System	4.3	1.0	8.5	4.0	4.6	3.4	4.5
14 Subdivide by Product Type	3.6	2.8	2.6	5.6	3.1	2.6	5.1
ALL MAIN ORGANISATION OPTIONS	100.0	100.0	100.0	100.0	100.0	100.0	100.0
DECISION STANDARD	✓	✓	✓	✓	✓	✓	✓
AGREEMENT	✓	✓	✓	✓	✓	✓	✓

5B ORGANISATIONAL CRITERIA

STRUCTURAL CRITERIA	PRIORITIES (%)
1 Scientific Motivation Maintained	16.8
2 Scientific Expertise Enhanced	16.2
3 Co-operative Culture Enhanced	15.3
4 Effectiveness & Ease of Operation	10.4
5 Communication Enhanced	8.5
6 Flexibility	7.4
7 Stability over Time	4.9
8 Integration with other Disciplines	4.4
9 Balanced Age & Grade Profile	3.7
10 Understandable Structure	3.4
11 Easy Absorption of New Scientists	2.9
12= Limit Extra Work	2.4
12= Less Strain	2.4
14 Opportunities for Career Development	0.7
15 Minimal Barriers	0.6
ALL CRITERIA	100.0
DECISION STANDARD	Consistent
AGREEMENT	Much

TABLE 6. ACCOMMODATION STRATEGY

SITE EXPANSION PRIORITIES

SITE UNITS	SPACE PRIORITIES (%)
Site Service Rooms	24.9
Science B - Offices	10.2
Science A - Development Rooms	8.8
Science A - Test Rooms	8.7
Science B - Development Rooms	7.1
Science C - Experiment Rooms	7.0
Science B - Experiment Rooms	5.4
Special Rooms	5.3
Science D - Offices	5.1
Science B - Test Rooms	5.1
Science E - Offices	5.0
Science A - Experiment Rooms	3.5
Science D - Development Rooms	2.2
Science C - Test Rooms	1.8
Science D - Test Rooms	0.1
ALL SITE UNITS	100.0
DECISION STANDARD	Consistent
AGREEMENT	Much

TABLE 7. INFORMATION TECHNOLOGY (IT) STRATEGY
(SAMPLE RESULTS)

7A IT OBJECTIVES

	IT OBJECTIVES	PRIORITIES (%)
1	Reposition Company in the Market	16.1
2	Enhance Consumer Satisfaction	14.8
3	Pre-emptive Strikes on the Market	14.3
4	Product/Service Differentiation	13.0
5	Organisational Integration/Control	12.1
6	Enhance New Developments	7.2
7	Improve Specific Functions	6.0
8=	Improve Problem-solving Skills	5.0
8=	Improve Effectiveness of Specific Jobs	5.0
10	Distribute Field Units	4.5
11	Improve Internal Communications	2.0
	ALL IT OBJECTIVES	100.0
	DECISION STANDARD	Consistent
	TEAM AGREEMENT	Much

7B. IT CRITERIA

IT CRITERIA	PRIORITIES (%)
1 Individual Development/Effectiveness	13.9
2 Organistaional Control/Integration	13.4
3 Innovation	10.4
4 Relevance to Existing Work	8.3
5= Speed/Immediacy	8.1
5= Flexibility	8.1
7 Control of Complexity/Large Volumes	6.0
8 Cost Effectiveness	5.1
9 Increased Reliability	5.0
10 Staff Satisfaction	4.1
11 Power Redistribution	3.6
12 Individual Developments	3.5
13 Time Independence	3.1
14 Improved Communications	3.0
15 Location Independence	2.3
16 Accessibility and Participation	1.2
17 Organisational Image	1.0
18 Clarification	0.1
ALL IT CRITERIA	100.0
DECISION STANDARD	Consistent
TEAM AGREEMENT	Much

TABLE 8A. RESOURCE PLAN DATA

```
DEVELOPMENT PROJECTS:   RESOURCE ALLOCATION DATA
```

FROM: Oct. 85   EMPHASIS-PRIORITY: 34.7%
TO: April 86   -DEMAND   : 65.3%
TOTAL AVAILABLE MONEY: £840,000

	PROJECTS (names)	PLANNED PRIORITIES (%)	PLANNED UNIT COST (£000)	DEMANDS (schemes)	MINIMUM (schemes)	MAXIMUM (schemes)
1	Project B	29.4	120	1	1	1
2=	Project D	26.5	360	1	1	1
2=	Project C	26.5	100	3	1	3
4	Project A	11.8	160	2	0	2
5	Project E	5.9	140	3	0	3
	ALL PROJECTS	100.0	–	10	3	10

TABLE 8B. RESOURCE PLAN

```
DEVELOPMENT PROJECTS:   RESOURCE ALLOCATION
```

FROM: Oct. 85   TOTAL AVAILABLE MONEY: £840,000
TO: April 86

	PROJECTS (names)	HANDLE (schemes)	POSTPONE (schemes)	ALLOCATION (£000)	REQUIRED MONEY (£000)
1	Project B	1.0	0.0	120.0	120
2=	Project D	1.0	0.0	360.0	360
2=	Project C	1.6	1.4	159.7	300
4	Project A	0.7	1.3	114.5	320
5	Project E	0.6	2.4	85.8	420
	ALL PROJECTS	4.9	5.1	840.0	1520

TABLE 9A. RESOURCE EVALUATION DATA

DEVELOPMENT PROJECTS: MONITORED RESOURCE DATA

FROM: Oct. 85　　　　　　　　EMPHASIS-PRIORITY:　34.7%
TO:　 Jan. 86　　　　　　　　　　　　　　-DEMAND :　65.3%
TOTAL MONEY SPENT: £380,000

PROJECTS (names)	HANDLED (schemes)	DEMANDS (schemes)
1　Project B	0.5	1
2=　Project D	0.5	2
2=　Project C	1.0	3
4　Project A	0.5	2
5　Project E	0.0	3
ALL PROJECTS	2.5	11

TABLE 9B. RESOURCE EVALUATION

DEVELOPMENT PROJECTS: RESOURCE EVALUATION

FROM: Oct. 85　　　　　　　　TOTAL MONEY SPENT:　£380,000
TO:　 Jan. 86　　　　　　　　EMPHASIS: Unchanged

PROJECTS (names)	IMPLIED PRIORITIES (%)	IMPLIED UNIT COSTS (£000)	IMPLIED ALLOCATION (£000)	REQUIRED MONEY (£000)
3　Project B	19.5	104	52	104
1　Project D	39.0	344	172	688
2　Project C	25.3	84	84	252
4　Project A	16.3	144	72	288
5　Project E	0.0	140	0	420
ALL PROJECTS	100.0	-	380	1752

TABLE 9C. PLAN & EVALUATION COMPARED

| PROJECTS

(names) | PRIORITIES || UNIT COSTS ||
	PLANNED (%)	IMPLIED (%)	PLANNED (£000)	IMPLIED (£000)
Project B	29.4	19.5	120	104
Project D	26.5	39.0	360	344
Project C	26.5	25.3	100	84
Project A	11.8	16.3	160	144
Project E	5.9	0.0	140	140
ALL PROJECTS	100.0	100.0	–	–

TABLE 10A. WORK PLAN DATA

DEVELOPMENT PROJECT WORK ALLOCATION DATA

FROM: Oct. 85   EMPHASIS-PRIORITY: 35%
TO: April 86   DEMAND: 66%
TOTAL AVAILOABLE TIME: 210 man-weeks

PROJECTS (names)	PLANNED PRIORITIES (%)	PLANNED UNIT TIMES (man-wks)	DEMAND (schemes)	MINIMUM (schemes)	MAXIMUM (schemes)
Project B	29.4	30	1	1	1
Project D	26.5	90	1	1	1
Project C	26.5	25	3	1	3
Project A	11.8	40	2	0	2
Project E	5.9	35	3	0	3
ALL PROJECTS	100.0	–	10	3	10

TABLE 10B. WORK PLAN (NON-INTEGRAL

DEVELOPMENT PROJECTS: WORK ALLOCAION

FROM: Oct. 85   TOTAL AVAILABLE TIME: 210 man-weeks
TO: April 86

PROJECTS (names)	ALLOCATION (man-wks)	HANDLE (schemes)	POSTPONE (schemes)	REQD. TIME (man-wks)
Project B	30.0	1.0	0.0	30
Project D	90.0	1.0	0.0	90
Project C	40.0	1.6	1.4	75
Project A	28.6	0.7	1.3	80
Project E	21.4	0.6	2.4	105
ALL PROJECTS	210.0	4.9	5.1	380

TABLE 11A. WORK MONITOR DATA

DEVELOPMENT PROJECTS: WORK EVALUATION DATA

FROM: Oct. 85
TO: Jan. 86

TOTAL TIME SPENT: 95 man-weeks

PROJECTS (names)	ACTUAL HANDLED (schemes)	ACTUAL DEMAND (schemes)
Project B	0.5	1
Project D	0.5	2
Project C	1.0	3
Project A	0.5	2
Project E	0.0	3
ALL PROJECTS	2.5	11

TABLE 11B. WORK EVALUATION

DEVELOPMENT PROJECTS: WORK EVALUATION

FROM: Oct. 85
TO: Jan. 86

TOTAL TIME SPENT: 95 man-weeks
EMPHASIS; unchanged

PROJECTS (names)	IMPLIED PRIORITIES (%)	IMPLIED UNIT TIMES (man-wks)	IMPLIED ALLOCATION (man-wks)	REQD. TIME IMPLIED (man-wks)
Project A	19.4	26	13	26
Project D	39.0	86	43	172
Project C	25.2	21	21	63
Project A	16.3	36	18	72
Project E	0.0	35	0	105
ALL PROJECTS	100.0		95	438

REFERENCES

[1] J. Algie   *Management Technology*, MSC, HMSO, 1986.

[2] L. Philips   Computing to Consensus, *Effective Decision Support*, Unicom Seminars, 1986.

[3] F. Newman   Speeding up the Board's Decisions, *Micro Decision*, July 1985.

[4] M. Bywater   Mind Set, *Punch*, 1 May 1985.

[5] J. Algie & W. Foster   *Priorities* (2nd Edition), BIOSS, Brunel University, 1987.

[6] Work Sciences   *Priorities*, 1986.

[7] Work Sciences   *The Budget Priority System* (BPS), 1985.

[8] Work Sciences   *The Work Priority Syste* (WPS), 1985.

[9] J. Algie & W. Foster   Seams of Agreement, *New Statesman*, 23 November 1984.

[10] J. Algie   Weighing up Priorities, *Community Care*, 11 September 1986.

[11] J. Algie   Budgeting Priorities, *Accountancy Age*, 12 September 1985.

[12] J. Algie & W. Foster   Ways to Cope with Council Cuts, *Local Government Review*, 25 May 1985.

7 Relationships between Reliability and Management

I. A. Watson
Systems Reliability Service, UKAEA

INTRODUCTION AND BACKGROUND

The various accounts and official reports describing events during the major accidents at Bhopal, Flixborough, Chernobyl and on the Challenger, as well as in other man-made catastrophes, eg the sinking of the titanic, show that management played an important part in the accident sequences. Reliability is important from a safety viewpoint and in the economics of plant operation. These aspects can be in conflict and management has an important role to ensure that a correct balance is obtained. There is no doubt however tht major accidents should be avoided because of their personal, ethical, political and economic consequences. Management has a role of assuring reliability but there is also the question of the role management itself plays in plant reliability. How reliable is mangement itself and what precise role should it play in plant operation and organisation, so as to avoid damaging accidents?

It is now commonly accepted by concerned professionals that human factors (HF) can have a significant impact on the safe and reliable operation of technological plant. This understanding is manifest across a variety of industries and technologies e.g., chemicals, processing, nuclear power, aviation, mining, computers and so on. What has been puzzling and controversial is how the matter can be wholly effectively dealt with.

This common concern was expressed in a paper produced on behalf of the Commission of European Community (CEC)[1] surveying research on human factors and man machine interaction and proposing a European Community collaborative research programme. Many probabilistic risk assessment (PRA) reports in the nuclear power industry[1][2] have shown the tremendous significance of HF and man machine interaction/interfaces (MMI) in nuclear power plant accident sequences. Also HF plays a considerable role in software reliability and common cause failures[3]. Its significance now in human computer interaction/interfaces (HCI) is being appreciated in the field of advanced information technology, so it has become a recognised research category in the huge UK, European, USA and Japanese 5th generation computer research projects now underway until 1990. It is well known in the case of aviation that over 70%[4] of accidents are due to crew error and similar figures apply to the shipping and chemical industries. The experience of the systems reliability service (SRS) in carrying out reliability assessments for the process industries is that human error (HE) can figure significantly somewhere in many plant or system safety/reliability assessments.

Reliability considerations that need to be taken into account are shown in outline in Figure 1. These usually start with the system or plant description, specification and performance. Design, degradation mechanisms, operations and maintenance are taken into account together with data on random failures and more systematic types of failures from data banks eg the NCSR Data Bank[5] and specific data collection and analysis campaigns. Methods of dealing properly with human factors/reliability are slowly emerging and work is in process[6]. The management factor has become apparent from many accident reports[7][8] including those highlighted above, but also from work on the analysis of common mode failures[9]. However there are at present no formal methods of dealing with this and its consideration is entirely subjective and a matter of judgement. The environment of the plant affects its operation and many of the factors shown in Figure 1. Finally there is bound to be degrees of uncertainty associated with all the considerations which will produce an overall uncertainty that can to some extent be expressed in statistical and mathematical terms.

A model which shows the interconnectedness of management, operators, plant and the tasks involved is shown in Figure 2. This was produced as a result of an analysis of industrial fatal accidents performed by SRD[10]. Accident causes arising from management errors were found to be significant by comparison with the other factors shown. There is a view held by members of regulating agencies, which is supported by some data, eg aviation accident rate spread between airlines that the variation in accident risk between good and bad mangement can be at least an order of magnitude.

It can thus be understood that the relationship between plant reliability, human reliability and management needs to be understood more explicitly than is now apparent. This will be done by showing specifically and analytically links between reliability analysis methods, operator tasks, human action theory and management structural analysis. A review of the Challenger accident report[7] and of a study of the Bhopal disaster[8] will follow this to illustrate the organistion and mangement links to safety and reliability.

RELIABILITY

Definition & Procedure

The requirements for reliability in technological systems and plant are summarised in Table 1. There is a need to balance the economic and safety requirements, but catstrophies need to be avoided with a very high degree of confidence. When a plant is not sufficiently reliable it will be unsafe or uneconomic or both. In order to decide this it is necessary to be able to quantify reliability. To do this requires an appropriate definition of reliablity as follows:-

"The characteristic expressed as a numerical probability of a system that it will perform a defined function in the required manner under all relevant conditions wherever it is required to do".

TABLE 1

THE NEED FOR RELIABILITY

IS THE PRODUCT RELIABLE?

- MANAGEMENT REQUIRE VALUE FOR MONEY
- IS PRODUCT SAFETY AFFECTED?
- MINIMISE PENALTIES AND DANGER!

IN THE PAST "WAIT AND SEE" METHODS WERE OFTEN USED

MODERN TECHNOLOGY DEVELOPMENT/LIFE-CYCLE

IS TOO SHORT FOR THIS

EG   CHEMICAL PLANTS
COMPUTERS
AIRCRAFT
POWER PLANTS
OIL RIGS
INGEGRATED MANUFACTURING

IS THE PRODUCT RELIABLE ENOUGH?
LEADS TO
QUANTIFICATION OF RELIABILITY

In order to be able to use this definition, analytical and modelling techniques are of course required. However for these to be used properly and to greatest advantage, an evaluation procedure is required starting at the definition of the plant or system under consideration. Such a procedure is tabulated below as a series of questions to be answered.

- WHAT ARE THE SYSTEM BOUNDARIES?
- WHAT IS THE SYSTEM'S REQUIRED FUNCTIONAL PERFORMANCE?
- UNDER WHAT CONDITIONS IS THE SYSTEM REQUIRED TO PERFORM?
- IS THE SYSTEM CAPABLE OF FULFILLING ITS REQUIREMENT?
- WHAT QUANTIFIED MEASURES OF SUCCESS CAN BE USED?
- WHAT LEVEL OF DETAIL IS REQUIRED IN THE ASSESSMENT?
- CHOOSE APPROPRIATE MODELLING TECHNIQUES
- WHAT ARE THE REQUIREMENTS FOR RELIABILITY DATA AND INFORMATION?
- HOW SENSITIVE IS THE SYSTEM TO THE RELIABILITY BEHAVIOUR OF ITS CONSTITUENT PARTS?

Reliability Analysis

Figure 3 shows this procedure more specifically for high reliability systems such as reactor trip systems (RTS) or other such high integrity plant protective systems. The initial steps enable a thorough understanding of the system and its operation together with decisions about the extent of the evaluation and the data requirements. The failure modes effects and criticality analysis enable the assessor to understand the types of hazard which system failures could lead to. The most widely used type of reliability modelling is fault tree analysis. A simple example of this for the redundant pump system shown in figure 4 is illustrated in Figure 5. This shows no operator action since it is not specified whether the system is automtic or manual. Clearly in practice the fault tree would need to be expanded to include this and to show further detail eg electric motors driving the pump. An example of the type of data which would be used in quantifying the component and fault tree reliability is shown in Table 2 and the following Table 3 shows the tpe of calculation which in principle would be done for each component. The calculation for the fault tree as a whole follows from the laws of logical algebra and would produce figures for the unavailbility or probability of failure of flow from valve X.

TABLE 2

EXAMPLE OF RELIABILITY DATA FROM SRS DAT BANK – (ELECTRIC MOTORS)

DESCRIPTION:	THREE PHASE MOTOR FEED FOR FEED PUMP FREQUENCY 60 CYCLES/SEC, 26HP, 415V
MANUFACTURER:	"X"
LOCATION:	"Y"
NUMBER OF ITEMS:	12
MEAN OPERTING TIME:	2.28 YEARS
SAMPLE SIZE (OPERATING TIME):	27.4 ITEM YEARS
MEAN HISTORY TIME:	10 YEARS
NUMBER OF FAULTS:	2
MEAN FAILURE RATE (OPERATING TIME):	8.33 FAULTS/MILLION HRS
UPPER FAILURE RATE (OPERATING TIME):	30.1 FAULTS/MILLION HRS
LOWER FAILURE RATE (OPERATING TIME):	1.01 FAULTS/MILLION HRS
CONFIDENCE BAND:	85%
DISTRIBUTION:	POISSON
APPLICATION:	AVERAGE INDUSTRIAL
INFORMATION TYPE:	FIELD, CORRECTLY REPORTED

TABLE 3

BASIC UNAVAILABILITY MODE

FORCED UNAVAILABILITY $\quad U_F = K \cdot \lambda \cdot t_R$

FAILURE RATE
APPLIES TO A COMPONENT
OR SYSTEM $\quad \lambda$

a Single Components } Non-Redundant
b Parallel Components
c Redundant Parallel Components

MEAN RESTORATION TIME
DEPENDS ON REPAIR STRAGETY $\quad t_R$

a Immediate Restoration $\quad t_R = t$, t = repair time

   Deferred Restoration $\quad t_R = \frac{\tau}{2}$, τ = time between tests or maintenance

FRACTIONAL OUTPUT REDUCTION FACTOR K
DEPENDS ON DEGREE OF OUTAGE

a Complete Outage $\quad K = 1$

b Partial Outage $\quad 0 \quad K \quad 1$

An example of a so-called enhanced fault tree where potentially important human influences are included in the fault tree is shown in Figure 6. This is an illustration of the so-called SHARP (Systematic Human Action Reliability Procedure), step 1 the object of which is to ensure tht important human influences are included in plant risk and reliability assessment.

The SHARP framework is shown in Figure 7 which shows the links between the seven steps involved. The objective of the first step is to ensure that potentially important human influences are included in plant logic diagrams such as fault trees (FT). An example of an enhanced fault produced after undergoing the detailed procedures of the definition step is shown in Figure 6. The failure "types" referred to in this figure are defined in the SHARP report, but are self-explanatory in the fault tree. In step 2 the objective is to reduce the number of human interactions identified in step 1 to those that might be significant. The application of coarse screening is shown in Figure 8 which is the same fault tree as the previous figure where the analyst has applied generic equipment data and a fixed human error probability, e.g., 1.0. Coarse screening takes into account only those system features that diminish the impact of human interactions on accident sequences. Fine screening goes beyond this by also applying probabilities to human actions. Various examples of suggested screening data have been given in the literature[11]. Figure 9 shows a graph based on the Rasmussen model of human action processes and typical malfunctions described in reference (6). The application of such error rates to the fault tree shown in the previous figures is shown in Figure 10. The impact of failure to maintain the breakers is thus seen to be very significant relative to the combination of the failure to scram automatically and manually.

The objective of step 3 is to amplify the qualitative description of each key human interaction identified in step 2. This is essentially done by means of some form of hierarchical task analysis[12]. Influence parameters, performance shaping factors, ergonomic features (or lack of them) etc., need to be considered to establish a basis for selecting a model basis for representation of the human interactions. This would include organisational factors, quality of information, procedural matters as well as personnel factors.

Task Analysis

An illustration

To illustrate this process consider an operation that might be carried out as one of the duties of a chemical plant operator - 'ensure caustic concentration is within limits specified by manufacturing instructions'. By questioning an informant competent at this operation, we may be able to say that the five sub-ordinate operations in Figure 11 need to be carried out.

But simply listing these five sub-ordinates does not provide a complete redescription of the operation being examined. Their plan must be stated. In this case the plan is most clearly stated in the form of the algorithm in Figure 12.

The same process of redescription can now be applied to each of the five sub-ordinate operations identified in Figure 11. Figure 13 shows how some of these subordinate operations may be carried out. Some of the operations so derived may also be treated in a similar fashion.

Two important themes emerge from what has been described so far. One of which accords with common experience is tht the tasks affecting plant operation (and design) are made up of many human actions in complex, but analysable patterns. Secondly since these may occur in many parts of a fault tree, the possibility of <u>common influences affecting them ie dependencies between them must be of great concern</u>. In order to consider this further the nature of human action needs to be carefully examined. Before this however it is worth noting that the repsonsibility for oganising and supervising all the tasks identified in the reliability model, eg fault tree lies with management in some shape or form. It is of course possible for tasks to be organised, ie managed, so as to reduce error, eg as shown in figure 14 where the aim is to educe engineering error by how many checking functions. The meaning of the "AND" gates is notionally the same as in fault tree terminology.

HUMAN ACTION

A general theory of the structure of action has been produced by John Searle in the 1984 Reith Lectures[13]. This theory makes sense of the many issues involved especially the anomalies, it can underpin some of the useful aspects of current human error models and can be specialised so as to be useful in understanding MMI and the occurrence of human error[14].

The relationship of this theory to human performance and reliability modelling has been extensively discussed in reference 16. These show that the theory provides a firm basis for the useful models and explains many anomalies particularly relating to data. However one purpose of this paper is to show how O&M relates to human action specifically. This is through the network of intentional states described in <u>Principal 7.</u> Other parts of the theory are briefly outlined below.

<u>Principles of the theory of the structure of Action</u>

Principle 1:

ACTIONS characteristically consist of two components viz:-

- <u>a mental component</u>
  and
- <u>a physical component</u>

Suppose an operator is closing a valve or paginating a computer visual dispay, he will be conscious of certain experiences. If he is successful then the valve will close or the correct screen page is displayed. If he is not successful then he will still at least have had a mental component, ie, the experience of attempting to close the valve or paginate the VDU (or a misplaced intention, ie, a mistake leading to an error) together with some physical components such as turning switch handles or pressing keys which may itself be in error due to a slip. This leads to:-

Principle 2:

The mental component is an INTENTION ie, it has intentionality.

To say that a mental state has intentionality means tht it is about something. For example, a belief is always that such and such is the case, a desire requires that such and such happen as in the examples above. Intentional states have three key features:-

1   They have a content in a certain mental type. The content is what makes it about something, eg, closing a valve. The mental type is whether it is a desire or belief, eg, the operator wants to close the valve or the operator believes he will close the valve or the operator intends (in common parlance) to close the valve.

2   They determine their own conditions of satisfaction, ie, they will be satisfied or not depending on whether the world (out thre) matches the content of the state. Sometimes when errors referred to as mistakes occur this is the result of a misplaced intentions leading to inaproprite physical components.

3   They cause things to happen (by way of intentional causation) to bring a match between their content and the state of the world. There is an internal connection between the cause and the effect, because the cause is a representation of the very state that it causes. the cause both represents and brings about the effect. This kind of cause and effect relationship is called intentional causation and is <u>crucial to both</u> the <u>structure and explanation of human action.</u> The mind brings about the very state that it is thinking about (which sometimes may be mistaken).

Principle 3:

The kind of causation which is essential to both the structure of action and the explanation of action is INTENTIONAL CAUSATION.

The physical components of actions are caused by intentions. Intentions are causal because they make things happen. They also have contents and so can figure in the process of logical reasoning.

Principle 4:

The explanation of an action must have the same content as was in the originator's head when the action was performed or when the reasoning was carried out tht lead to the performance of the action. If the explanation is really explanatory the content that causes behaviour by way of intentional causation must be identical with the content of the explanation of the behaviour.

In this respect actions differ from other natural events in the world. In the explanation of an earthquake or electricity the contents of the explanation only has to represent what happened, ie, a model, and why it happened. It doesn't actually have to cause the event itself. But in explaining human behaviour the cause and the explanation both have contents and the explanation only works because it has the same contents as the cause.

Principle 5:

There is a fundamental distinction between those actions that are premeditated which are the result of advance planning and those actions which are spontaneous and which we do without prior reflection.

Principle 6:

The formation of prior intentions is, at least generally, the result of practical reasoning. Such reasoning is always about how best to decide between alternative (sometimes conflicting) possibilities and desires.

The motive force behind most human action is desire based on needs or requirements. Beliefs function to enable us to figure out how best to satisfy our desires. Tasks are generally complex and involve practical reasoning at a high level on the way forward and intentions in action and many physical components (often repetitious) at a lower level. Take for the example the response of control room operatives to a simulated LOCA in a nuclear reactor. Without going into technical detail it can be seen from Figure 15 that the methods chosen by various operatives were different, although all were considered acceptable. If one particular strategy were preferred then all others could be considered to be in error ie, mistaken unless there is some overriding criterion, such as keeping below a maximum operating temperature. Notice also that errors ie, slips, could occur at the detailed level in not correctly operating pumps or valves.

Principle 7 :

An intentional state only 'functions' as part of a network of other intentional staes. 'Functions' here means that it only determines its conditions of satisfaction relative to many other intentional states. The example given above and illustrated in figure 15 indicates some of life's typical complexities. One doesn't have intentions by themselves. The operatives are in the control room for many reasons, personal, organisational, technical etc. The desire to successfully control the LOCA functions against a whole series of other intentional states eg, to maintain the reactor working, the quality of its output, please the boss, maintain the integrity of the plant, keep their jobs, job satisfaction etc. They characteristically engage in practical reasoning tht lead to intentions and actual behaviour. The other intentional states that give the intentional state particular meaning is called the network of intentionality.

Principle 8:

The whole network of intentionality only functions against a background of human capacities that are not themselves mental states.

Our mental states only function in the way they do becaus they function against a background of capabilities, skills, habits, ways of doing things etc, and general stances towards the world that do not themselves consist of intentional staes. In order for example to form the intention to drive a car somewhere one must be able to drive, but this ability doesn't just consist of a whole lot of other intentional staes. A skill is required of know 'how' rather than 'that'. Such skills, abilities, etc, against which intentional states function is the "background".

Principle 9:

The formation and development of intentions is affected by the results of our actions which are continually evaluated.

This is an additional principle to Searle's theory but is essential if we are to take into account practical experience of doing things and of correcting (or <u>not</u> correcting) errors. Even the simplest actions such as pressing a computer key has some form of feedback (touch, sight or sound) if they are to be fully satisfactory. More complicated tasks involve much more elaborate evaluation for their progress. This is illustrated in Figure 15 where continual adjustments are being made during the process of controlling the LOCA. At an even higher level strategies may be evaluated and modified to obtain desired results. Unless actions are continually corrected to satisfy Principle 6 (prior intentions) then intentions in action (Principle 5) may be mistaken. Practical reasoning arising from Prinicple 6 is continually modified by evaluations required by Principle 9.

In the case of technological systems, apart from internally derived mental states eg the desire to please, satisfaction, <u>most if not all the intentional states in the network are aspects of organisation and hence to management</u> (responsible for setting up and running the organisation). Events the internally derived states, so called, relate to aspects of O&M, thus the operator function as part of a network of other intentional states involved in running the plant. These need to be properly managed for continued successful operation of the plant.

Management Assessment

This is the most problematic and least developed area from a risk and reliability viewpoint. It is a common influence affecting all aspects of plant operation. Some authorative sources believe that the range from very good to very poor management can produce an order of magnitude increase in risk of accidents. Some analysts believe it can best be dealt with by considering the effects of supervision, training, working environment, etc., and other management controlled factors at the detailed task level. Indeed the existence and performance of overall controls and monitoring as previously described is clearly a major management responsibility in reducing risk and improving reliability. In the aviation world[15] the flight crew training programmes are expanding beyond the traditional role of maintaining piloting skills and providing instruction orientated towards flight deck management crew co-ordination, teamwork and communications.

Flight simulator training[15] now include management programmes focusing on communications and management practices e.g.,

- managerial philosophy
- individual work styles
- communications
- integration of the "four" foundations of management - planning, organising, leading and controlling
- management skills and involvement practices
- specific strategies for the effective exertion of influence.

Flight experts tend to relate aircraft accidents to interpersonnel and management factors far more than lack of systems knowledge or to aircraft related factors. Studies[15] identify a "safety window" in which nearly 83% of accidents involving professional pilots occur beginning at or about the final approach fix and extending through approach and landing. 90% of the accidents that occur in this window appear not to be aircraft related, they are pilot caused and seem to reflect failure to manage properly. As a result in training pilots a role change is occurring converting the pilot from a control manipulator to an information processor.

A technique which has been developed to model and assess management from the risk viewpoint is the Management and Oversight and Risk Tree (MORT)[16]. This system safety programme has been developed and refined by the US Department of Energy (DOE). MORT is a systematic approach to the management of risks within an organisation. It incorporates ways to increase reliability, assess risks, control losses and allocate resources effectively.

The acronym, MORT, carries two primary meanings:

1   the MORT "tree", or logic diagram, which organises risk, loss, and safety program elements and is used as a master worksheet for accident investigations and program evaluations;

and 2   the total safety program, seen as a sub-system to the major management system of an organisation.

The MORT process includes four main analytical tools. The first main tool, Change Analysis, is based upon the Kepner-Tregoe method of rational decision making. Change Analysis compares a problem-free situation with a

Table 4: **Comparison of Demand characteristics of tasks facing personnel capabilities required in representing management decision**

Level number	Typical management role name	Timespan inherent in management tasks represented at given level	Demand tasks facing with responsibility given level
1	Chairman M/D of corporate group.	20 - 50 years	Anticipation of changes in sociological, demographic and political developments; strategic development to meet them.
6	Corporate group/ sector executive.	10 - 20 years	Co-ordination of social and theoretical of corporate strategic development into
5	Direction of NDT enterprise.	5 - 10 years	Problem not dealt with in context set modify boundaries of NDT business within
4	General management	2 - 5 years	Detachment from specific inspections. examples of issues calling for development
3	Inspection management	1 - 2 years	Control of trend of tasks and problems from trend to ways of formulating problems.
2	Front-line management	3 months - 1 year	Can anticipate changes in tasks due to any object, production resources, pathways, or
1	Operational	less than 3 months	Limited task to concretely and physically

having management responsibilities at a given level with structuring problems at that level

characteristics of personnel at	Structuring capabilities required in representing management decision problems at given level
technological leading corporate	Isomorphic with level 2, except can conduct sensitivity analysis simulating changes in level 5 representations; assessing their impact.
systems; translation business direction.	Isomorphic with level 1, except such node is now a level 5 problem representation within fixed cultural structure.
wholly from above can policy.	Articulation of principles conditional (goal) closing of an open system, and/or re-opening of a conditionally closed system (eg through scenario generation).
seeing then representative of a system.	Selecting/interfacing capability between frames represented in different organisation dimensions (requires use of problem structuring language).
arising. Extrapolation	Re-structuring capability within a frame represented in a single organisational dimension.
one of: demand, pathway resources.	Manipulation of data on one variable at a time within fixed structure (eg sensitivity analysis).
at hand.	Assessed/reporting of valves of nodes within fixed structure (eg calibration systems).

problem (accident) situation in order to isolate causes and effects of change.

The second tool, Energy Trace and Barrier Analysis, is based on the idea that energy is necessary to do work, that energy must be controlled, and that uncontrolled energy flows in the absence of adequate barriers can cause accidents.

The third, and most complex, tool is the MORT Tree Analysis. Combining principles from the fields of management and safety and using fault tree methodology, the MORT tree aims at helping the investigator discover what happened and why.

The fourth tool, Positive (Success) Tree Design, reverses the logic of fault tree analysis. In positive tree design, a system for successful operation is comprehensively and logically laid out. The positive tree, because it shows all that must be performed and the proper sequencing of events needed to accomplish an objective, is a useful planning and assessment tool. An illustration of a MORT "tree" or logic diagram is shown in Figure 16.

ANALYSIS OF MANAGEMENT STRUCTURE

Having shown

1   that O&M is a common factor in the many tasks which can affect plant/system reliability/safety

2   that human actions function in a network of intentional states mainly determined by O&M, how can we carry the analysis into O&M structures in order to see in any partiuclar case how that affects individual tasks or types or sets of tasks from a reliability viewpoint.

Generally technological management is hierarchically organised (cf management charts). So the generic problem is to relate the functions of this hiearchy to the tasks which affect plant reliability safety. A model[17] for describing the operations of such organisational decision making has been derived from the theory of cognitive problem solving. This is a multi-level approach to the representation of decision problems. The scheme is represented diagramatically in Figure 17 and is discussed below.

Levels of Abstraction in Representing Decision Problems

This decription is derived from tht given in reference (17). Two points should be made at the outset about the formal characteristics of this multi-level problem representation scheme. The first is that the elements modelled at each level are operations performed by the decision maker in developing a problem representation, rather than the substantive content of the representation thus developed.

The second point concerns the relations between the levels. In a "two level" decision-making scheme, what is represented as form at the first level can be manipulated as content at the second level. But this relation may be continued through further levels of abstraction, that is, what is represented as form at the second level can be manipulated as component at

the third level, and so on. This implies, of course, that the content
manipulated at each level is qualitatively different, as are the
progressively more powerful operators that become available to a person who
can understand the principles underlying their employment within the
calculus formalised at each progressive level of abstraction.

Level 1: Concrete Operations-Making "Best Assessments"

The operations actualised at this level are limited to providing
assessments of quantities to be represented as components at a defined mode
in a task structure that has been fixed a priori. Typically these would be
on-line tasks in plant operation.

Level 2: Formal Operational-Sensitivity Analysis

Moving up to Level 2 involves understanding the principles underlying what
is called formal operational thought. Piaget[17] describes the fundamental
characteristic of cognitive abilities at this level as the "capacity to
deal with hypotheses instead of simply objects", hypotheses that are
expressed as propositions rather than facts.

The key formal operations at Level 2 comprise: operationalising principles
relating to inversion, negation, reciprocity and correlation. Although
each of these types of operations may be involved in a decision maker's
attempt to provide "best assessments" in Level 1 problem solving, it is at
Level 2 that these properties as a group are first understood and exploited
in exploring aspects of a (prestructured) representation of a decision
problem.

This type of exploration of aspects of a problem is generally referred to
as "sensitivity analysis": exploring "what if?" questions about changing
values at nodes in the structure eg, the probability of an event in an
act-event sequence to see what effects are propagated throughout the
structure. Hence, at Level 2 the content manipulated within the structure
is not "facts" by hypotheses (opinions, views, etc). It is explicitly
recognised that probabilities can vary in reflecting the range of specific
participants' interests and preferences in group decision making.

Level 3: Developing, Structure within a Single Structural Variant

Fundamental activities in structuring and restructuring decision problems
involves processing a decision problem at Level 3 and above. At Level 3,
we move beyond Piaget's account of operations dictating the form of the
current problem representation. They now become content manipulated within
operations aimed at developing the structure of the problem under the
constraint that the variant of structure used to represent the problem
remains the same.

Level 4: Problem-Structuring Languages

Decision problem-structuring activities at level 4 involve the articulation
of principles that enable the manipulation of complete Level 3
problem-structuring systems as content. There is, however, no formal
language within decision theory that articulates Level 4 principles, as
they are superordinate to the forms addressed by that theory, hence, in
working at Level 4 a decision maker has either to articular these
principles within his or her own natural language or to learn a new
language for generating systems linking Level 3 (sub)problem

representations into a structure comprising the whole range of aspects of the problem under consideration. In practice, the language employed by the decision maker serves as a generative problem-structuring calculus at this level.

Level 5: Scenarios Exploring Small Worlds

Level 4 problem representations often appear to decision makers to be "complete" descriptions of the structure of the decision-making problem they are facing. yet these Level 4 descriptions are themselves situated within what Savage (1954) described as the small world encompassing the decision maker's problem-structuring activities and the knowledge representations that he or she believes to be relevant to these activities. This "boundary setting" for a decision problem changes with changes in motivation, as does the nature of the structures the decision maker will consider requisite in handling any decision problem.

Decision making at levels higher than Level 5 is concerned with choosing between courses of action that, when supported at lower levels, will lead to the generation and re-ordering of the cultural structures within which individuals find and exercise their identities. Few decision makers occupy roles with the scope and levels of organisational support that permit them to handle decision-making tasks effectively at these levels of abstraction.

IMPLICATIONS OF THE MULTI-LEVEL SCHEME FOR SUPPORTING ORGANISATIONAL DECISION MAKING

Table 4 shows the correspondence between the levels of abstraction involved in conceptualising decision problems described here and Jaques's[17] levels of abstraction of the demand characteristics of the tasks carried out by decision makers located at the various levels within the hierarchy of a bureaucratic organisation.

According to Jaques, the qualitative differences between the levels of organisational roles shown in the first column can be understood in terms of progressive levels of abstraction in the symbolic construction of actions that may be carried out by executive at each level. Moreover, these levels are not viewed as a specific product of organisational forms; rather, bureaucratic levels are parasitic on levels of abstraction of (idealised) tasks within organisations.

The second column in Table 4 gives the typical time span in the problem representation that is requisite for a task carried out by an executive at each level. the time span indicates how far away the decision horizon (Toda, 1976) is usually set for tasks for which the decision maker is held responsible within the organisational context.

The third column in Table 4 summarises the description of the demand characteristics of the tasks facing personnel with responsibility at a given in an organisation. In any actual organisational context we may find personnel at particular organisational levels also responsible for carrying out tasks at lower levels (rather than delegating them to sub-ordinates). Executives may be able to take initiatives at more than one level in organisations where the role structure permits this (for example, as "consultants" or "problem fixers").

In a practical analysis the scheme in table 4 will also be divided horizontally into columns representing different management activities or agencies such as resource management, safety assurance, QA, personnel operations etc. The communications between these vertical "lines" of management as well as between levels will be of crucial importance to the success of plant operation. This theoretical framework is now being developed in a study of the management of inspection processes.

CASE STUDIES

The management issues arising from two recent catastrophic accidents will be reviewed and related to the foregoing theory on the connectivity in reliability/safety/O&M.

The Challenger-Shuttle 51-L Loss[7]

Loss of the space shuttle challenger and its crew on January 28 occurred in part because of an ineffective "silent safety programme" within the National Aeronautics and Space Administration (NASA). The Marshall Space Flight Centre project managers failed to provide full and timely bearing on the safety of Flight S1-L to other vital elements of Shuttle programme management. Thus overall there was an absence of one essential line (or column in the multi-level scheme) of O&M concerning safety and a failure to communicate between lines. this is supported by the following quotation.

Review of shuttle management - "Project managers for various elements of the shuttle program felt more accountable to their center management than to the shuttle program organisation. Shuttle element funding, work package definition and vital program information frequently bypasses National Space Transportation System program manager (Arnold D Aldrich). A redefinition of the program manager's responsibility is essential", the commission said. "This redefinition should give the program manager the requisite authority for all shuttle operations. Program funding and all shuttle program work at the centers should be placed clearly under the program managers authority".

Specific Recommendations were:-

- Increase astronaut managers - The commission specifically recommended that NASA increase the number of astronauts in management positions so that astronaut experience could benefit overall agency decisions.

- Formation of new safety organisation - NASA should establish an Office of Safety, Reliability and Quality Assurance to be headed by an associate administrator, reporting directly to the agency's administrator. The office should have direct authority for safety issues throughout the agency.

- Formation of shuttle safety panel - "NASA should establish a shuttle Safety Advisory Panel reporting to the shuttle program manager", the commission said. The charter of this panel should include review of shuttle operational issues, launch commit criteria, flight rules, flight readiness and risk management. The panel should include representation from safety organisations, mission operations and the astronaut office, the commission said.

- Improvement in management communications - "A policy should be developed that governs the imposition and removal of shuttle launch constraints", the commission said. The Rogers group was concerned that Marshall mangers - specifically solid rocket booster project manager Lawrence B Mulloy - first imposed a launch constraint on the booster joint because of concern over the component, then waived that constraint on six consecutive flights. Neither the launch constraint, the reason for it nor the six waivers were known to Jesse W Moore, who headed the shuttle program at the time, nor to Aldrich in Houston or James A Thomas, the lead Kennedy launch commit official for Mission 51-L.

Increase maintenance safeguards - Installation, testing and maintenance procedures for critical items such as the booster joints must be especially rigorous, according to the commission. "NASA should establish a system of analysing and reporting performance trends of such items", the commission said. The agency has to develop a comprehensive maintenance inspection plan for shuttle orbiters, perform structural inspections when scheduled and not waive them as has been done in the past. The spare parts program needs to be restored and the practice of cannibalising orbiter parts at Kennedy halted.

The recommendations thus include new lines of management and improved links between specific lines criticisms of various levels of management were as follows:-

The commission said that the safety organisations in place during the Apollo program had been dismantled and overall safety monitoring at NASA had become ineffective. Deficiencies in NASA's safety program included a "lack of problem reporting requirements, inadequate tend analysis, misrepresentation of criticality and a lack of involvement in critical decisions. A properly staffed, supported and robust safety organisation might well have avoided that faults", the commission said.

"Kennedy Space Center has a myriad of safety, reliability and quality assurance organisations that report to supervisors who are responsible for processing. The clear implication of such a management structure is that it fails to provide the kind of independent role necessary for flight safety", the report said. The commission had the same criticism for Marshall.

Commission members believe a key management level decision at Johnston Space Center in 1983 played a role in the accident by modifying the requirement that shuttle Level 3 managers - such as those in the booster project at Marshall - report all critical safety issues to Johnson Level 2 managers overseeing the entire program.

Prior to 1983, Level 3 at Marshall was required to report all problems with flight critical hardware, such as the boosters, to Level 2 at Houston. A 1983 revision, however, "substantially reduced this requirement to include only those problems, that dealt with common hardware items, or physical interface elements", the report said.

The revision to streamline the reporting system was submitted by Martin Raines, director of safety, reliability and quality assurance at Johnson and approved by Glynn Lunney, who at the time was the senior Level 2 manager as shuttle program director at Johnston.

"With this action, Level 2 lost all insight into safety, operational and flight schedule issues resulting from Level 3 problems', the commission said.

The lack of flight safety trend analysis of the booster joint after evidence of O-ring seal erosion was found on several flights was also criticised by the committee. A series of changes to booster processing procedures at Kennedy "may be significant" in creating the booster anomalies that had been seen with more regularity in the latter flights, but never tracked in detail by the shuttle program.

The changes at Kennedy included a discontinuation of prelaunch O-ring inspections, a doubling of pressure in the O-ring seal test process that blew holes through the boosters' protective putty and changes to the putty positioning pattern and type of putty used. In addition, the use of previously flown booster segments was increasing at Kennedy, and a significant management change occurred at the launch site when Morton Thiokol took over responsibility for booster assembly from United Space Boosters, Inc.

Other specific findings by the commission include:

Launch constraint waivers - "The waiving of launch constraints appears to have been at the expense of flight safety", the commission found.

Marshall's attitude - "The commission is troubled by what appears to be a propensity of management at Marshall to contain potentially serious problems and to resolve them internally rather than communicate them forward", the commission said.

Thiokol management - "Thiokol management reversed its position and recommended the launch of 51-L at the urging of Marshall and contrary to the views of its engineers in order to accommodate a major customer", the commission said.

The commission found that NASA and Thiokol discovered a booster O-ring design problem as early as 1977 and that Thiokol then began treating it as an acceptable risk, while some Marshall managers at the time thought a redesign was essential. Although the commission has placed the primary burden of blame on Marshall managers, they also found that an August, 1985, O-ring briefing to shuttle Level 1 management, including L. Michael Weeks, deputy associate administrator for space flight, "was sufficiently detailed to require corrective action before the next flight".

In future the flight rate should be limited. NASA's resources were increasingly unable to keep up with the planned flight rate.

Poor risk assessment - "NASA and Thiokol accepted escalating risk apparently because 'they got away with it last time'," the Rogers commission said.

The commission found that with an ineffective safety system, pressures on the shuttle project were magnifying other problems. "In establishing the shuttle flight schedule, NASA had not provided adequate resources for its attainment. As a result, the capabilities of the system were strained by the modest nine-emission rate of 1985, and the evidence suggests the agency would not have been able to accomplish the 15 flights scheduled for 1986", the commission said.

"At the same time that the flight rate was increasing, a variety of factors reduced the number of skilled personnel available to deal with it. The flight rate did not appear to be based on the assessment of available resources and capabilities and was not reduced to accommodate the capacity of the work force.

"At Kennedy the capabilities of the shuttle processing and facilities support work force became increasingly strained as the orbiter turnaround time decreased to accommodate the accelerated launch schedule. This factor resulted in overtime of almost 28% in some directorates. Numerous contract employees worked 72 hr per week or longer and frequently 12 hr shifts".

It appears there are enormous differences of opinion as to the probability of fail rate with loss of vehicle and human life, with estimates ranging from roughly 1 in 100 to 1 in 100,000. "The higher figures come from working engineers, and the very low figures from management".

It was found that flight readiness review certification criteria often develops a gradually decreasing strictness. "The argument that the same risk was flown before without failure is often accepted as an argument for the safety of accepting it again. Because of this, obvious weaknesses are accepted again and again, sometimes without a sufficiently serious attempt to remedy them, or to delay a flight because of their continued presence".

Clearly there was a problem of adequate resources to meet the launch rate demand, the availability requirement affected management decision making concurrently with inadequate safety management arrangements.

BHOPAL DISASTER

Nine conditions have been analysed[8] as necessary and sufficient for the accident scenario and at least 5 of these were directly attributable to human error/management decisions involving design, maintenance and operational errors.

Possible Causes of Error

Lack of Design Support Emphasises Human Safety System

One of the Areas where the Bhopal plant was criticised in the literature is in terms of its lack of automatic devices to help maintain the system within tolerable limits (eg Bowonder, 1985). It is said that safety systems had to be manually switched on, there was a general lack of automatic warning systems, and safety interlocks were not provided for critical systems. If this is the case then the operator does not appear to have been given much support from the designer.

Safety Role Ambiguities

Possible primary candidates with responsibility for safety were identified as:

- Operators
- UCIL supervision and management
- The parent company in the US
- The Madhya Pradesh inspectorate
- The Indian Government

A conclusion was reached that safety roles were probably highly ambiguous (lack of proper specification of safety duties). Potentially independent human safety systems could also fail to "audit" each others decisions and enforce safety. The implications of the report literature were that it could not be clearly established who was responsible for:

- Ensuring that the established procedures of the plant were followed.

- Ensuring that plant management, supervisory and operations personnel had sufficient plant knowledge, training and experience to operate the plant safely.

- Ensuring that the original design of the plant was safe.

- Ensuring that the plant was maintained in a safe condition.

- Defining the safety criteria and ensuring that they were maintained.

- Providing information about risk, such as MIC toxicity, and who should be informed. It should be noted that in the USA there is as yet no requirement to inform the local public of toxicity effects of plants and in the UK this has only recently become a requirement.

- Ensuring that if plant procedures or design were changed they met the safety criteria.

- Identification and notification of unsafe practices or design and whom should be notified.

- Evaluating plant siting and risk to the public.

- Ensuring the enforcement of health and safety legislation.

The execution of these roles represent the primary and back up human safety systems.

Lack of Knowledge, Rules and Procedures

It is possible that operational and/or critical decision making personnel at Bhopal could have lacked sufficient system knowledge. Such knowledge enables the consequences of actions or system state changes to be anticipated during the lifetime of a process plant. It would therefore be important to consider whether operators, supervisors and management at UCIL had sufficient training, experience and formal procedures to enable them to operate the plant safely.

Lack of System State Information

Just after washing of the filter RV lines began at 9.15pm on 2 December it is reputed that an operator noticed that the bleeder valves were blocked. The situation could have been recovered but, if the reports are correct, the supervisor apparently ordered washing to continued. Another event occurred an hour later. Pressurisation of tanks for transference of MIC to the Sevin plant began but pressure in tank (2 psi) failed to rise.

Fifteen minutes later there was a shift change. this shift was said to have observed leaks of MIC, a pressure rise in tank 610, and ultimately the catastrophic discharge.

A detailed examination of the report literature led to the following questions arising:

1   Was there a reliable indicator to provide information on the considerable temperature rise from the exothermic reaction in the tank?

2   Were the tank pressure and level indicators working correctly and did operators consider that readings taken from them were reliable?

3   Were sufficient warning information systems available and in operation (temperature, pressure and leak alarms)?

4   Did the operators have sufficient information on MIC toxicity and the behaviour of MIC on contact with water to enable accurate perception of risk?

Economic Pressure

If, as has been reported in the media, pesticides sales in India had been sinking then economic pressures would exist to minimise the costs of pesticides production. Human error in response to pressures of one sort or another is a common contributory factor in major accidents.

If the Bhopal plant was subject to economic or production pressures, one would expect to find certain indicators of this, principally:

- A decrease in production
- Reductions in manning and/or manning costs
- Reductions in downtime and/or attempts to reduce downtime
- Reductions in costly equipment
- Shortcuttings such as reduction in time consuming procedures
- Priorities of production over safety
- Attempts to increase efficiency.

The report literature, if correct would supply supporting evidence for each of these indicators, except the last. For example, the introduction of a jumper line would enable either the process vent header on the relief valve vent header to be used for venting and relief whilst the other was being maintained, without the need for plant shutdown.

It is also estimated that savings from switching off the refrigeration unit would be about $50 a day.

If economic pressures existed at the time that it was decided to have MIC storage, then such pressure may have influenced this decision. Storage has the following advantages:

- Reductions in downtime
- Fluctuations in the process can be evened out
- Ease of operability

The nine conditions which were necessary and sufficient at the time of the accident were the result of decisions taken over a considerable period of time. The decision to store large quantities of MIC was part of the design concept. The jumper line between header lines was introduced sometime during operation as was the removal of the refrigeration of the tanks. The magnitude of the MIC/water reaction that occurred was not foreseen in the design of the tanks, plant or vent gas scrubber nor in the inadequacy of the procedures or in the ability of the operators to cope at the time of the accident.

CONCLUSIONS

The accidents considered have similar generic features eg resource problems, safety management inadequacies, communication problems, design issues, and inadequate information. These could potentially have been assessed and led to accident prevention by the methods discussed in the paper. The O&M assessment would have enabled common features that could have affected many aspects plant operation eg demand pressures/resources, possible deterioration of maintenance standards, limitations of design, to be considered in the task analyses and the effects to be allowed for in the safety/reliability analysis and assessment. It is clear that major accidents cannot be accounted for on the basis of a snapshot approach. Variation over a long period of time has to be considered. This means continual review of safety and reliability assessment. It also means that reliability data based on certain standards of plant maintenance for instance are not applicable at potential accident instances. Thus not only are there increasing dependencies but item failure rates are likely to be increased also.

These analyses of O&M influences on plant reliability will be mainly qualitative. This is because of their mainly mental and social characteristics which make quantitative data collection and analysis fundamentally difficult. this also applies to the reliability of management itself eg in the communication process or in controlling resources properly that may affect plant reliability. The issue of avoiding catastrophic accidents is too important to thereby downgrade the importance of performing such analyses since they can point to ways of preventing common influences which give rise to unforeseen dependencies.

REFERENCES

1 WATSON I A et al "Criticality Survey of Research on Human Factors and the Man-machine Interaction" IAEA-SM-26B/29. Interntional Atomic Energy Agency (1984).

2 "The German Risk Study" Rep EPRI-NP-1804 SR Electric Power Research Institute Palo Alto (1981).

3 EDWARDS G T and WATSON I A "A Study of Common Mode Failures", The Safety and Reliability Directorate UKAEA SRD R146 (1980).

4 Flight International 22, January (1975).

5 Contents of the NCSR Reliability Data Bank NCSR/DB/40.

6 WATSON I A "Review of Human Factors in Reliability and Risk" Assessment I Chem E SYMPOSIUM Series No 93.

7 COVALLT Craig "SHUTTLE 51-L Loss" Aviation Week and Space Technology/June 16, 1986.

8   BELLAMY L J "The Safety Management Factor: An Analysis of the Human Error Aspects of the Bhopal Disaster".

9   EDWARDS G T et al "Defences Against Common-Mode Failures in Redundancy Systems" SRD R196 January 1981.

10   "Human Factors in industrial Systems - Review of Reliability Analysis Techniques". (Draft available from the HSE, Bootle, Liverpool).

11   "Systematic Human Action Reliability Procedure (SHARP)" EPRI NP-3583 Interim Report, June (1984).

12   DUNCAN K D et al "Task Analysis". Training Information Paper No 6, (1971), HMSO London.

13   SEARLE, John "Minds, Brains & Science". The 1984 Reith Lectures. Published by the British Broadcasting Corporation.

14   WATSON, I A "Fundamental Constraints on some Event Data" Proceedings of the 5th EuReDatA Conference Heidelberg, April 1986.

15   Aviation Week & Space Technology. October 1, (1984) Page 99. "Cockpit Crew Curriculums Emphasise Human Factors".

16   "MORT Management and Oversight Risk Tree". International Risk Management Institute, Vol Vi, No 2, October (1983).

17   HUMPHREYS P & BERKELEY D "Handling Uncertainty Levels of Analysis of Decision Problems" in G Wright (Ed) "Behavioural Decision Making" London: Plenum Press 1985.

FUNDAMENTAL FACTORS IN SYSTEM RELIABILITY

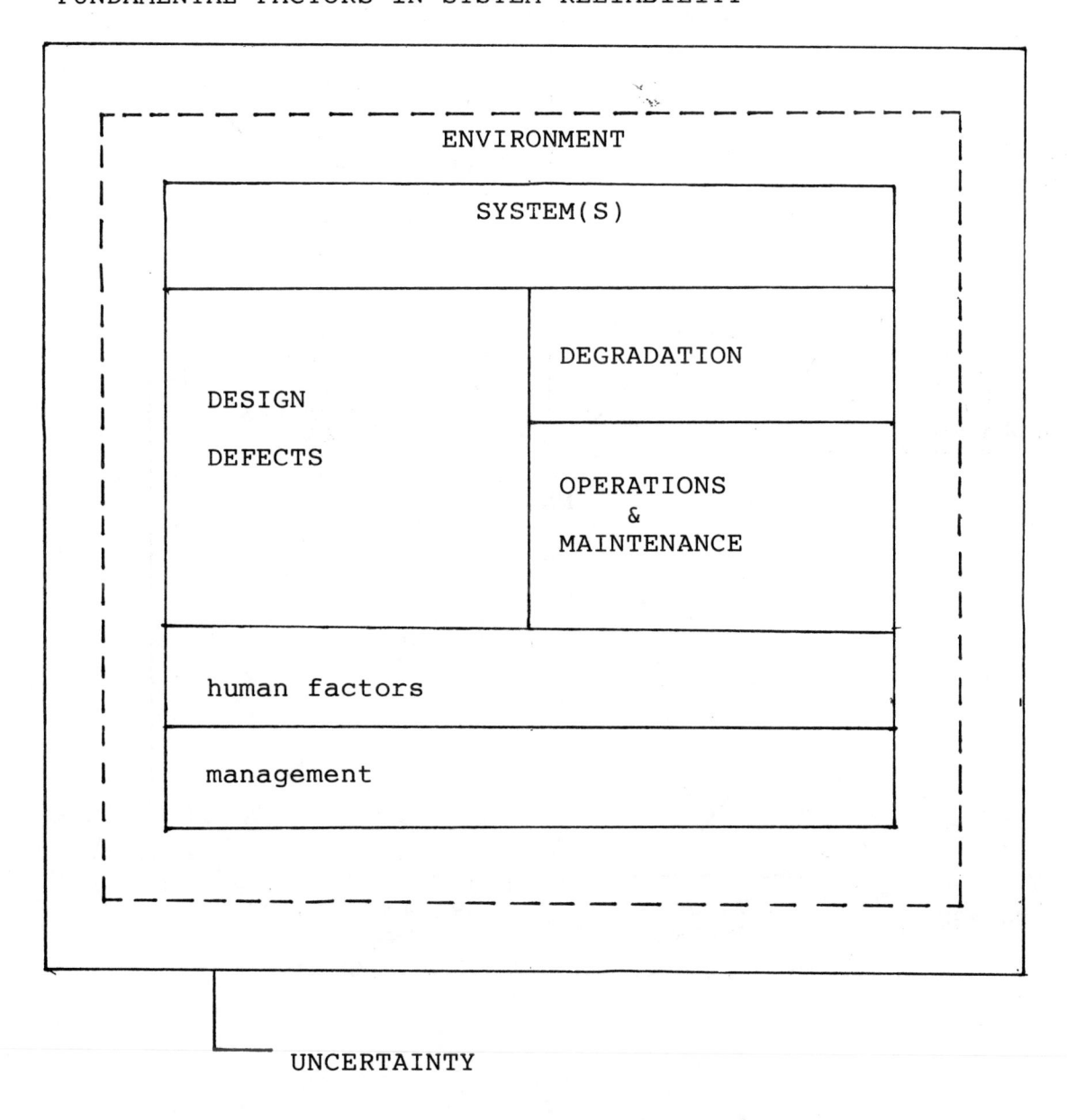

```
┌─────────────────────────────────────────────┐
│   ┌─────────────────────────────────────┐   │
│   │            ENVIRONMENT              │   │
│   │   ┌─────────────────────────────┐   │   │
│   │   │          SYSTEM(S)          │   │   │
│   │   ├──────────────┬──────────────┤   │   │
│   │   │              │  DEGRADATION │   │   │
│   │   │   DESIGN     ├──────────────┤   │   │
│   │   │   DEFECTS    │  OPERATIONS  │   │   │
│   │   │              │       &      │   │   │
│   │   │              │  MAINTENANCE │   │   │
│   │   ├──────────────┴──────────────┤   │   │
│   │   │      human factors          │   │   │
│   │   ├─────────────────────────────┤   │   │
│   │   │      management             │   │   │
│   │   └─────────────────────────────┘   │   │
│   └─────────────────────────────────────┘   │
└─────────────────────────────────────────────┘
     └── UNCERTAINTY
```

Figure 1

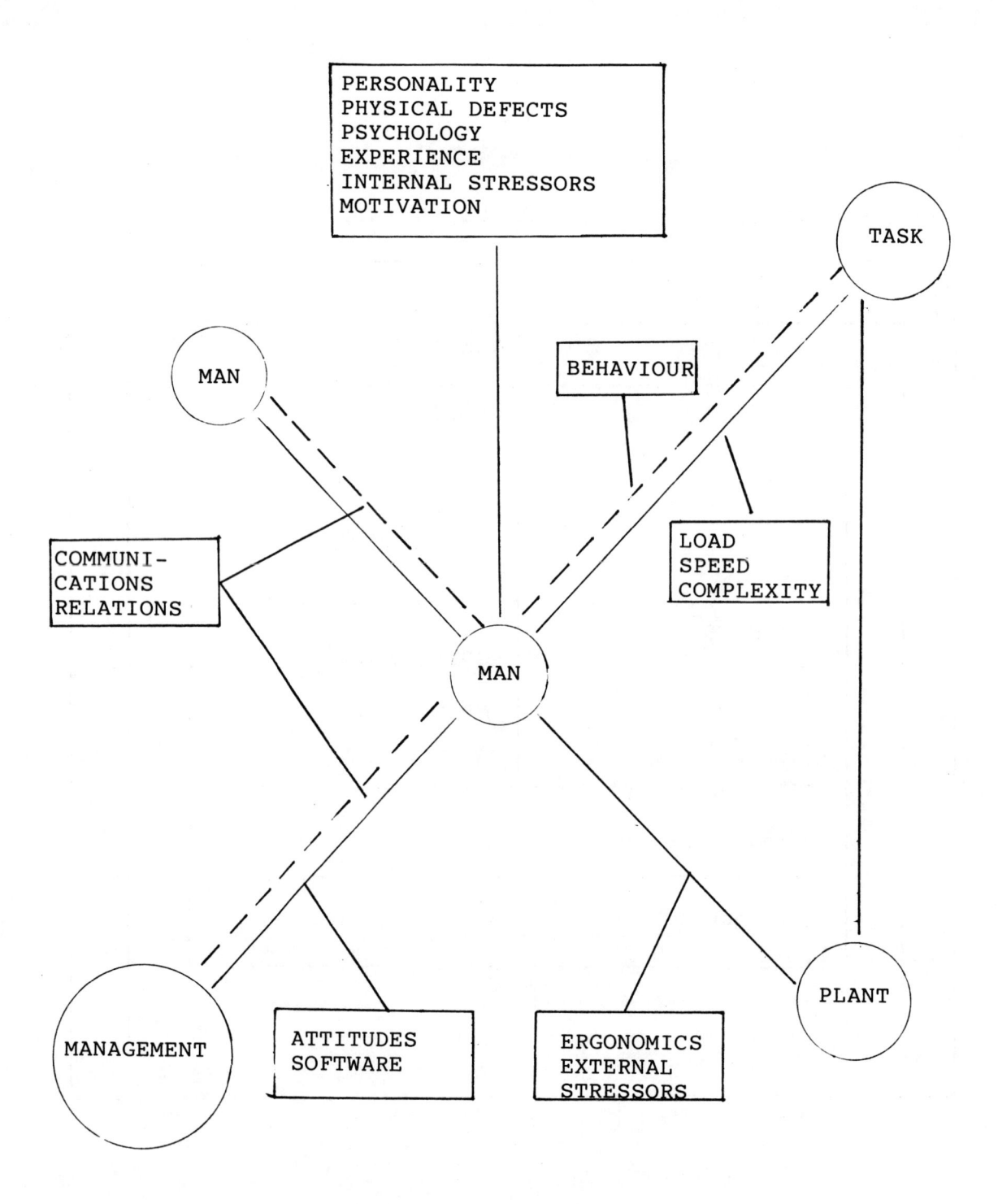

Figure 2   Influences on man in industry

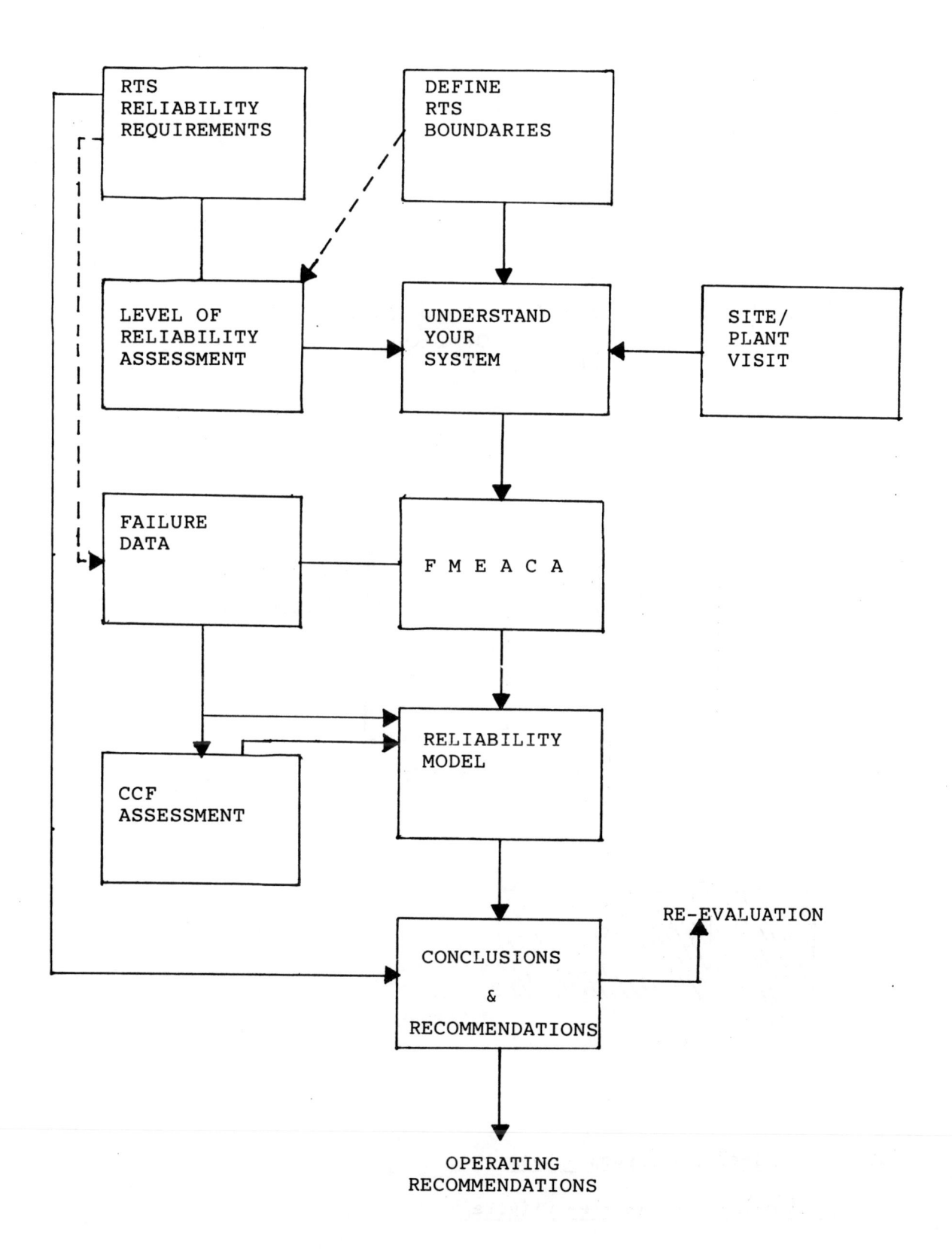

Figure 3   Overall reliability assessment procedure

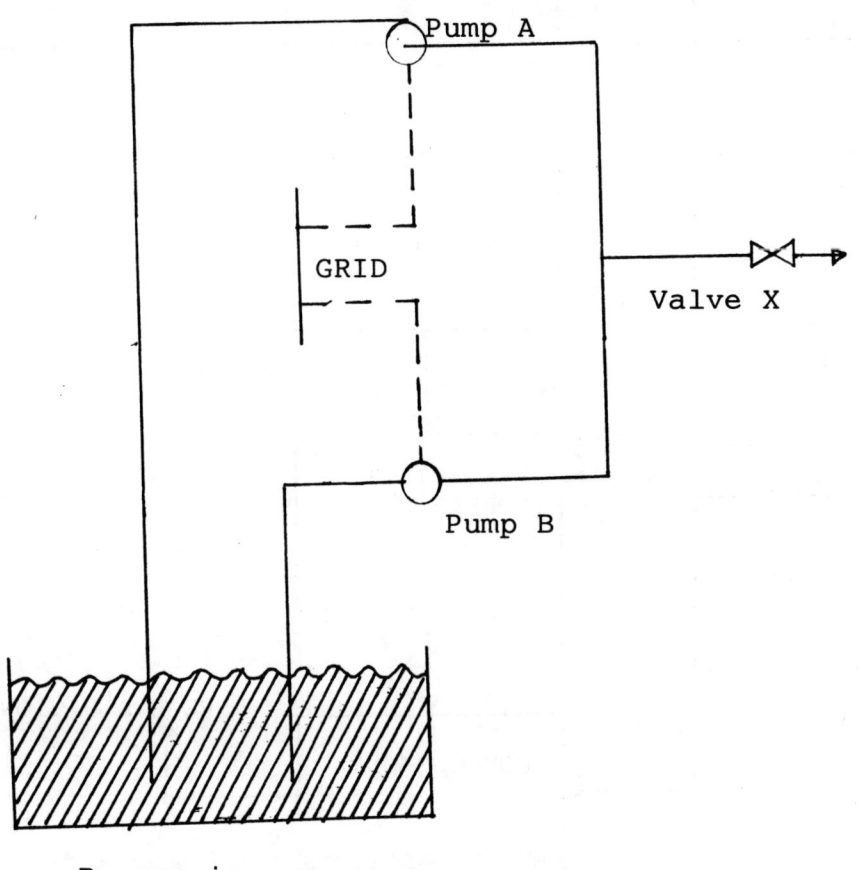

Figure 4   1-out-of-2 Pump System

Subject for fault tree (figure 5)

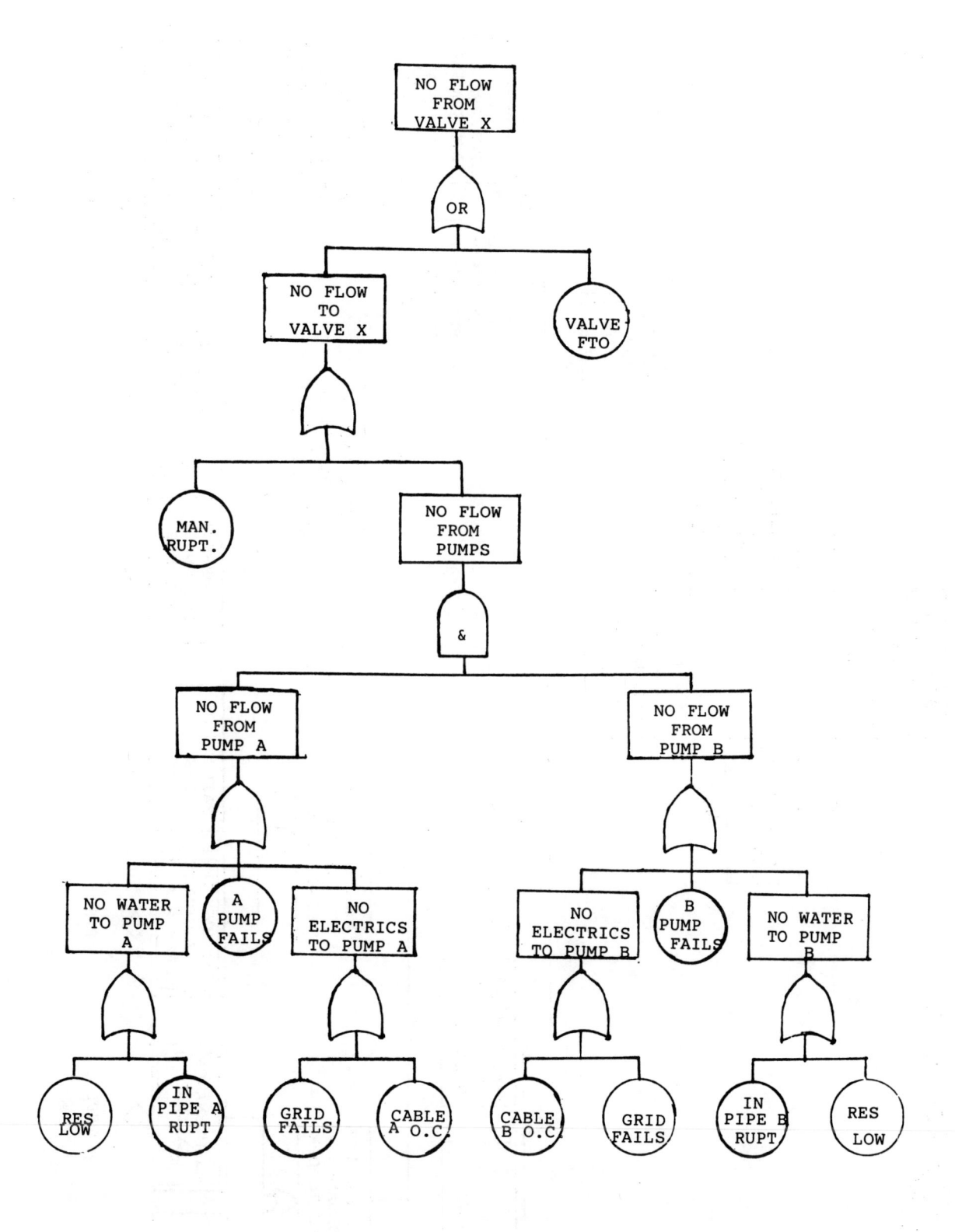

Figure 5   Fault tree for 1 out of 2 pump system

Figure 6 Enhanced fault tree

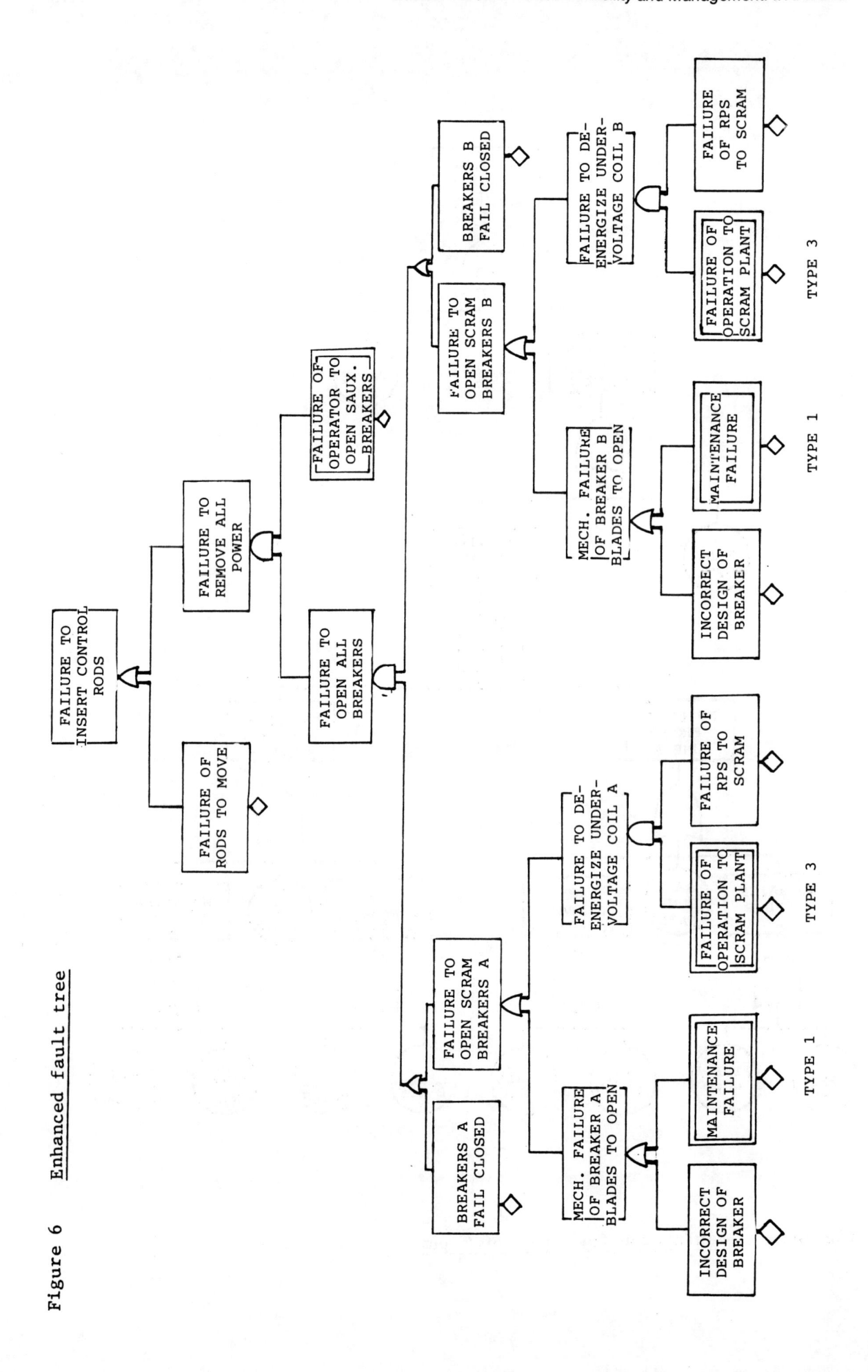

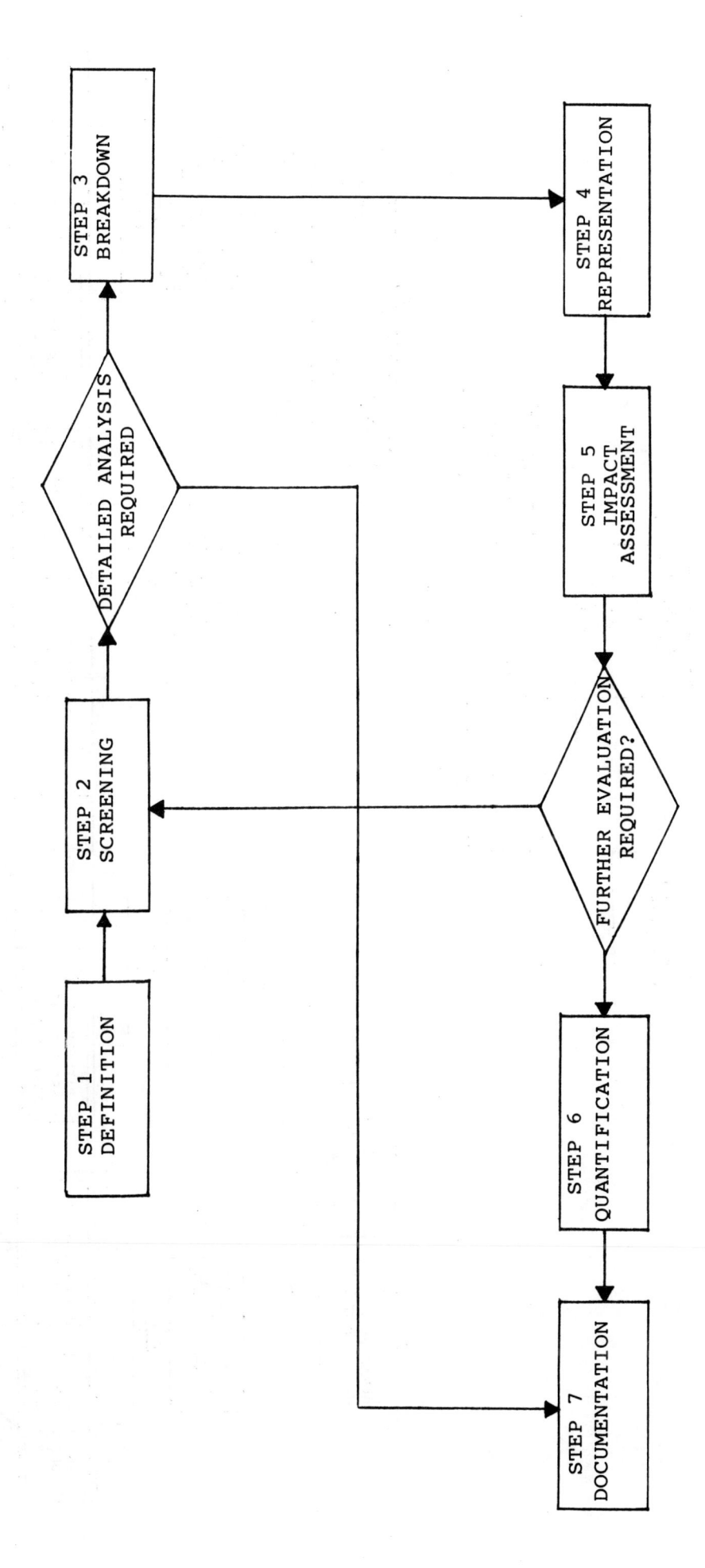

Figure 7 Links between SHARP steps

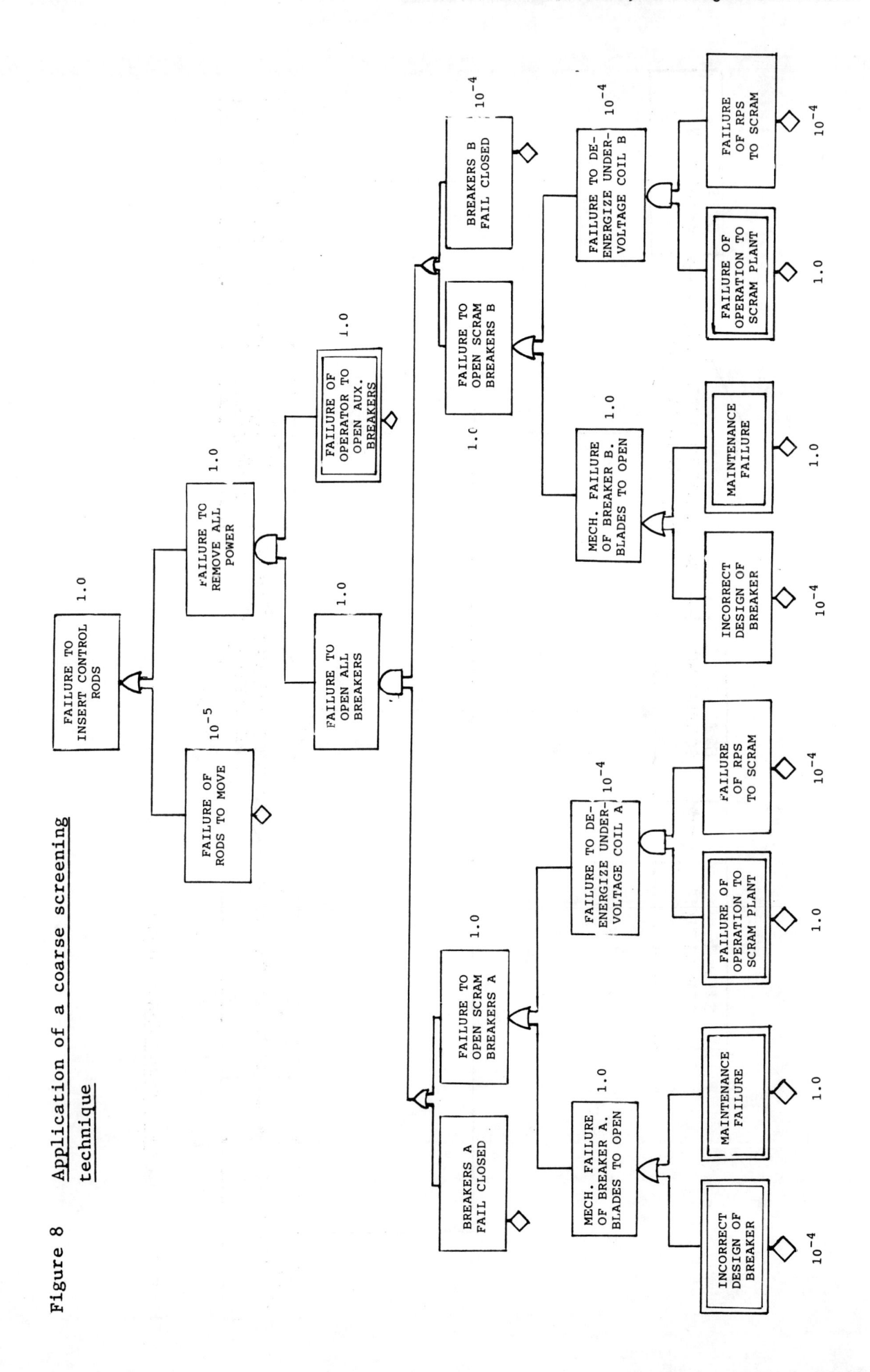

Figure 8 Application of a coarse screening technique

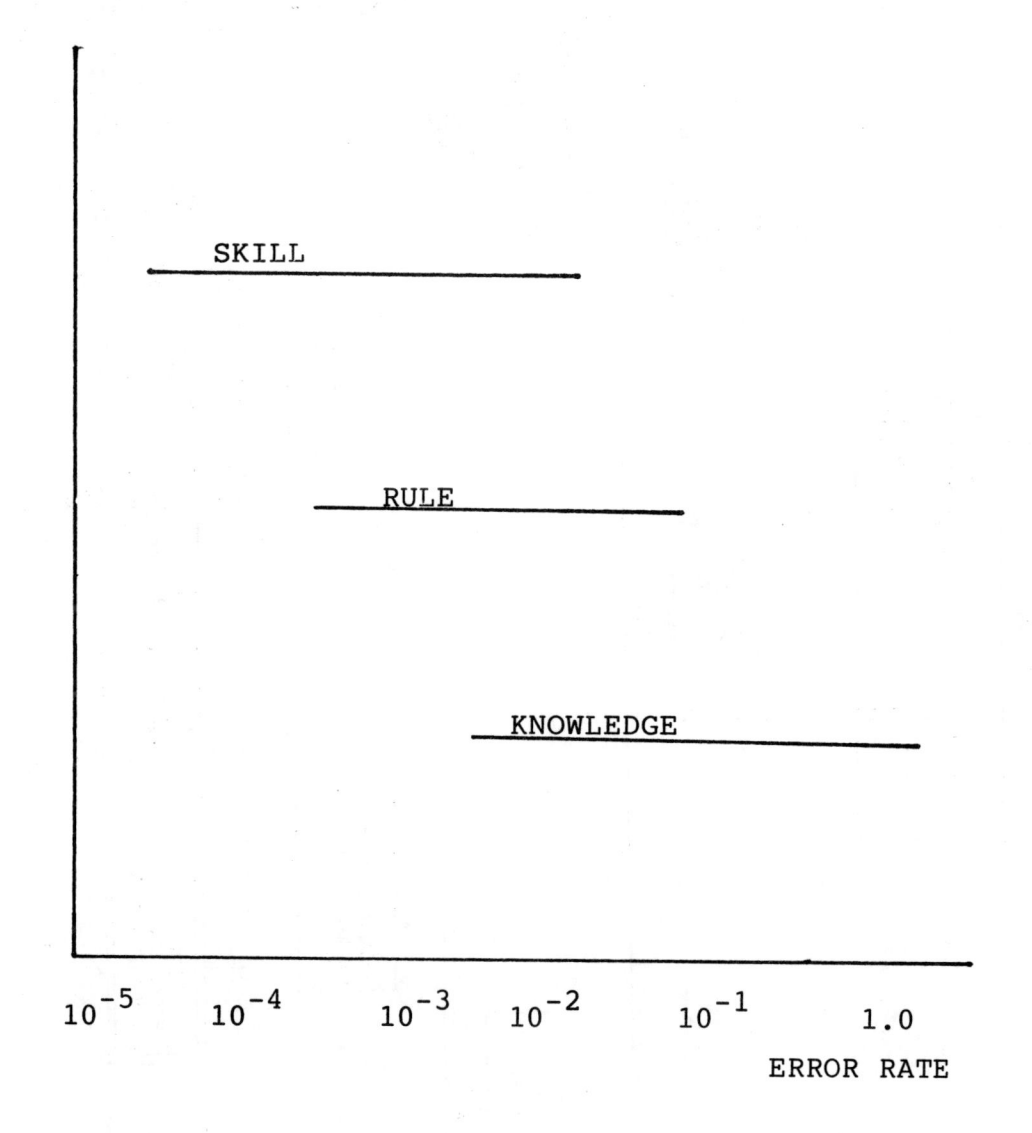

Figure 9   Error rate ranges associated with human behaviour

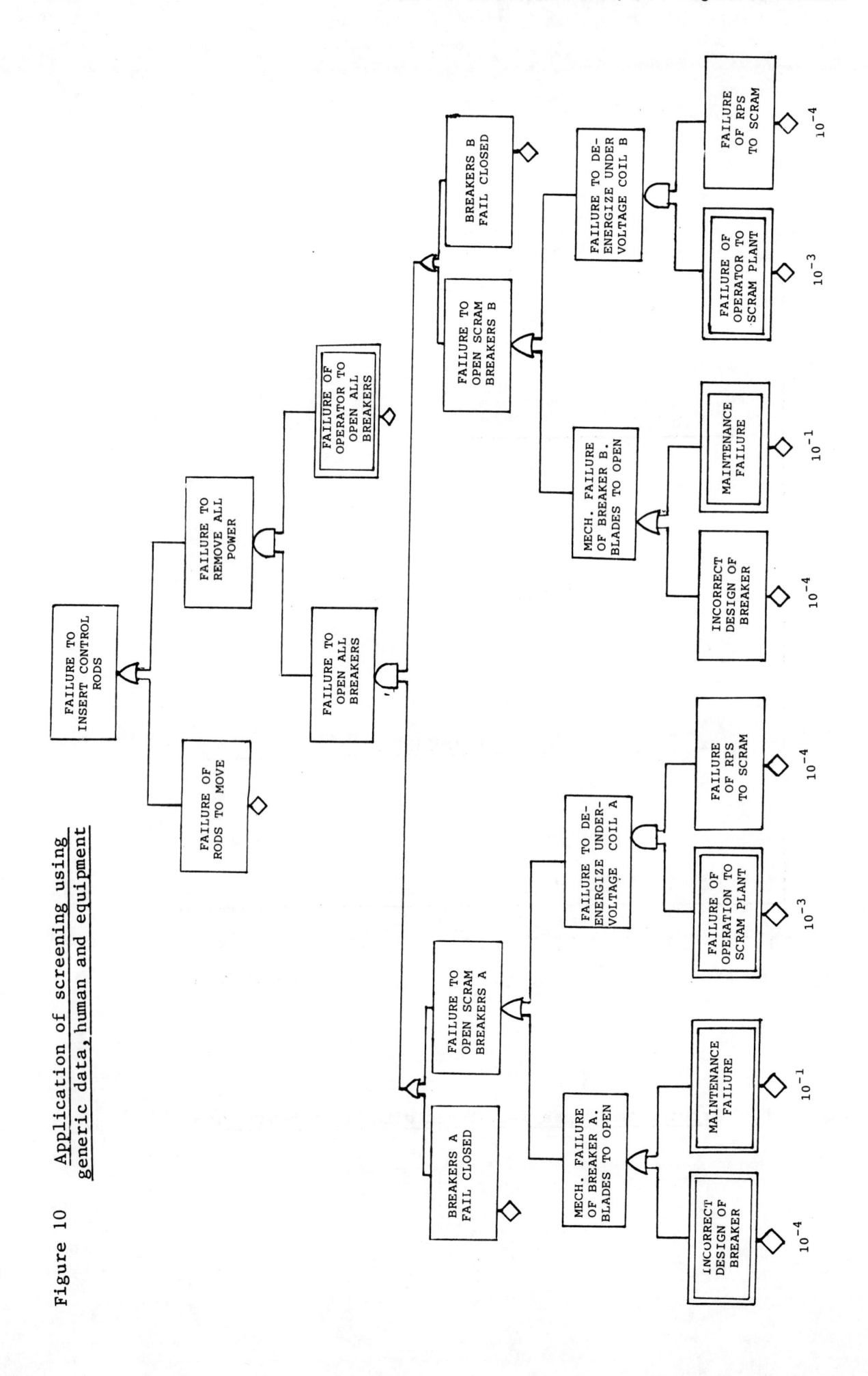

Figure 10   Application of screening using
             generic data, human and equipment

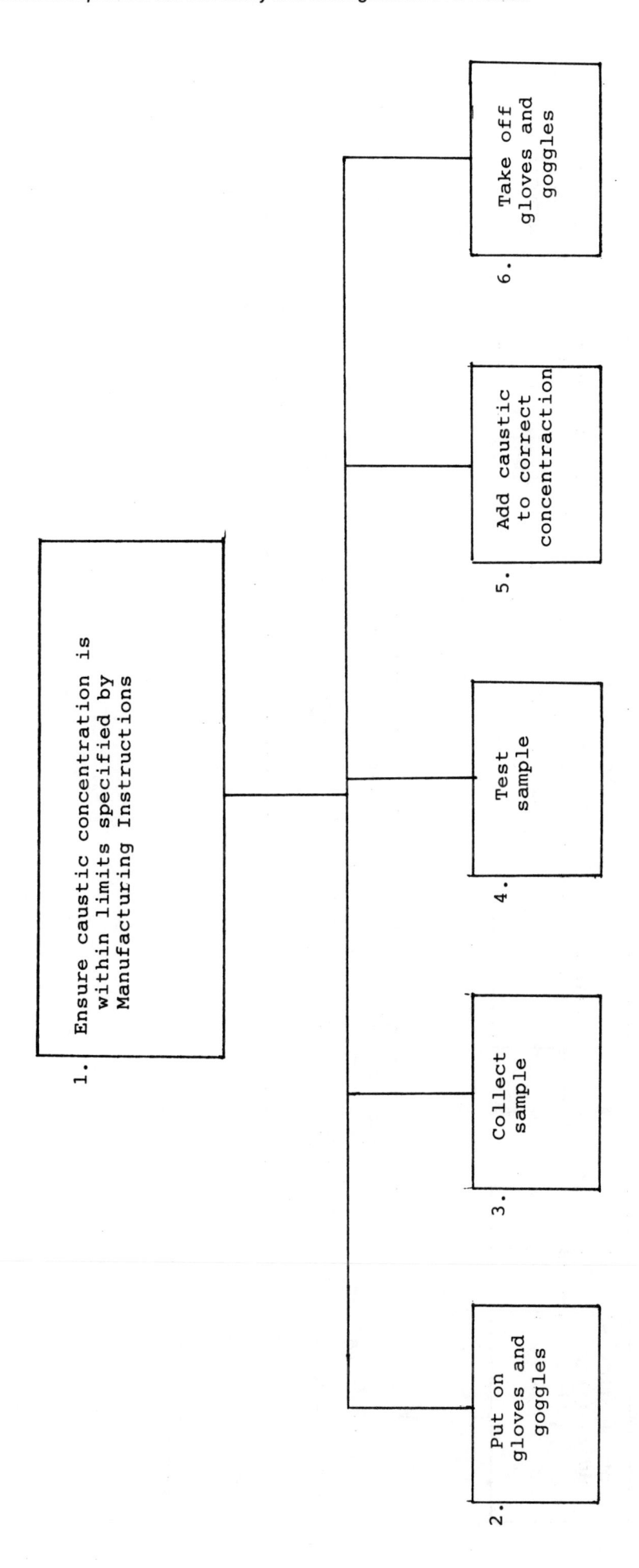

1. Ensure caustic concentration is within limits specified by Manufacturing Instructions

2. Put on gloves and goggles
3. Collect sample
4. Test sample
5. Add caustic to correct concentration
6. Take off gloves and goggles

Figure 11

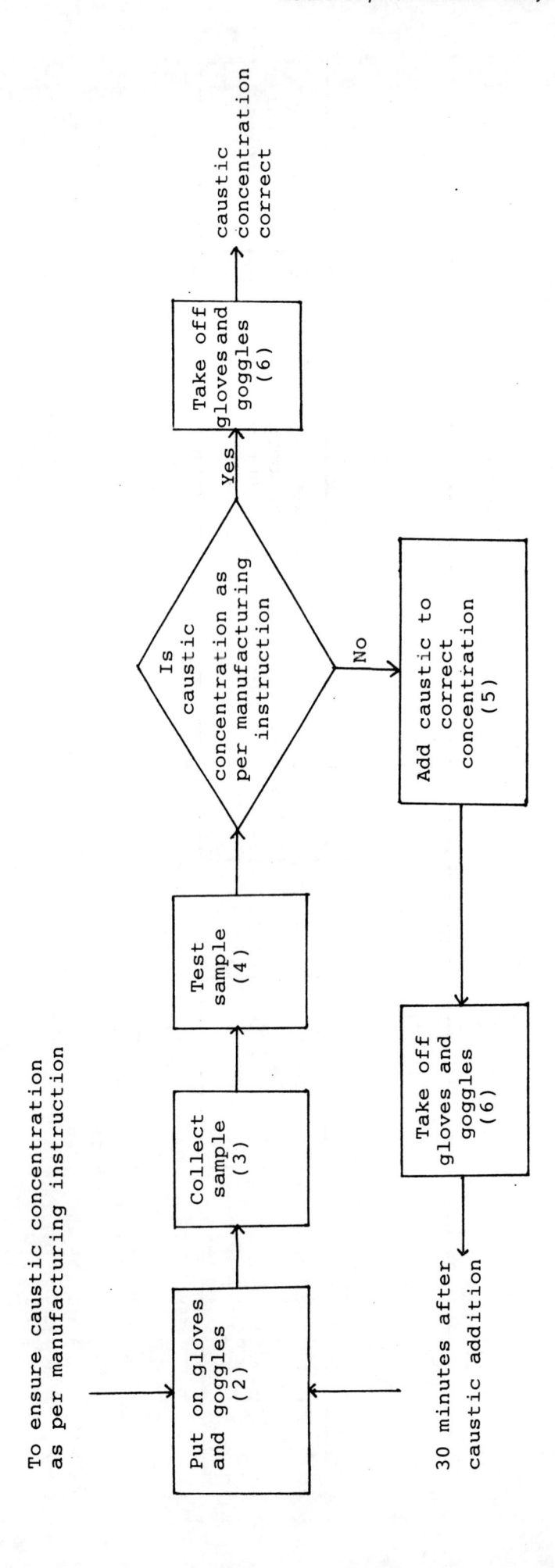

Figure 12

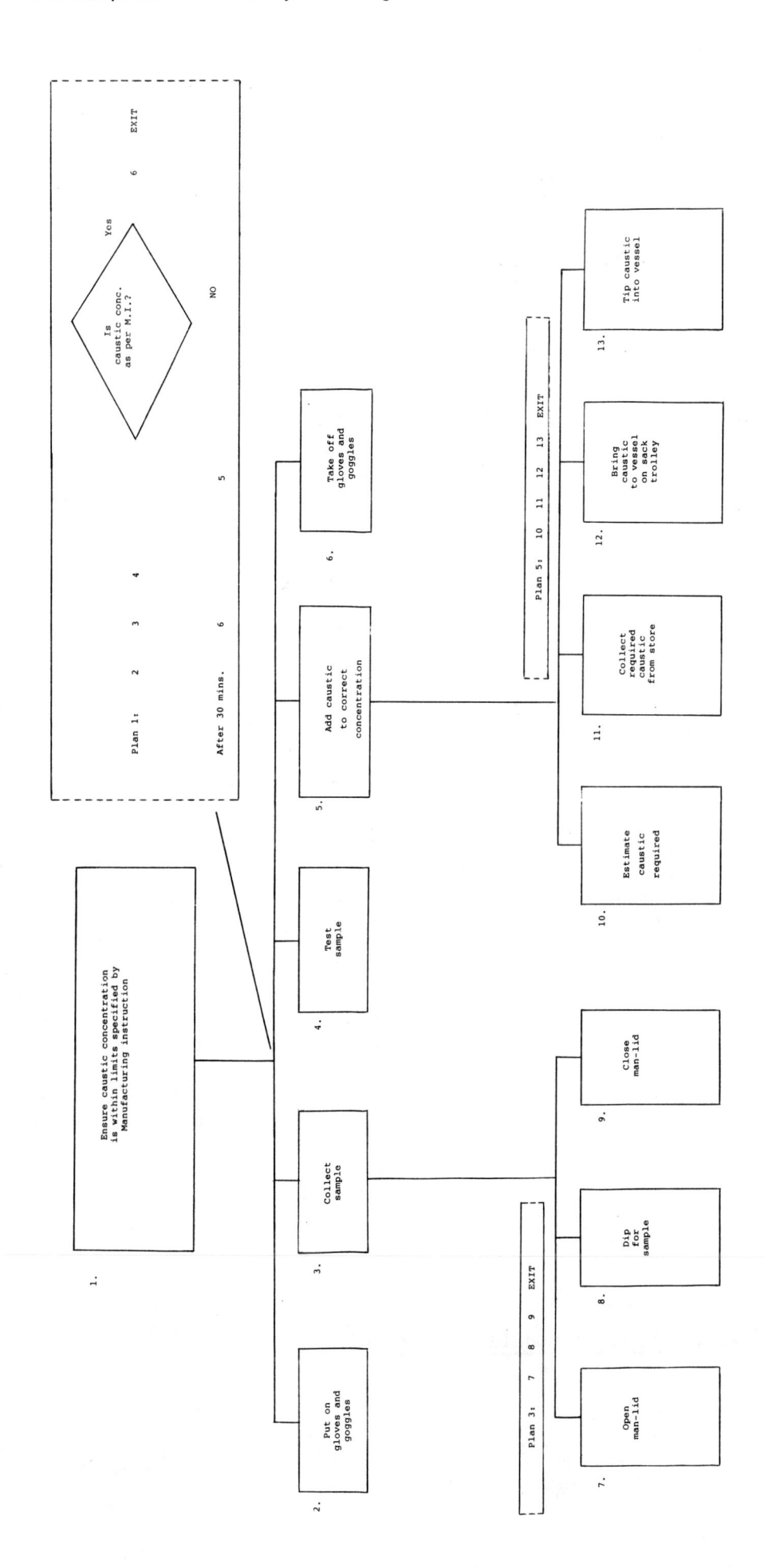

Figure 13

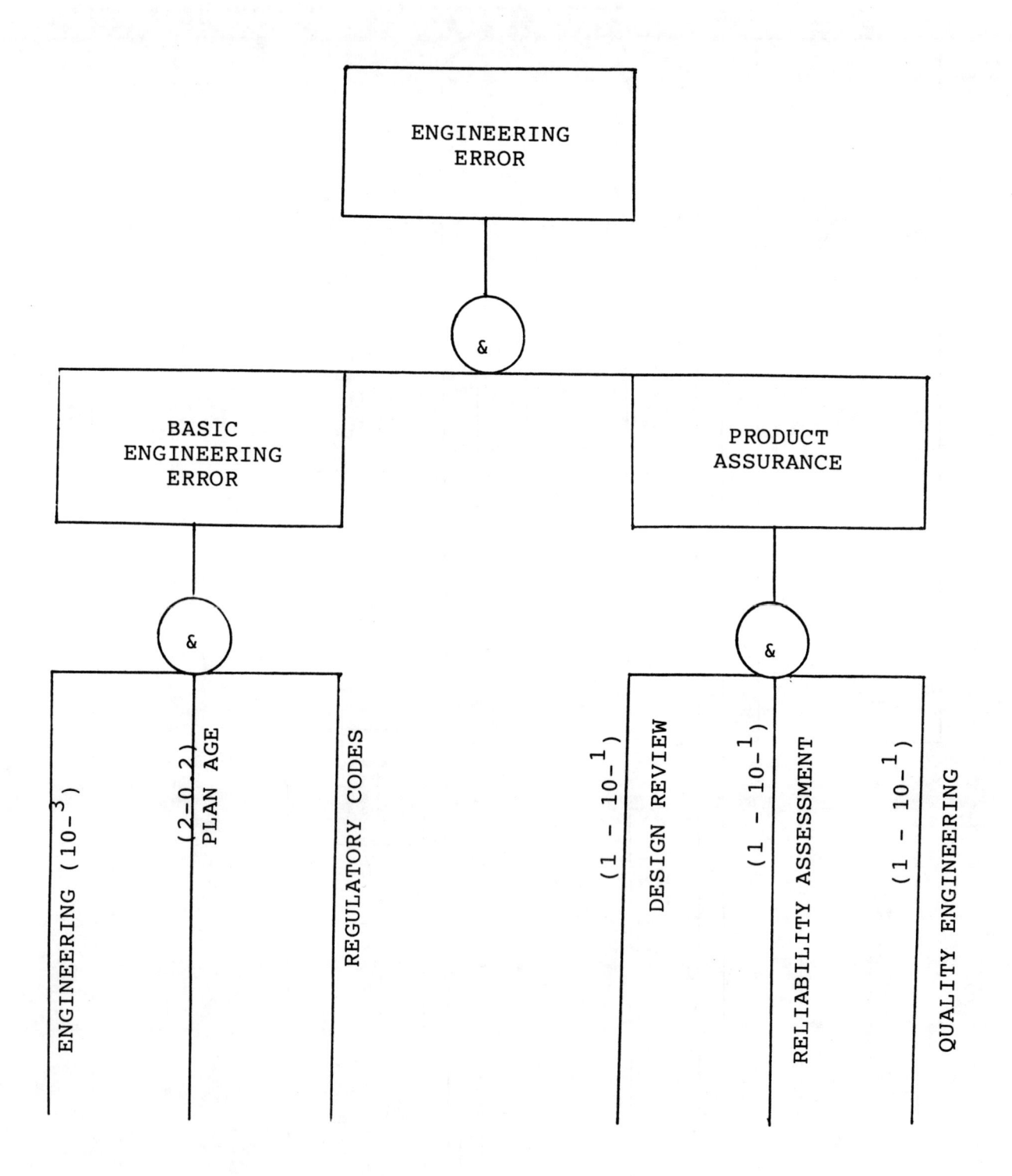

Figure 14   Part of a subsystem modelling structure

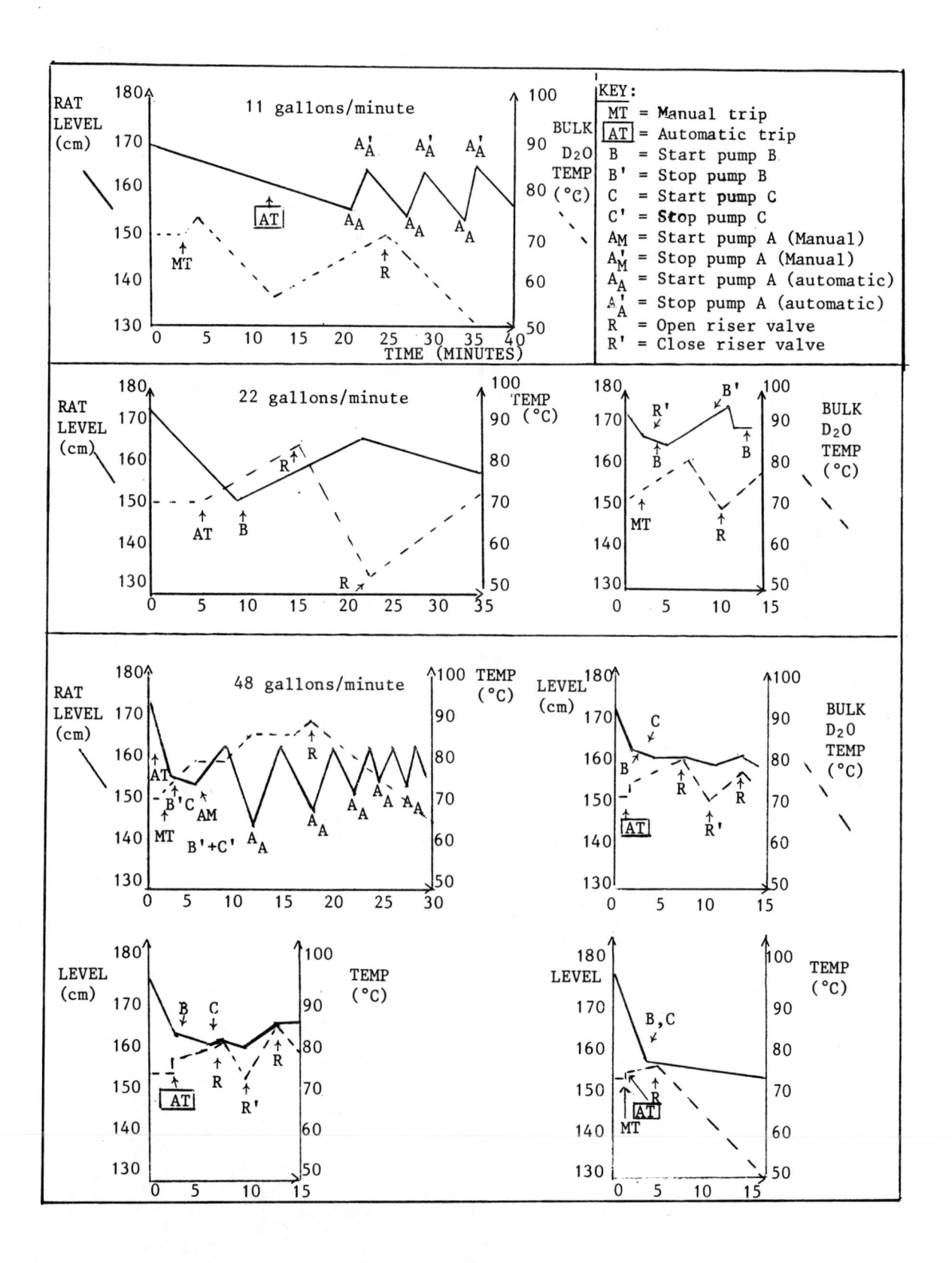

FIGURE 15 Various Strategies for Controlling a Simulated LOCA

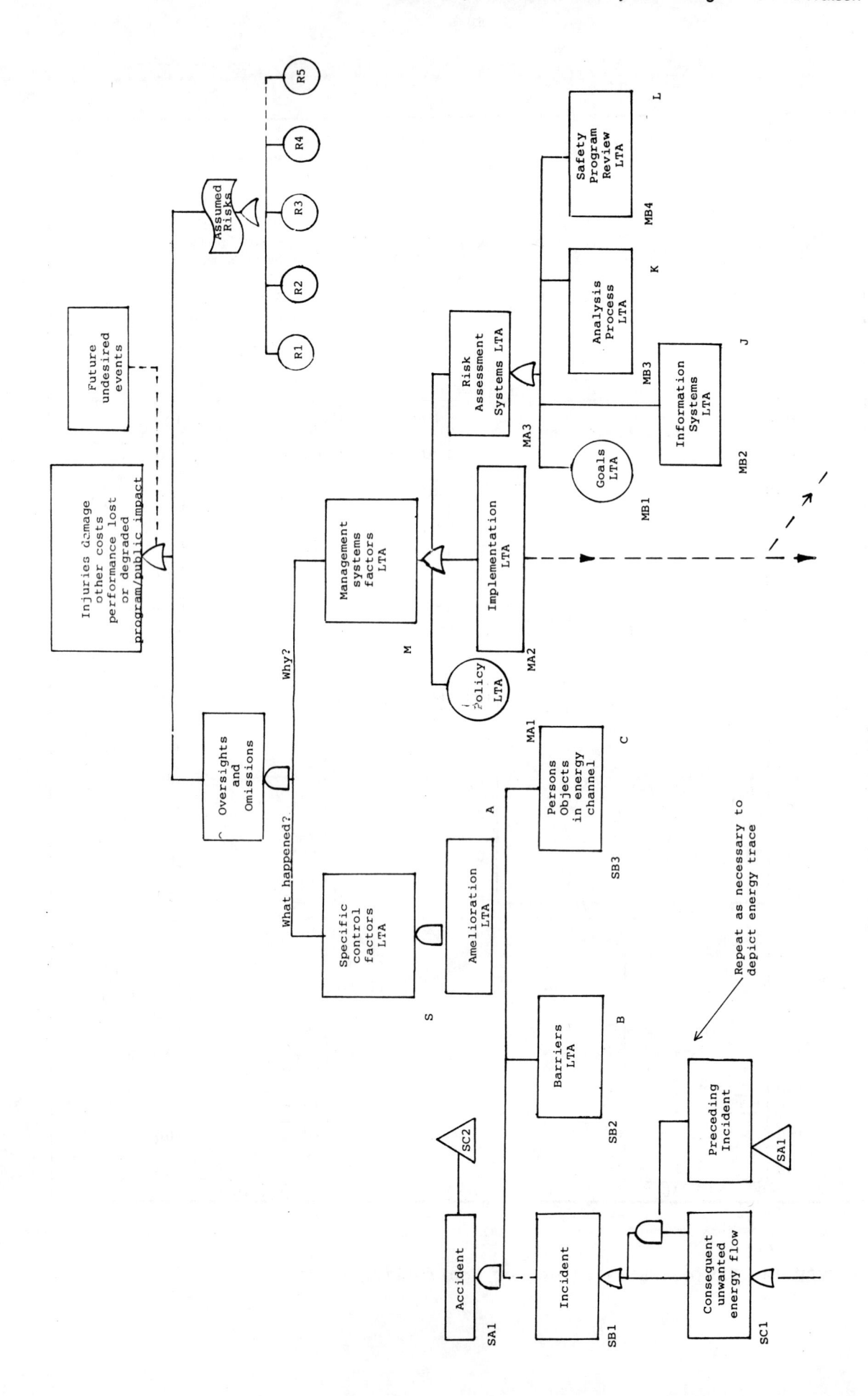

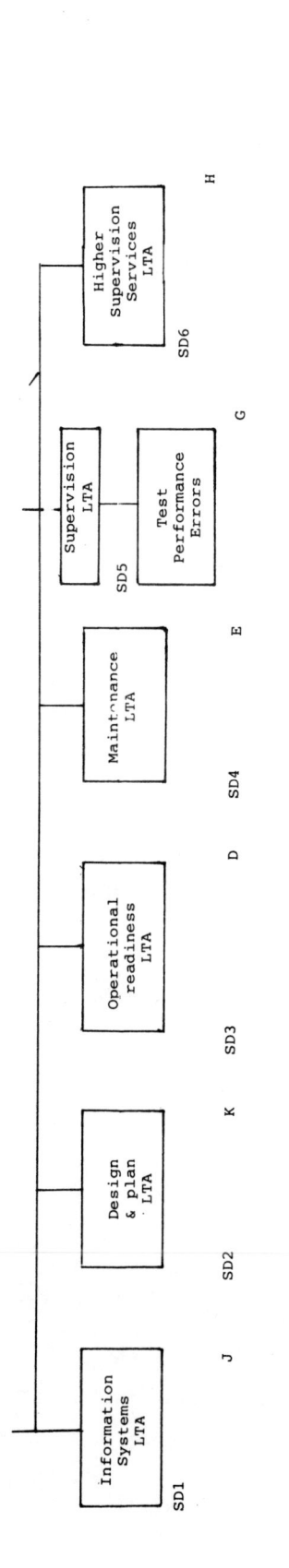

LETTER ABBREVIATIONS

D/N	-	DID NOT
D/NP	-	DID NOT PROVIDE
ERDA	-	ENERGY RESEARCH & DEVELOPMENT ADMINISTRATION
F/	-	FAILED FAILURE
F/M	-	FAILED TO MONITOR
F/M&R	-	FAILED TO MONITOR & REVIEW
F/T	-	FAILED TO
HAP	-	HAZARD ANAL. PROCESS
JSA	-	JOB SAFETY ANAL.
LTA	-	LESS THAN ADEQUATE
OSHA	-	OCCUPATIONAL SAFETY & HEALTH ADMINISTRATION
RSO	-	REPORTED SIGNIFICANT OBSERVATION
W/	-	WITH

Figure 16   MORT: Management oversight and risk tree

Cognitive Problem Solving

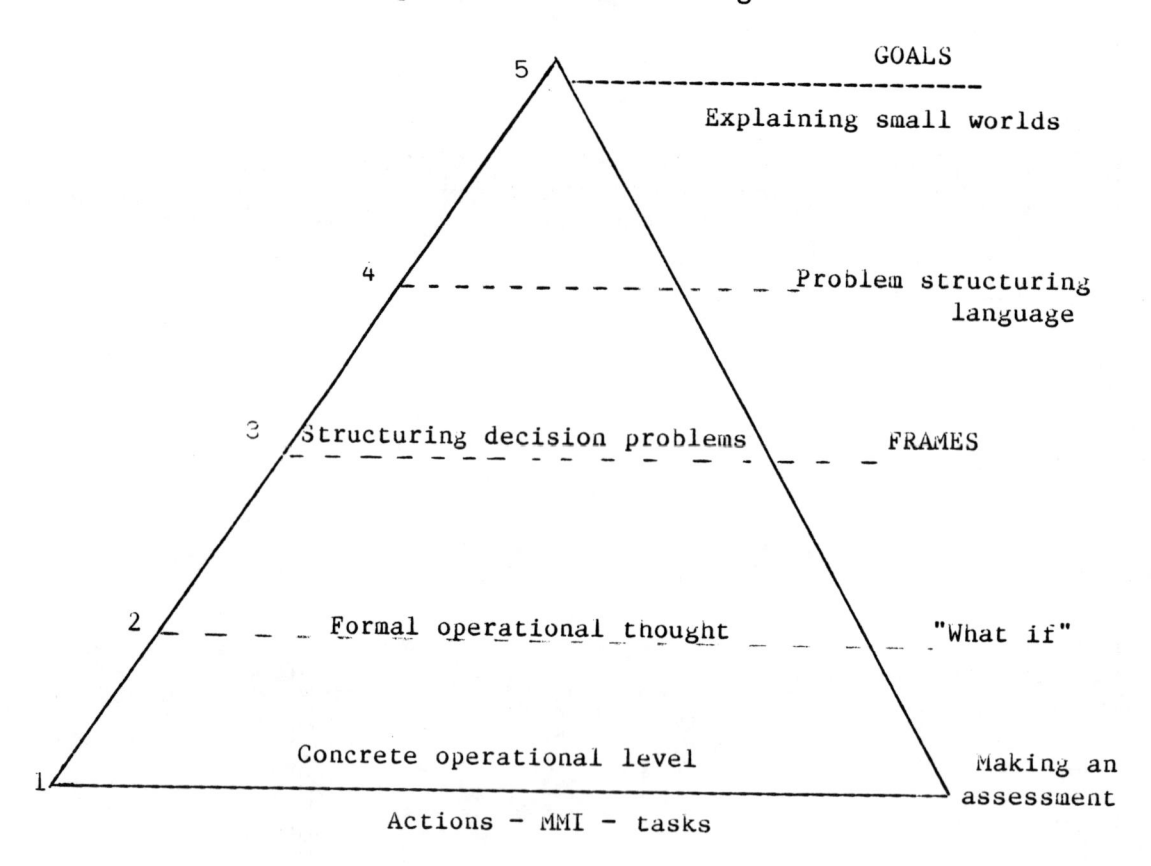

```
                    5 /\                      GOALS
                     /  \ ----------------------
                    /    \      Explaining small worlds
                   /      \
                4 /- - - - \- - - - - - - Problem structuring
                 /          \                       language
                /            \
             3 /Structuring decision problems\      FRAMES
              /- - - - - - - - - - - - - - - \
             /                                \
          2 /- - - Formal operational thought - \    "What if"
           /                                    \
          /                                      \
       1 /____Concrete operational level_____\  Making an
                                                     assessment
               Actions - MMI - tasks
```

Figure 17

8 Early Experience in the Application of Decision Analysis to Selected CEGB Problems

K. G. Begg
Central Electricity Generating Board

1. INTRODUCTION

The activity of the CEGB in the area of decision analysis (D.A.) described in this paper is mainly confined to the Environmental Studies Section which is responsible for advising on the policy implications of environmental developments and activities associated with fossil fuel power stations. D.A. is used to some extent in other areas of the Board's activities but these tend to be applications to specific operating problems.

Historically our interest has stemmed from the Acid Rain question. In the early 1980's within the UNECE, under the Convention on Long Range Transboundary Air Pollution, there was a great deal of conflict because of the range of scientific opinion on effects. When the Executive Body for the Convention moved from a cost benefit analysis (CBA) approach to a Decision Analysis (DA) approach this conflict within the meetings was reduced because it was known that all opinions would be taken into account. The DA approach was therefore attractive in that it was a much more structured procedure for evaluating strategies and it appeared capable of taking account of the differing international views and putting them into perspective.

The UK Government (DoE) took the initiative and started to develop a UK model on Acid Rain which could be input to the UNECE CBA Group of Experts (Watson 1986). In collaboration with Dr. Watson's team at Cambridge and Department of Environment the CEGB assisted in the preparation of the detailed specification of the UK model and have continued to contribute to the development of the model along with other UK experts. To be able to contribute to this development and to assess the models in this field being produced by IIASA and EPRI (Boyson et al 1982) we have had to become familiar not only with the background science of the Acid Rain Issue but also problem structuring for decision analysis. This has involved, in the very early stages of the work, the construction of a small acid rain model called DAS at the Central Electricity Research Laboratories. This allowed us to gain valuable experience in modelling the issue and provided a large data base on emissions and transport, and on the health, materials, lake and crop impacts.

In the environmental field, which tends to be rather subjective, there are many problems which seem to be amenable to the technique of Decision Analysis and where conventional cost benefit analysis is difficult to apply. The main advantages of the technique are that,

1. it forces the decision maker to consider a more comprehensive view of the problem

2. it ensures discussion in some depth

3. it forms a rational framework for a decision which can then be justified more openly and easily.

2. APPLICATION OF DECISION ANALYSIS TO CEGB

The Board faces problems which differ in scale and complexity. At one end of the scale are decisions which involve large scale technological developments involving many sections of the community, such as building a new power station, and at the other we have small internal decisions, some of which may input to large scale projects. An example of this is selecting a pipeline route.

Decision Analysis may offer a way forward on all these areas but in these early stages we tend to concentrate on the smaller scale problems. However there are difficulties in gaining acceptance within the Board for this type of approach, which we have to deal with.

2.1 Early Experience

When Decision Analysis was in its infancy in the late 1960's the technique was applied to some major problems such as coal or nuclear generation choices. The attempt to use DA was unsuccessful for a number of reasons, but one of the main problems was in the estimation of probabilities associated with particular values of variables. In some cases no probabilities could be assigned, but were insisted upon, thus building up a prejudice against the technique. At these early stages, before the development of experience of many case studies, consultant advice, and computer decision aids, it is not surprising that in a particularly complex problem there was great difficulty in applying the technique.

2.2 Use of Subjective Probabilities

Another major problem is the use of subjective probabilities. In the nuclear industry generally, engineers have become used to fault trees and probabilistic risk assessments, but have received criticism on the use of subjective probabilities as inputs to these methodologies. This has led the industry and the CEGB to become wary of the whole concept. The nuclear industry is at present straining every other technique to substitute for subjective probabilities in risk assessments, in order to base the results on engineering knowledge and therefore, they believe, to make them more acceptable. There is consequently a genuine resistance and distrust of the use of subjective probabilities in Decision Analysis.

3. CURRENT PROGRAMME

To gain some acceptance of the technique, we have chosen to build up a toolkit of decision aids which we can apply to a range of environmental problems, but which we hope can be applied throughout the CEGB. In this way some sort of foundation can be built for expansion in the use of the approach and this will also allow us to incorporate consultant input to specific larger scale problems.

Three main problem types have been examined so far.

1. Decision/Event Tree Structure with many end points

2. Standard Decision Tree Approach

3. Selection of Options.

This toolkit is comprised of some external models and in-house models which we are in the process of developing.

3.1 In-House Model Development

The reason for attempting to build some of our own models is driven by the need to have models appropriate to the industry. External models have a "black box" image which can be unsatisfactory for a technological industry. On a personal level, it is less than convincing when trying to persuade someone to use a model, if the details behind it are not known. There is a problem in presentation for external models whereas a flexible approach can appeal to certain people and be more tailored to their perceptions of a problem.

Another advantage is that experience and expertise is developed in setting up models. However one of the main problems is in rationalising the different theoretical frameworks for the different models available on the market. On one hand the Keeney and Raiffa approach (Raiffa 1969, Bell et al 1977) demands a rigorous treatment of utilities, the shape of utility functions, models for combining utilities, lotteries to derive attribute weights, in addition to specific rules such as weak conditional utility independence or preference independence. On the other hand, the difficulty of applying the theory in practice has been to some extent overcome by the current models on the market. In gaining some ease of use, different compromises are made by different models and these compromises are validated either in the theory or by experience in practice. However it can be difficult to judge how valid and how extensive these compromises are. Building a model from basics has the advantage that any compromises are explicit. Nevertheless, as we are at the start of this work, we are aware that the models described are not at all sophisticated in terms of decision theory, and we have still to address many of these issues.

3.2 Event Tree Model

The first category of problem we have examined applies to very large scale issues such as acid rain as well as to more localised engineering types of problems. In these cases there are many possible branches in the tree structure which may or may not include decision nodes, as well as probability nodes. In the case of acid rain, in addition to the early work on DAS, we have the EPRI ADEPT model and the UK model which have been built to handle this specific issue, and for these two models we have confined ourselves to user feedback on the use of these models and the provision of basic data.

For other in-house problems such as the costing of wind generators a small model for general use is being developed using the CEGB IBM mainframe system, and an IBM Graphics Terminal. It is written in APL and uses the IBM chart facility. The tree is constructed initially with only

probability nodes and a limit of three possible values with associated
probabilities per variable. The calculation required for the final result
is input and the output can be produced in several ways. The minimum,
maximum, mean and median with the value, probability and pathways to
produce these results are listed (figure 1). A bound such as 1% can be
set up to limit the number of paths round the values of interest. A
cumulative probability graph is drawn from the end point results.

A second method is also incorporated into the model where, given the
initial points on the distribution for a variable, a curve is fitted
through these. The variables are then combined in the calculations along
with their distributions, described by a number of points which are
selected at the start of the run. At the end, a cumulative probability
graph is drawn based on the number of points specified. This takes
account of the problem of 'fixing' the minimum value, rather than having a
small chance that the actual minimum may be less than the value given.
There are problems in the approach, where a variable is being assessed
purely by subjective methods, in biassing the probability distribution in
the first place by having three values with minimum, medium and maximum
labels already in place rather than eliciting probabilities. In fact the
model also allows this type of input in another option where several
points describing the probability distribution on a variable can be input
ignoring the limit of the three original points. A graph can be produced
to compare the effect of these changes on the final distribution
(figure 2).

This model is by no means complete and is still under development. The
output from these considerations can then be fed into the decision making
process in terms of the probability that the cost will be between certain
values or less then specific values. These latter problems are not
concerned with multiple and conflicting objectives; nevertheless we regard
the model as a first step in decision support which opens the way for a
much wider input to decisions.

3.3 Decision Tree Model

The second category of model is a simple decision tree model. It uses our
mainframe system and is APL based as before. This has been formulated and
tested using mainly standard problems such as the LSE Graham problem, or
using decisions already taken in the Board such as that to proceed with
Heysham Power Station. It obviously involved multiple and conflicting
objectives. As an example, a section of this problem is shown in figure 3
using demonstration input. At the moment the model can handle only 1 page
of a tree, which limits the present model to about 10 or 12 end points.
There is no real restriction on the size of the tree but we have still to
tackle the practicalities of more than one page. The tree is drawn by the
user on the screen and criteria assigned to evaluate each end point. The
criteria are scored and weighted and the probabilities on each branch are
elicited as the tree is drawn. Utilities and expected utilities can be
used to store sets of scores, probabilities and weights to call up for
sensitivity analysis. Some of the output features include the facility
for exploring the effect on the utility or expected utility of a node, of
continuously changing the weight on one criterion (figure 4). Different
sets of weights representing different viewpoints can be tabulated to see
the effect on utilities, and the sensitivity of the decision to key
probabilities can be examined.

3.4 Selection of Options

The third type of problem concerning the selection of one option from many applies across the Board's activities, from selecting a power station site to interview sessions for job candidates. At the moment we have the LSE model MAUD 6 which we find very useful (Humphreys et al 1979). The model has been set up to explore a part of the site selection problem, for example the range of environmental effects which could occur at particular sites and to rank these in terms of minimum effect. This is still at a very early stage but there are two aspects to the work.

At the interface with biologists and other environmental specialists, there can be a resistance to the use of the model in terms of the time needed to have attributes elicited and trade-offs made. In many cases the difficulty of scoring and making trade-offs is increased when there is no scale on the attributes. The person has to know that, for example, he is trading off 2 broadleaved trees and ½ mile of hedges against 10 broadleaved trees and 3 miles of hedges. Quantitative aspects are at the root of the trade-offs in this situation.

Another factor is in the underlying structure of the model which appears to impose a framework which does not correspond to the user's own conception of the problem. The user in this case is immersed in a mass of detail which can be ordered in different ways. At the moment our attempts to order the information using MAUD6 have not been particularly acceptable and different approaches are being explored to try to solve this problem. One option is to provide a small model with an acceptable presentation at the front end, but with verification of the scoring and the trade-offs being carried out using MAUD6. There has been a great deal of work done on the problem of site selection, particularly in the USA and we hope to make full use of the experience gained (Keeney, 1980).

3.5 External Models

There are many decision analysis models on the market and we already have OPCOM and MAUD6 from LSE and are considering PDS from Works Science Associates. The main justification for developing our own models has already been discussed, but in addition, it was considered that none of the current decision tree models really were able to fulfill what we perceived to be our needs, particularly in presentation. Nevertheless there are some problems which would be better handled with external models. Hence the acquisition of external models which can also accommodate for the fact that different people find different approaches more or less attractive.

3.6 Gaps in the Current Approach

3.6.1 Policy Generation

In examining some of the more complex issues in the environmental field, such as the Acid Rain Problem and the Greenhouse Gases Problem, Decision Analysis has proved to be very useful in structuring an approach. However there is the additional area of policy or option generation. One can for example analyse some of the implications of a 30% reduction in SO_2 emissions in terms of costs and benefits. However for the issue to really progress a series of options need to be generated which can address some of the specific problems. In a similar manner, the Greenhouse or Trace

Gas Issue is such an enormous global issue that it is imperative that policies and strategies be generated to ameliorate the problem. Even in the literature, the development of D.A. structures for policy generation is well behind other aspects of Decision Analysis. Indeed it may not be appropriate to impose too much structuring into an essentially creative area of planning. However some way of avoiding the same old paths and synthesising appropriate strategies to suit the problem are required.

3.6.2 Risk of the Decision

In an organisation such as the CEGB, it is important to know much more about the risk associated with a decision than can be obtained using the output from current models. The risk associated with a decision may be related to many factors, including uncertainty in input data and uncertainty on probabilities. Sensitivity analysis can help, but other methods such as risk profiles on all the options may be required. EPRI have taken up this problem and are developing an approach to planning called CHOICE which, it is claimed, can integrate the technical analysis of individual options with the planning process. We intend to investigate this area in more detail and hopefully provide a package of decision analysis approaches suitable for most problems in the Board.

4. CONCLUSION

There is no doubt that decision analysis techniques could usefully be applied to many areas within the CEGB. In the Environmental Studies section exploration of the available approaches is at a very early stage. As our experience is limited, we need to interact with Decision Analysts and Consultants in the field, and to exchange views with other organisations on the problems involved in the introduction and application of the technique.

5. ACKNOWLEDGEMENTS

Thanks are due to Mr. R. Bowman for his excellent computer modelling work and for many helpful discussions to which Ms J. Bliss also contributed. This paper is published by permission of the CEGB.

6. REFERENCES

1. Bell, D.E., Keeney, R.L., Raiffa, H., 1977,
   Conflicting Objectives in Decisions, John Wiley

2. Boyson, W.E., Boyd, D.W., North, D.W., 1982, EPRI Report.
   Acid Deposition: Decision Framework EA 2540.

3. Humphreys, P., and Wisudha, A., 1979,
   Multi Attribute Utility Decomposition,
   DA Unit Brunel University Technical Report 79-2.

4. Keeney, R.L., 1980, Siting Energy Facilities, Academic Press.

5. Raiffa, H., 1968, Decision Analysis, Random House NY.

6. Watson, S.R., 1986, Modelling Acid Deposition for Policy Analysis,
   J. Oplres Soc 37, 9, 893-900.

```
                    VALUE      PATHS

    MIN   .000245   .000245   1 1 1 1 1
                    .000264   1 2 1 1 1
                    .000265   1 1 2 1 1
                    .000275   1 1 1 2 1
                    .000284   1 3 1 1 1
                    .000286   1 2 2 1 1

    MAX   .002361   .002361   3 3 3 3 3

    AVG   .000912   .000883   2 3 2 3 2
                    .000894   2 1 1 3 3
                    .000895   2 3 3 2 2
                    .000901   2 3 2 1 3
                    .000910   2 2 3 3 2
                    .000921   2 3 1 2 3
                    .000927   2 2 2 2 3
                    .000934   2 2 3 1 3
                    .000952   2 2 1 3 3
```

Figure 1: Wind Cost With Path Information

WINDY WITH PROBABILITY DISTRIBUTION

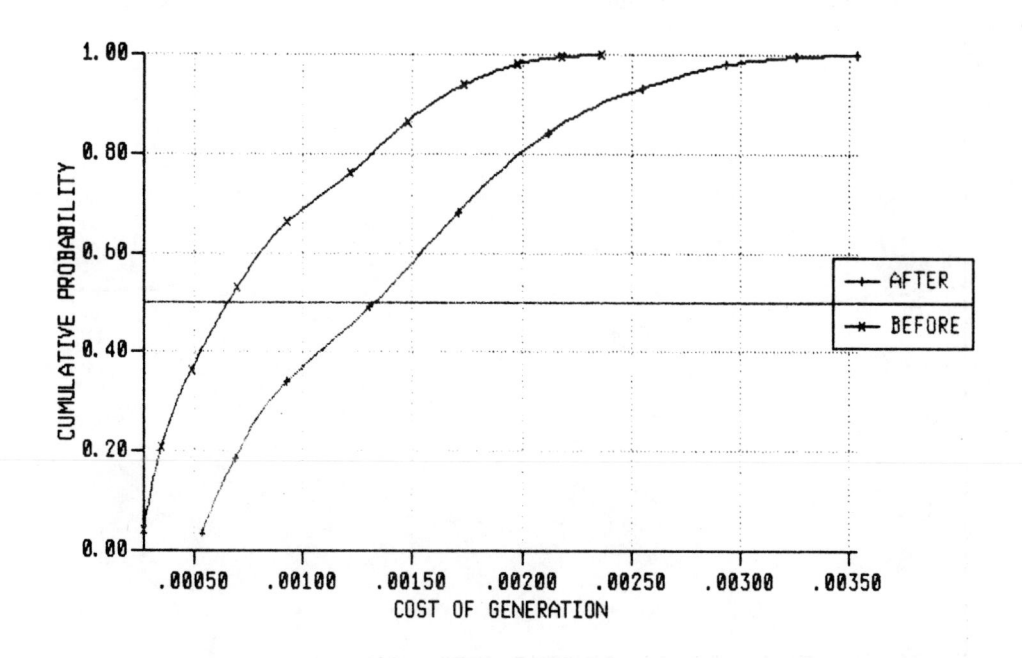

Figure 2

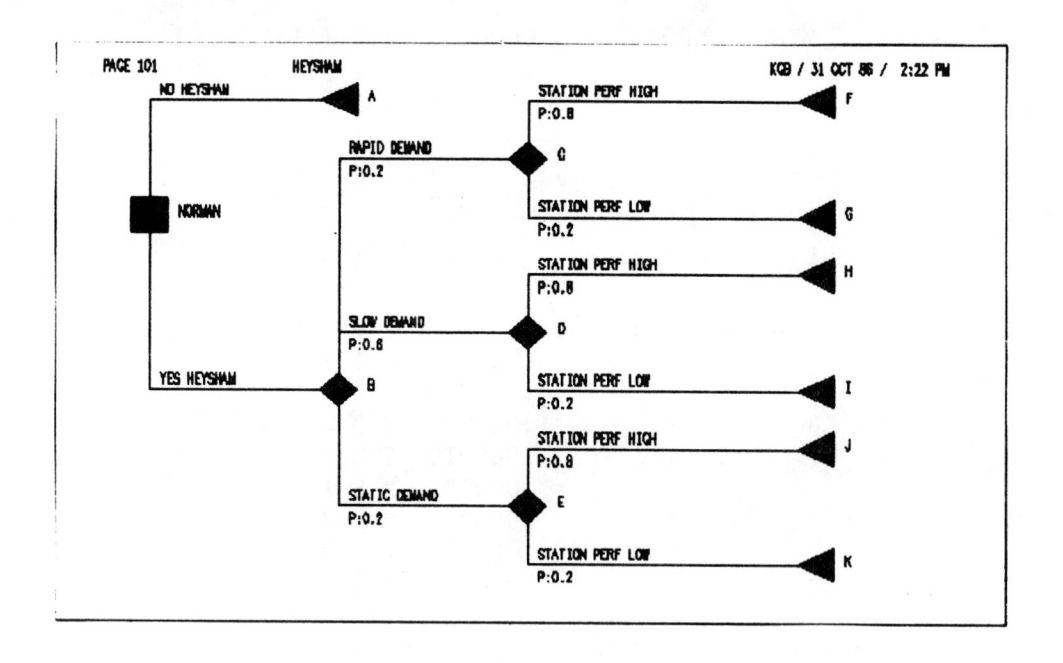

Figure 3: Decision Tree for Example Problem

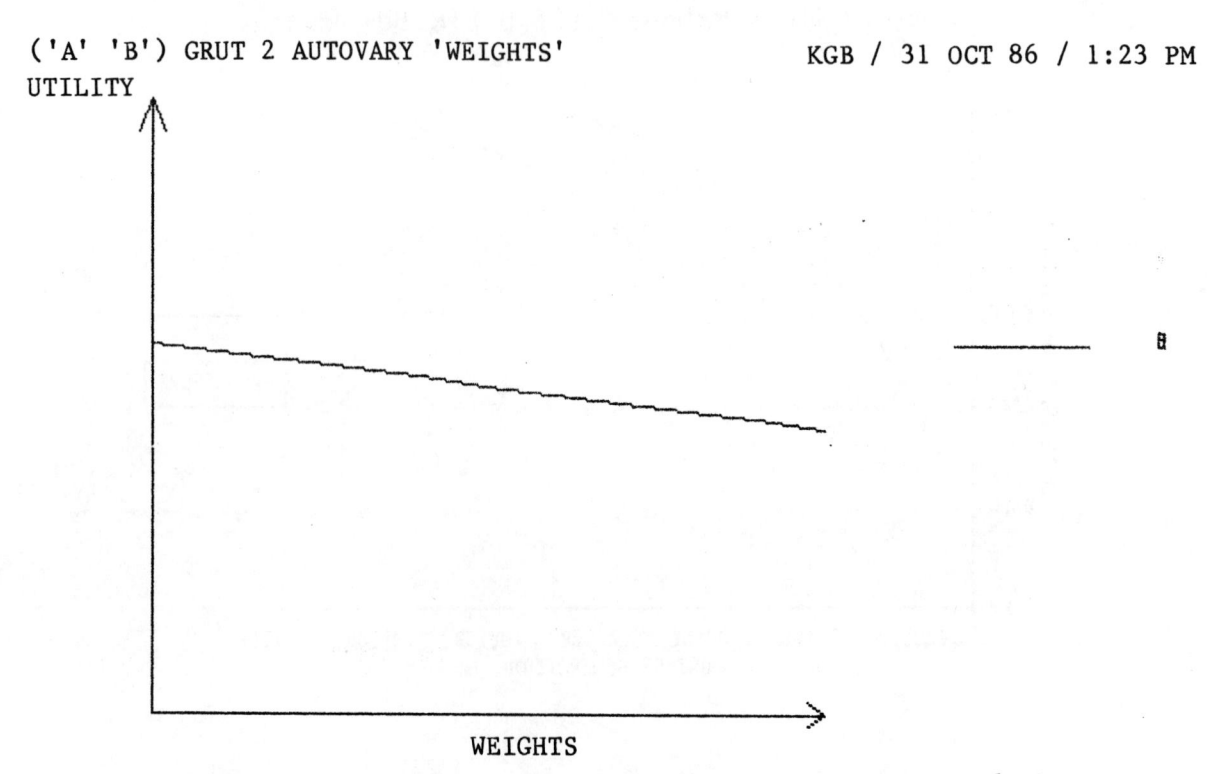

Figure 4: Effect on Nodes 'A' and 'B' of continuously varying one criterion

9 Competitor Marketing Analysis and Planning

R. S. Stainton
Henley Management College and Brunel University

INTRODUCTION

There is a large multi national company which has its head office in New York. Above the reception door it boasts the title "World Trade Headquarters". Employees of the company seldom notice it. They take it for granted that because the company trades on a world wide basis, they work in World Trade Headquarters. But they deal with only their own subset of the world market, despite their illusions of grandeur.

A company in the South East of England has signs posted on its main corridors. They point the ways to Western Europe, to the Middle East and Asia, and to America. The company trades in these areas and the signs refer to those locations where the respective management teams reside. Each team behaves as though what it does is all that ever happens in those regions.

Let us now turn to resolving problems with multiple and conflicting objectives, the title of this seminar. Some we can resolve, perhaps, but certainly not all. With a title like this, we could not ask for greater coverage. Problems with multiple and conflicting objectives include the universe of problems. So which are the ones with which we are concerned? What is the subset of problems which forms our market? How can we identify them, before we too assume the mantle of omnipotence?

There is no clear answer, other than claims by some that most problems can be knocked into the shape they require in order that their solution procedures can be adopted. This is cart before the horse, or solution before the problem situation is known, perhaps. Yet obviously, those specific problems for which the technique was designed are well catered for. They are ones which are properly defined and about which their structure is known. In short then, we can resolve a subset of structured problems with multiple and conflicting objectives.

PROBLEM STRUCTURE

The emphasis is upon structured problems, which leaves us with a myriad of unstructured problems, with which the world abounds. Obviously, if we can force a given problem situation into a structured form, particularly one for which a known solution technique exists, we are in a much better position to solve it. Yet the solution of the wrong problem by a conveniently available technique is no solution at all.

Unstructured problems do not allow for such ease of procedure. Indeed, the most important and difficult aspects of this procedure relate to the definition and description of the problem. If we reflect for a moment upon current issues, be they international or within our own personal domestic environs, we shall quickly see that those who are in conflict are in that state because they perceive their situations in different ways. Just like beauty, reality is in the eye of the beholder and we each work from differing understandings of rationality.

Any technique we might devise to deal with problems which have multiple objectives must, by definition, have their own built-in rationale. Unless we can convince the parties to a problem that their rationales are the same as those of the problem solving vehicle or mechanism, we have no hope of finding an acceptable solution. If we recognise too that each party has his or her own rationale anyway, that the problem situation is unlikely to be well defined and there will be inevitable difficulties of interpretation, prospects of a solution being reached are poor indeed.

It is prudent then to repeat the caveats that we must not claim more for our techniques than is justified and that we must be crystal clear about the structure of the problems we tackle and their relationships to the structure of the techniques we are propogating. Let us take care that when, for example, we show interest in a particular solution package, we are not more impressed by its packaging, presentation and sophistication than by its problem solving capabilities.

SEMANTICS AND SYNTAX

The difficulty lies perhaps in a lack of appreciation of the difference between semantics and syntax. By its nature, any solution technique has a far greater share of syntax than it does of semantics, whereas a problem situation is the reverse. Once translated into syntactical form, i.e. stripped of its meaning and presented as an interrelated precise logic, a problem loses substance and both the opportunity for deeper understanding as well as wider interpretation.

There are many examples we might cite, but one which is

topical is the current excitement about the use of computers for trading in the financial world. Some experts are predicting that in the near future, financial deals will be made entirely by computer, based upon the most up to date and instant information, determined by decision rules set by common practice. If all financial dealers were to use such systems, each with its own characteristics, advantages and therefore disadvantages, there would inevitably emerge a winning system which could establish itself in any given sector of the financial market. Initiative and creativity would no longer find their rightful places and the natural logic, to some perhaps illogic, of the competitive market place would disappear.

THE MARKETING FUNCTION

If we take the marketing function in any company in its broadest sense, it is clear that it includes problem situations which can be handled in highly structured analytical ways, as well as problem areas which are best suited to creative and entrepreneurial flair. The more a market becomes established and the sooner companies achieve recognisable market shares, the less room there is for innovation. Naturally, there are always exceptions and AMSTRAD in the personal computer market may be one. But in the main, marketing models can be designed and built which relate the various aspects of marketing, such as pricing, advertising, consumer attitudes and product positioning.

In general, these models are mostly useful to demonstrate academic principles and are seldom used to aid real world marketing decisions, for which there are a number of reasons we could propose: competitive situations change; personnel move on, within organisations and without; technology creates natural and inherent obsolescence. A marketing department must therefore try to balance these matters and incorporate experience into the actions that it takes. But with changing circumstances, how does it manage to capture that experience?

Of major concern in most marketing departments is the desire to understand and pre-empt the actions and decisions of its competitors. However, in order to do so, often it must rely to a considerable extent upon a company marketing philosophy, much of which is anecdotal. For example, advice might be given to keep prices higher than those of competitors or perhaps to promote one's own products immediately following an advertising campaign mounted by a major competitor. One might be told too that it is necessary to sell one's wares to the end user or consumer so that the goods are pulled through the distribution network, rather than the products be pushed through from the manufacturing end. These statements, based on experience, are not universal truths; but he who contravenes them does so at his peril. Each one occurred in particular circumstances which may not subsequently apply. Yet experience, custom and convention dictate.

EXPERIENCE SYSTEMS

Obvious questions arise. To what extent is it possible to try out various strategies in advance, recognising that competitors may adopt different approaches in different environmental states? Can each strategy in each circumstance be explored in advance? Can established marketing expertise be incorporated?

If affirmative answers to these questions could be given and a supporting system devised, there would be created an Expert System of a special kind, one which might be better named an Experience System. It would need memory, deductive capabilities and an inference engine not dependent on event probabilities from the past (they would not exist), but upon activities believed to be relevant for the future.

Such a concept is far from new. The armed forces have for many years played out their battles both on manoeuvres and through simulated war gaming. They explore, in these ways, the effectiveness of new weapons (an addition to the company's product range) and the deployment of their forces (channels of distribution for their products, promotion/propoganda spends). They try out their strategies under different conditions, making various assumptions about the actions and reactions of the enemy (analysing competitor behaviour).

The designers of war games devote much energy and effort to establishing rules by which each game proceeds. They must be reasonable and realistic. They must be devised with experience and with opportunities to react sensibly and appropriately in unforseen circumstances and to unexpected events.

The terminology of the market place is often associated with military conflict. There are fights to secure market share; customers who are captured from the opposition; attacks on competitor activities. Experienced marketeers have their own perceptions of how the market place behaves and they are convinced of underlying relationships between the factors which influence market behaviour. Just as experienced military personnel are able to construct battle rules, so is it possible to develop a model of a particular market, incorporating the issues which are considered to be relevant and important. Competitors can be identified, their span of discretion translated into decision factors and their activities in competition with each other can be recorded over time and subsequently analysed. In short, a company can play out its own market situation, with its own people taking the roles of its competitors and exploring the avenues open to each as a marketing situation develops.

SIMULATING REALITY

Each simulation produces different results. This is entirely expected and is indeed the very reason for experimenting in this way. As we have already identified, marketing abounds with unstructured problems, each of which has its share of multiple and conflicting objectives. Through the medium of simulation, we hope to build structure where it is possible to do so whilst at the same time allowing experienced people to behave and react in ways which suit their purposes. In so doing, they are balancing for themselves the conflicts and the objectives which pull in many directions. They are able to go some way towards resolving the cycle of events which begin with objectives, proceed to actions determined by those objectives, experience the consequences of those actions, then be forced to modify the objectives and continue round the cycle again.

The design phase of a simulation of a market is critical, of course. It must be thought through carefully and tirelessly, with total co-operation between those experienced in the market and those who are building the simulation. Appeals might be made to existing historical data, but such data can be misleading and relationships identified which might possibly explain the past, but provide no real indications about the future.

Past data allows one to predict and prepare for what becomes an inevitability (if the prediction is believed). It is far more important, particularly in a marketing environment, to design instead what that future should be and to take steps to achieve it.

Models of markets, similar in concept to war games and perhaps similar to flight simulators (in that experiencing a crash in simulation mode is far less troublesome than doing it for real), have been developed for companies in FMCG (Fast Moving Consumer Goods) and in Retailing. It is important that they be designed to be user friendly and flexible. They must be felt to be real by the participants and directly relevant to their own interests and experiences.

Each simulation session is carried out over a period of two or three days, when a group of senior managers develop strategies for their own company and for their competitors and play out the results of their decisions through the simulation. They are able subsequently to discuss their actions in detail, to understand their own behaviour and to recognise other actions that might have been taken. They may then change roles and compete again, experiencing new circumstances and new events which become the basis for further discussion. Control over the simulation is exercised by individuals who ensure that the rules are properly understood and followed and that the simulated environment reflects that in which the companies expect to operate.

POWERS AND IMPORTANCES

Perhaps suprisingly, the most time consuming aspect of the design of a simulation is the method and means of input and the form of output so that it is readily understandable by participants. The market generation part of the simulation can be constructed with relative ease by identifying firstly the factors which are considered to be important, then by establishing their hierarchy of importance, then by determining the power that each one displays in the market place. These parameters, so called Powers and Importances, require much debate and discussion before they can be settled and agreed. But they are also a means by which the model itself can be modified in order to take full account of the beliefs and expectations of those who are experienced in the ways of the market place.

Each time the model is run, not only can different strategies be adopted, but the interrelationships between the factors which determine the market can also be changed. This allows for an analysis of sensitivity and an exploration of the robustness of the factors which influence the market.

CONCLUSION

So far, experience with the models has been good. It has been possible to draw up contingency plans to deal with future actions that it is thought competitors might take. It would be difficult to claim that financial benefit has yet been derived by the companies who have used the models since they are primarily tools for the development of strategies. Nevertheless, there has been more immediate tangible benefit in the guise of training in the ways of these companies.

Once a model has been developed for strategic purposes, it is possible to allow others within the organisation to compete and thereby learn more about their own markets and their own relationships within their companies. They are resolving for themselves the multiple and conflicting objectives which they experience in their normal working lives and the more they attempt to model their own situations in this way, the closer they come to a full representation of reality (defined each in his own particular way, of course) and the resolution of their own problems to their own best advantage.

10 A Methodology for Decision Support in Conflict Analysis

William L. Cats-Baril
School of Business Administration, University of Vermont

1. INTRODUCTION

Attitudes toward conflict have shifted over the past couple of decades. Conflict is perceived today as a potentially positive and creative force. With the recognition that conflict can be useful, the emphasis has shifted from the elimination of conflict to the management of conflict. In order to manage conflict effectively, however, one must understand what sort of analysis is most likely to lead to constructive outcomes.

Sometimes conflicts become so heated and embedded that rational approaches to reduce them don't work. Often, however, all sides realize a decision needs to be made and that a better understanding of each other's positions is essential. In that case, it becomes helpful for the parties to know: the goals, attitudes, values, motivations, and levels of aspiration of the parties in conflict; the nature of the issues underlying the conflict and the options available to resolve them; as well as, the consequences involved in taking one course of action versus another. Unfortunately, research on policy formation suggests that people are inconsistent in their judgement, unaware of their values and unable to explain accurately not only their opponents' positions but theirs as well [2, 6].

This article proposes that a decision analysis framework can provide a useful structure within which conflicts can be examined. This idea is not new. Theoretical models with specific prescriptions have been discussed in the literature for a long time [9, 12]. This article, however, does not suggest a specific model but presents an entire methodology to bring greater understanding of the conflict at hand to the different parties involved. It is a methodology to support the process of conflict resolution. The methodology is based on addressing the basic sources of conflict: lack of understanding, lack of information, and distorted communication among parties.

The conflict analysis methodology presented here is based on the assumption that de-escalation of conflict will occur when the participants in a situation of conflict understand the real issues, their position as well as the position of the "other side" on those issues, and the possible trade-offs among them. The idea is to resolve conflict through a better understanding of its foundations. This better understanding comes through a process of breaking down the "whole" conflict into specific issues that can be traded-off.

The methodology can be used in situations where two or more constituencies recognize there is a conflict to be resolved and are willing to take the necessary steps to solve it, or in situations where one of the constituencies involved in that conflict is interested in developing a deeper understanding of the conflict in order to manipulate it.

The basic premises behind this conflict analysis methodology are the following: a) a conflict situation is easier to grasp when it is broken down into specific elements (some of which may be less, or not at all, conflictive); b) people have cognitive biases that become more acute under conflict or crisis situations; c) preconceptions and false assumptions blur the ability to make trade-offs; d) individuals can specify their values and prioritize as long as they are given a structured process to do it; and e) the analyst has access to all views involved in the conflict to be studied, i.e., access to people representing each and every side of the problem, or to knowledgeable observers that can role play the values, preferences and priorities of those parties that cannot be involved or may not be willing to participate in the conflict analysis effort.

2. CONFLICT ANALYSIS: THE METHODOLOGY

The methodology of conflict analysis consists of five major phases as shown in Exhibit 1. The constituencies involved and/or affected in the conflict to be studied (stakeholders), the spokespersons that will represent these constituencies in the conflict analysis process, their goals, values and assumptions are identified in the two first phases. These phases are aimed at providing the analyst with an understanding of the underlying issues and a general perspective on the background of the conflict.

The third phase is aimed at exploring the problem. It consists of refining the preliminary goals obtained in the first phase and of decomposing those goals into more specific components. We will call these components, issues. Moreover, these issues can be resolved through different approaches (e.g., actions, laws, services, programs, etc.). We will call the various potential solutions to an issue, levels of resolution. The levels of resolution are also identified in this third phase.

The fourth phase, analysis of treaties, is aimed at exploring the solution to the conflict as a whole. The analysis begins by having the stakeholders give relative importance weights to the different issues and state their preferences for the various levels of resolution. The analysis consists in packaging a level of resolution for each and everyone of the issues into a "treaty". A given treaty represents a possible resolution to the "whole" conflict. Each treaty is then scored. The total score is obtained by multiplying for all issues the importance weight of an issue by the preference value assigned to the specific level of resolution chosen to address that issue, and adding across all issues. That is,

$$\text{Score of Treaty}_k = \sum_{i=1}^{n} W_i U_{ij} \quad \text{where} \quad (1)$$

k   is a specific treaty consisting of a set of levels of resolution for all n issues
W_i is the importance weight of issue i
U_{ij} is the preference, or utility, of level of resolution j to issue i.

Exhibit 1
Conflict Analysis Methodology

Understanding the Problem
1. **Identification of Stakeholders**
   *General understanding of problem through informal and brief interviews
   *Identification of Stakeholders
   *Selection of Spokespersons

2. **Identification of Assumptions**
   * Assessment of Importance and Certainty
   * Analysis of Catchwords

Exploring the Problem
3. **Identification of Goals, Issues and Levels of Resolution**
   *In-depth interview with one or more objective outsider
   *Identification of Goals, Issues and Levels of Resolution with Stakeholders

Exploring the Solution
4. **Analysis of Treaties**
   *Quantitative Estimates for Goals, Issues and Levels of Resolutions
   *Form and Score Treaties
   *Develop Set of Feasible Treaties

5. **Negotiate Differences**
   *Classify sources of Disagreement
   *Develop Strategy of Resolution
   *Recommend Course of Action

The next step in the analysis of treaties is the application of several methods to obtain the best treaty possible for all parties involved (or for a specific party if that is the purpose of the analysis).

The fifth phase of the methodology is to bring all the parties together in an effort to obtain a consensus resolution. In an environment that can be at times explosive, choosing what issue to debate first can be crucial to the rest of the conflict resolution effort. A set of criteria, to classify the sources of disagreement surrounding issues and levels of resolution, is presented to determine a sequential order in which issues should be discussed.

The identification and quantification of goals, issues and levels of resolution as well as the analysis of treaties is performed for each group of stakeholders representing a point of view in the conflict. There is no exchange or interaction between opposing groups in these phases. The identification and quantification sessions as well as the analysis of treaties should be done separately for each stakeholder group. If access to one of the groups is impossible, an objective outsider could be used as proxy. The groups of spokespersons are brought together to discuss the model of conflict, the treaties, and decide on further actions only in the last phase of the process. It is important to note that even if the stokespersons agree on a final treaty, they still must go and "sell" that treaty to the constituencies they represent. Agreement among spokepersons does not imply an end to the conflict at hand. An example of this, is the now famous Strategic Arms Reductions Talks "walk-in-the-woods" agreement reached by the two chief negotiators representing the USA and USSR which was later disavowed by their respective governments.

Each of these phases of the methodology is described in detail in the following sections. It may be useful to remind the reader that the methodology can be applied in several different ways. One possible application is to use the methodology to bring together parties in conflict to develop general areas of agreement. Another possible application is to have a neutral observer/mediator use the methodology to develop an understanding of the issues and priorities of the different groups involved in a conflict. Finally, the methodology can be used by one party in the conflict to clarify its own position and to role-play and simulate the opposing parties' positions.

Throughout the rest of the article, we use as an illustration of the application of the methodology the issue of whether to provide family planning services for adolescents with or without parental consent. We have assumed that the person ordering the conflict analysis is a member of Congress interested in knowing how to vote on allocating funds for those services. He has instructed his policy analysis team to develop a politically tenable position, i.e., a position that does not alienate any major interest group.

2.1 Preliminary Analysis: Identification of Stakeholders, Spokespersons and Goals

Stakeholders are those people who stand to gain or lose something as a result of the conflict. There are several ways to identify stakeholder groups. For example, one could ask a number of recognized groups, associations and organizations to assign priorities to a set of goals underlying a specific conflict. Then, the groups with similar priorities could be treated as one "perspective". This empirical approach works well if all relevant groups are surveyed.

One should always go beyond canvassing the groups which are "lining up" against each other. A first observation may suggest that there are only two groups opposing each other. However, further analysis may identify other important players. For instance, on first view it appears that there are two groups involved in the conflict over what role, if any, family planning organizations should have with adolescents. Those two constituencies might be characterized as the "anti-abortion forces" and the "family planning advocates". However, a third group may appear upon further examination -- a "concerned parents group".

Often there will be many stakeholders from many different persuasions but their value systems may be similar enough to be characterized by just two or three models. For instance, in the family planning issue we may find parents, ministers, physicians, health educators, social workers, women's rights advocates, etc. While they may come from many different perspectives, the value system around this issue may fall into perhaps just two distinct models.

These models might be characterized by the goals each constituency has for family planning. Suppose Constituency I opposes family planning services being made available to adolescents without parental consent and Constituency II favors them. Furthermore, suppose that their goals are those shown in Table 1. To the right of the goals are two columns of numbers. The numbers are relative importance weights (in percent) assigned to the four top goals of each group of stakeholders or constituency. Note that both constituencies feel goal "b" is important. However, there is much disagreement on the importance of goals "a", "c" and "d".

This information can be obtained through interviews with individuals knowledgeable about the issue to be studied (the individuals may or may not be the same people that will be interviewed later in greater depth and be part of the conflict analysis process.) These interviews should be informal and their main purpose is for the analyst to get acquainted with the conflict.

Table 1
Goals and Importance Weights for the
Two Constituencies in the Issue of
Family Planning

Goals	Constituency I	Constituency II
a) Reduce Unwanted Pregnancies	.13	.36
b) Teach Children to Be Responsible	.32	.33
c) Preserve the Family	.43	.10
d) Reduce Number of Abortions	.12	.21

At this early stage, the weights are preliminary approximations that may be refined in later phases of the conflict analysis process. At this point, however, since only an estimate of the importance of each goal is needed, a simple method can be used in determining the relative importance of each goal (e.g., the method of splitting 100 points among the most important goals is good enough [5]).

The emphasis at this stage is to be comprehensive about listing the goals. That is, one must try to discover as many goals as possible in order to obtain a realistic perspective of the problem and start diagnosing the sources of conflict and division among the different stakeholder groups. Later, certain goals may be dropped if they are found to be redundant, have low priority, or turn out to be, after close analysis, irrelevant to the conflict at hand. After having listed the goals identified in the early interviews, a rough rating of the goals can be performed. The most important goals (four is a good number, but no more than ten) can be weighed for preliminary analysis.

The preliminary data shown in Table 1 are just the start of the formal conflict analysis but they already provide much useful information. We now understand which goals are important to each side. We also begin to understand where opportunities for compromise might exist. For instance, goal "a" is crucial to Constituency I but relatively unimportant to Constituency II. Goal "c" is very important to Constituency II but unimportant to Constituency I. This means that Constituency I may be willing to give a lot on goal "c" to get what it wants on goal "a", and the other way around for Constituency II.

Some people feel that this type of information is not surprising. They say that any good politician thinks of these things intuitively. Unfortunately, we are not all good politicians. Furthermore, even good politicians are busy people who may not have the time to carefully examine the true position of both sides. The result is that the intuitions they have could be based on inadequate information and, thus, their intuitive assessment of the stakeholders may be inaccurate.

After this preliminary analysis to get acquainted with the conflict has been performed, we need to identify a group of spokespersons representing each stakeholder group that will participate in the conflict analysis process. There are at least three types of spokespersons' groups that need to be identified: the proponents of the issue; the opponents; and objective outsiders.

The reason for identifying the third group may not be obvious. Objective outsiders are needed because these people often see the proponents and opponents in a conflict situation in a different way than the proponents and opponents see themselves and each other. Where differences in perception occur, it may be important to understand why. Also, in certain instances, policy makers may not want to get involved in negotiations with another constituency but may still like to increase their understanding of the conflict. The most important time to use only objective outsiders is when involvement of stakeholders is likely to influence the conflict in an undesirable way. In those situations, conflict analysis can be performed with a group of objective outsiders only.

In selecting the spokespersons, the analyst should look for individuals that are good identifiers of issues and solutions and comfortable with the tasks of quantifying their preferences. While at later stages of the process we may want to include individuals with institutional power and influence in order to implement a compromise, in the conflict analysis phase we need individuals with a strong analytical mind. In general, in this early stage of the process, we want to involve individuals who are considered to be sensitive, insightful, verbal and very familiar with the conflict situation.

An effective means of identifying spokespersons is to use a nomination process. The nomination process begins by identifying five or six nominators -- individuals who are well-connected in the arenas of interest and can identify individuals who could be good spokespersons to represent the various stakeholder groups. The nominators are contacted and asked to name several individuals who could effectively reflect the positions of each stakeholder group. It is good practice to select only nominees who are suggested by more than one nominator because multiple nominations are likely to occur on people who are respected by different constituencies. The nominees should then be contacted by phone or letter and asked to participate in the conflict analysis process. Their participation is more likely to occur if they are told:

   -who nominated them (get permission to use the
    nominator's name);
   -what the project is about;

- why it is important for them to participate;
- what will and will not be done with the results;
- how their name will be used;
- what tasks are expected of them;
- how long each task will take;
- when each task will occur;
- what payment (if any) they will receive.

There may be good reasons to identify more nominees but if properly selected, three spokespersons from each constituency are sufficient. As mentioned before, in some situations it may make sense to involve only objective outsiders and usually three of them are enough.

2.2 Identification of Assumptions

After the preliminary analysis has been performed and the participation of the spokespersons has been secured, the analyst has to do some homework. Often when significant conflict exists between parties regarding the definition of a problem or its solution, it is because of a disagreement over something a much more basic preamble which is not immediately apparent or obvious even to the stakeholders themselves. This "something" is made of the differing assumptions which parties inevitably bring with them to the definition and analysis of all conflicts.

The analyst should proceed to force to the surface, for explicit examination, the underlying, often unconscious assumptions that stakeholders bring with them. The purpose of this phase of the process is threefold: to be able to compare and to evaluate systematically the implied assumptions of different sides of an issue; to examine the relationship between underlying assumptions and the resultant policies advocated by each stakeholder group, and to attempt to formulate policies that are acceptable in light of the various sets of assumptions.

The stakeholders' assumptions can be classified on the basis of their relative importance and their relative certainty [10]. That is, the analyst should try to determine which assumptions are critical in supporting the position taken by a given stakeholder. In addition, the analyst must determine which assumptions the stakeholder feels most certain about, how great is his confidence in them, and what type of data, if any, does he have to support them. The analyst should study closely the assumptions that are important and uncertain. It is around these assumptions that the analyst may be able to find potential resolution breakthroughs.

In order to elicit the assumptions, the analyst should try and obtain as many items of information as possible describing the stakeholders views. Leaflets, brochures, commercials, any means of advertising their position, position papers, legislative hearings, data items used by the stakeholders to buttress their position, are all critical clues to discovering and understanding the basic assumptions.

Direct interviews may also be useful in identifying the assumptions behind the stakeholders' positions, but because of their implicit nature, individuals often have problems articulating them. More often than not, assumptions are so ingrained in a particular position that people espousing them accept those assumptions unconsciously. On more than one occasion, individuals have been surprised by their assumptions and have questioned those assumptions once they were made explicit to them.

Throughout this inductive process, the analyst should look for catchwords or slogans that appear frequently in the stakeholder's statement of the conflict. In the example of family planning services for adolescents, one of the opponent's (Constituency I) catchwords was: "I want my children to have the courage to say no", and one of the proponent's (Constituency II) was: "Let us stop children from having children".

While these statements may be a simplification of the actual issue, nonetheless they provide us with a flavor of the position of each constituency. Again, remember that at this stage, we are trying to <u>understand</u> where the different stakeholders are coming from and the summarization of their positions through slogans may help us in that task. Usually, slogans have a high emotional content, and may provide the analyst with a wealth of information on the stakeholder's values. Exhibit 2 shows some of the assumptions forming the worldviews of Constituencies I and II.

A close reading of Exhibit 2 shows that assumptions can be classified into contradictory and non-contradictory assumptions. An example of contradictory assumptions is the assumption held by Constituency I that access to contraceptives lures teenagers to sexual activities which clashes with the assumption held by Constituency II that access to contraceptives does not increase sexual activity. Clearly, one of the two must be unfounded. An example of a non-contradictory assumption is the assumption held by Constituency I that administration and red tape will take up to 90% of the funds. This assumption and the one held by Constituency II that the cost/benefit ratio in family planning programs is excellent can both be true at the same time.

It is crucial, then, before interacting with the stakeholders, for the analyst to have an understanding of all the assumptions involved in the conflict situation. Indeed, the stakeholders must perceive the analyst as a fair individual who is sensitive to their values. Thus, it is important that before conducting the sessions to identify goals, issues and levels of resolution, the analyst is sure that he can role-play the different value systems involved.

Exhibit 2
Catchwords and Assumptions of Two Constituencies
on the Family Planning Services Issue

Constituency I	Constituency II
Catchwords	Catchwords
- Too much government - I want my children to have the courage to say "no"	- Let us stop children having children - Contraception is better than unwanted pregnancies
Assumptions	Assumptions
- Administration and red tape will take up to 90% of the funds - Contraception is dangerous and people are misinformed about its effects - Parents do a better job providing sexual education - Morality is the best contraceptive - Access to contraceptives lures teenagers to sexual activities - The decision to have sex is a good opportunity for establishing communication between parents and children	- The cost/benefit ratio in family planning programs is excellent - Contraception makes it possible for minors to take advantage of other possibilities (education, employment, etc.) - Parents do not provide adequate sexual education - Counsellors in family planning agencies provide the most persuasive influence against premarital sex - Access to contraceptives does not increase sexual activities - Confidentiality is crucial in obtaining family planning counselling

2.3 Identification of Goals, Issues and Levels of Resolution

After the analyst has identified the conflicting constituencies and their general goals and assumptions, and once the spokespersons representing each constituency have been contacted and have accepted to participate, the next step is to model the conflict. The process of building a model of the conflict at hand consists of breaking down the conflict into more specific components and of quantifying those components. These components are: a) the goals that drive each constituency; b) the issues, i.e., specific aspects of the overall conflict, that must be addressed if the conflict is to be resolved; and, c) the possible levels of resolution for each issue.

It is important to identify the goals of each constituency because those goals will help explain why the conflict exists. When we understand "why", it becomes possible to identify ways of resolving the conflict. The list of goals that was obtained earlier in the preliminary analysis can be used as a starting point for the in-depth discussion on goals with the spokespersons. The set of goals of each constituency will indicate how resolving the conflict at hand fits in the overall agenda of that constituency.

Issues are the basic building blocks of conflict. They constitute the fundamental aspects that need to be understood and addressed if the conflict is to be resolved. Indeed, after decomposing the conflict into its smaller, more specific issues, the opposing constituencies may find that they agree on a number of issues, are mildly opposed on some others, and that the conflict really lies with just a couple of them, making the task of resolving the initial conflict a more manageable and focussed one. Classifying issues on a continuum of disagreement allows the analyst to concentrate his energies and resources on finding an acceptable compromise to those issues where disagreement is most intense.

If some of the issues where intense disagreement exist are not ripe for resolution (i.e., their political time has not yet come), or if the situation is such that the conflict on those issues is not likely to be resolved, the analyst can move to develop partial solutions to the conflict by concentrating on the issues where both parties have agreed. Either way, by decomposing the conflict into specific issues the analyst is able to localize conflict to smaller areas of disagreement and use the available resources for problem solving more effectively.

Finally, the levels of resolution need to be identified. The levels of resolution are specific actions, laws, services, etc., that deal with an issue. Typically, constituencies will identify levels of resolution that range from being optimal to unacceptable. This step in the methodology allows the analyst to identify what stakeholders are considering as suitable (or unacceptable) solutions to an issue, and to provide a foundation for generating new ways of resolving the conflict.

There are several ways of identifying the goals, issues and levels of resolution (e.g., questionnaires, surveys, Delphi, individual interviews), but structured group meetings, like the Integrative Group Process or the Nominal Group Technique, among the spokespersons of each constituency works well [1, 4].

At this point, separate group meetings should be arranged for each constituency. Bringing opposing parties together when the analyst does not have a measure of how deep the conflict is and on what issues may be risky and dysfunctional. Later on, but only after the conflict analysis model has been formed and some trade-off resolutions have been mapped out, the different constituencies may be brought together to try and reach a resolution. In the case where one of the constituencies cannot, or does not want, to participate in the conflict analysis process, a group of "objective outsiders" should be asked to role-play the missing constituency.
Some people may ask what the value of doing conflict analysis

is when not all of the conflicting parties are present? The answer is that conflict analysis is a process which increases the understanding of one's own position, increases the consistency of one's own choices in later negotiations, and identifies different ways of solving the conflict by defining areas of possible agreement. Indeed, conflict analysis is a useful process for understanding and clarifying the complexities of a situation and it is a positive preliminary exercise for any constituency or individual faced with conflictive decisions that will require negotiation. While refusal, or the inabilility, to participate of one or more of the constituencies involved may hinder the probabilities of a resolution being implemented, the "proxy" spokesperson approach is far superior to the alternative of performing the conflict analysis with a missing point of view. It is always helpful that those objective outsiders who are role-playing the missing constituency be individuals highly regarded and respected by that constituency.

An important preparation for the meeting with the spokespersons' groups is to do an in-depth interview of a few trusted objective outsiders. This strategy permits the analyst to rehearse the process that will be followed in the group sessions with the spokespersons representing each constituency; to obtain a preliminary conflict model that can be used as a starting point in the stakeholders' group sessions; and to develop a deeper understanding of the conflict by defining in detail the goals of each constituency and becoming familiar with the issues and levels of resolution connected with the conflict. The agenda for these interviews should be the same one used in the spokepersons' group sessions, and is the following:

1) The analyst should discuss the problem in general terms and note examples of goals, issues and levels of resolution. The analyst should ask questions of the "outsiders" to define the problem and to be sure the key elements of the conflict are understood.

2) The analyst should ask the "outsiders" to describe the opposing sides in the problem: Who are the proponents? Who are the opponents? How do they view the conflict? What would each side like to see in terms of a resolution to the problem? Why?

3) The analyst should ask the "outsiders" to specifically list the goals that drive the opposing sides on this conflict (give examples of what you consider to be goals so the "outsider" knows what you mean.) The "outsider" should be encouraged to brainstorm and generate a comprehensive list.

4) The analyst should ask the "outsiders" to specifically list the issues that divide the opposing sides and make sure that the issues are as independent from each other as possible (i.e., there is no overlap). Questions might include: what is the underlying conflict about? On which issues do the opposing sides agree? Disagree? In order for the opposing

sides to come to agreement, which issues need to be resolved? Again, the analyst should make sure that the list of issues is exhaustive.

5) Finally, the analyst should ask the "outsiders" to specifically list the levels of resolution for all issues. Each issue is likely to have several levels of resolution. Some levels will be preferred by the proponents and some will be preferred by the opponents. Other levels will be compromise positions not preferred by any side but acceptable to all. The analyst needs to identify as many levels of resolution as possible on each issue even though in the final analysis only a few levels may be considered. The analyst must try to keep the levels as independent from each other as possible, that is, no overlap should occur. The reason for seeking more levels than needed is to promote the creative development of levels of resolution not previously considered by either side. The "outsiders" should be asked: the proponents' preferred position on each issue, the resolutions they might be willing to accept and resolutions they could never accept, the explanations about why the levels are preferred, acceptable or unacceptable. Ask the "outsiders" to repeat the process for opponents on the issue.

Let us suppose that after performing these interviews with a couple of objective outsiders and the spokespersons representing each constituency on the issue of family planning services for teenagers, the list of goals and weights previously shown in Table 1 is confirmed. Those goals were to: reduce unwanted pregnancies; teach children to be responsible; preserve the family, and reduce the number of abortions. Furthermore, let us suppose that the interviews revealed that the focus of the conflict is which components of a family planning program should be made available to minors and under what conditions. Let us suppose too, that there was agreement among all parties that any family planning program must have at least three components -- education, counselling, and services -- and that those components can be defined as follows:

*Education: includes components such as values, morals, biological processes (e.g., sexual response, anatomy, etc.), birth control information, decision making and goal setting information, sex roles, pregnancy and parenting skills.

*Counselling: focusses on some of the same issues but involves more intensive interaction between provider and client on an individual or small group basis. The foci of counselling might include crises, pregnancy, pre/post abortion, elective non- parenthood, child birth preparation, etc.

*Services: includes the provision of services to the client that goes beyond education or counselling. Adolescents might receive birth control devices, adoption services, abortions, prenatal care, VD treatment/testing, financial assistance, etc.

With this information, the analyst is in a position to explore the specific issues underlying the conflict. In this example, some of the issues could be whether values and morals should be taught or not when delivering family planning services? Should counselling come from the perspective that adolescent sex is bad? Is it more important to have easy access to services (e.g., social service clinics, schools) or more important to have services under the control of organizations with high morals? What should the technical qualifications of the personnel providing the services be? Who, if anybody, should regulate the provision of family planning services to adolescents?

Once the issues have been identified, the objective outsiders and the spokespersons are asked, separately, to define a set of feasible resolutions for each issue. A set of assumed issues and their possible levels of resolution have been listed in Exhibit 3 in the format we will use to perform the next step in conflict analysis.

Once the issues and levels of resolution have been formulated by the objective outsiders, they must be checked, rephrased and detailed in separate group sessions with the spokespersons representing each constituency. It is very important to obtain a consensus on the phrasing and substance of all issues and all levels of resolution from all parties involved before proceeding to the next phase. It should be noted that at this time, the point is to have <u>all</u> the constituencies agree on the components that make-up the overall conflict and not on a solution to the conflict.

2.4 Analysis of Treaties

2.4.1 Eliciting Weights and Preferences. Model development should be the most time-consuming aspect of conflict analysis. The identification of the goals, issues and levels of resolution should involve about 70% of the total effort because model development requires a thorough understanding of the conflict. This section on quantitative estimates is certainly an important aspect of the methodology but should be much less time consuming.

To compute comparative "goodness" scores of different treaties, quantitative estimates are needed for each constituency's preference for all goals, issues and levels of resolution. The analyst should obtain the weights and preferences for goals, issues and levels of resolution by using again structured group processes and having separate sessions with the objective outsiders and the stakeholders' groups. Methodologies to elicit weights and preferences can be found in Huber [5] and Keeney and Raiffa [7].

Exhibit 3
Issues and Levels of Resolution

Issues	Levels of Resolution

A. To what extent should family planning programs attempt to <u>convince</u> clients that <u>adolescent sex is bad</u>?
- A1 — Should not be a part of program
- A2 — A program available to clients
- A3 — A program required of all clients
- A4 — A fundamental part of every component offered by family planning programs

B. To what extent should family planning <u>programming</u> be oriented <u>toward strengthening the family</u>?
- B1 — Not part of programming
- B2 — Available to clients
- B3 — Required of all clients
- B4 — Fundamental part of every component

C. What limitations to <u>access</u> to family planning programs should exist for adolescents?
- C1 — No notification
- C2 — Notification before counselling of services
- C3 — Permission before counselling of services

D. What <u>technical qualifications</u> should be required for people who provide family planning services to adolescents?
- D1 — Social work supervision
- D2 — Physician supervision
- D3 — Theologist supervision
- D4 — Past Parent of Adolescent

E. What <u>organizations</u> (with what <u>moral qualifications</u>) should be allowed to deliver family planning services?
- E1 — Non-profit
- E2 — Educational
- E3 — Governmental
- E4 — Health care (doctors' offices/hospitals)
- E5 — Religious organizations

F. Who should <u>regulate</u> the provision and quality of family planning services for adolescents?
- F1 — Peer review
- F2 — Local government
- F3 — State government
- F4 — Federal government
- F5 — Community

At this point, it is important to restate the goals of the constituencies because the levels of resolution and issues identified so far in building the model of conflict may only represent the most obvious subset of all existing issues and feasible levels of resolution. The analyst may be able to identify new issues and levels of resolutions by analyzing the implications of the goals of each constituency.

For instance, in our example we know that preserving the family is very important to Constituency I and of little importance to Constituency II (see bottom of Table 2). This suggests that new issues and resolutions that positively affect the preservation of the family might be sought for inclusion in the model as long as they do not negatively affect any other goals. For example, family planning organizations could begin to develop educational and counselling programs to teach adolescents how to get along with their families or teach parenting skills to parents of adolescents. The point is that understanding the goals may lead to creative ideas on how to add issues or levels of resolution that had not been considered before.

Goal review also insures that the analyst will not solve the wrong problem. By going back to the goals of each constituency and analyzing the impact of a given treaty on the constituencies' goals, the analyst can avoid the infamous error of the "third kind" [8]. After all, what the constituencies want is to further their goals and may not, inherently, want an agreement. When the analyst starts developing a negotiating strategy to bring all parties together to consider a small set of feasible treaties, he should recheck what the main goals of the constituencies are to determine areas of potential resistance and resolution.

Issues and levels of resolution along with their respective importance weights (in percentages) and utilities are shown in Table 2. Issue weights were obtained by asking the spokespersons in the group sessions to split 100 points among the issues. This assessment is then rechecked by asking them to assign 10 points to the least important issue, and by using it as a benchmark, to proportionally assign weights to the other issues. The weights are then normalized.

The levels of resolution were scored by asking spokespersons to assign a preference value or "utility" to each resolution level. The spokespersons were asked to assign numbers between 0 and 100 in the following way: 100 for the best possible resolution level advocated by their constituency; 0 for the least desirable (but still acceptable) resolution to their constituency. The levels of resolution in between were scored directly (e.g., if level of resolution x is the best possible resolution for issue i, and thus has a utility of 100, and level of resolution y is the worst but still acceptable resolution, and thus has a utility of 0, what is the utility of level of resolution z?). The assessments were then checked by using the mid-value splitting technique [7].

When the scoring of goals, issues or levels of resolution of
two or more spokespersons representing the same constituency
differ, the discrepancies should be discussed and explained.
If the differences remain, then the weights and values should
be averaged to obtain the values representing the position of
a constituency. However averaging should be done as a last
resort and only when the differences are relatively small.

It should be noted that during the discussion to resolve the
differences you might find that certain factions of a constituency are more amenable to compromise (their scores on issues
and levels of resolution might be closer to those of the
opponent constituencies) or in the extreme case, you might
find that the spokespersons represent two different positions
when originally it was thought they represented one and the
same. In this case the analyst should develop another model
and include it in the conflict resolution process.

The complete conflict model for each constituency is presented
in Table 2. It represents a consensus model of the conflict
at hand. What we have at this point in the process is a
consensus among all constituencies on the set of issues which
are at the basis of the overall conflict and the set of
feasible resolutions for each issue. There is also consensus
among the spokespersons of a given constituency on the
importance of each goal and issue, and their preference for
each level of resolution. What we don't have is consensus
across constituencies on the relative importance of the issues
and the attractiveness of the same level of resolution. It is
now that the analyst must look for the trade-offs that may
bring about a solution to the conflict as a whole.

2.4.2 Creating and Scoring Treaties. Let us consider Table 2.
If the values shown in Table 2 are an accurate reflection of
the two constituencies, it would be possible to calculate the
value of potential conflict resolution options. Indeed, if we
were to take a particular level of resolution for each issue,
multiply its value by the importance weight of the issue, and
do the same for all issues, a total score for a particular set
of levels of resolution could be obtained. A set of levels of
resolution is called a <u>treaty</u>. Typically, the number of
treaties is very large. In this example, there are 4800
possible treaties, and in general, the number of possible
treaties N is equal to

$$N = \prod_{i=i}^{n} x_i \qquad (2)$$

where x_i is the number of levels of resolution attached to
issue i, and n is the number of issues. But of that large
number of possible treaties, only a few are conducive to general agreement. In the next section, an analysis of the
various treaties is performed to find the ones more likely to
lead to a resolution of the conflict. Before we do that let
us give an example of how to score treaties.

Table 2
Importance and Preference Attached to Goals, Issues, and Levels of Resolution by Each Constituency

Constituency I Preference for Issue / Level	Constituency II Preference for Issue / Level	Issue/Level of Resolution
.14	.07	A - <u>IS ADOLESCENT SEX BAD?</u>
0	100	A1 -Not part of program
30	90	A2 -Programs available
80	20	A3 -Programs required
100	0	A4 -Built in to all components
.20	.04	B - <u>FAMILY</u>
0	100	B1 -Not part of program
30	90	B2 -Program available
90	20	B3 -Required
100	0	B4 -Built in to all components
.25	.48	C - <u>NOTIFICATION</u>
0	100	C1 -No notification
80	10	C2 -Notification
100	0	C3 -Permission
.11	.14	D - <u>QUALIFICATIONS</u>
0	100	D1 -Social work
60	50	D2 -Medical
100	30	D3 -Theological
50	0	D4 -Past parent of adolescent
.23	.16	E - <u>ORGANIZATIONS</u>
0	100	E1 -Non-profit
60	30	E2 -Educational
30	15	E3 -Governmental
80	10	E4 -Health care
100	0	E5 -Religious
.07	.11	F - <u>REGULATION</u>
0	100	F1 -Peer review
90	20	F2 -Local government
40	30	F3 -State government
10	40	F4 -Federal government
100	0	F5 -Community

Importance Weight	Importance Weight	GOALS
.13	.36	Reduce unwanted pregnancy
.32	.33	Teach responsibility
.43	.10	Preserve the family
.12	.21	Reduce number of abortions

A treaty is then a set of levels of resolution, one level of resolution per issue. Now, suppose legislation were to be passed on family planning with the following characteristics (the specific levels of resolution are taken from Table 2):

A_2 Program available aimed at the negative aspects of adolescent sex.

B_2 Programs available for strengthening the family required in any adolescent family planning component.

C_2 Notification of parents when an adolescent uses a family planning program.

D_2 All providers of family planning services must have medical qualifications.

E_2 Educational institutions must be responsible for family planning.

F_2 State governments must be responsible for regulating family planning programs.

The value of any treaty, as mentioned above, is calculated by multiplying the relative importance weight assigned to a given issue by the utility assigned to a specific level of resolution to that issue and adding across all issues.

That is, the score of treaty k for Constituency c is equal to,

$$\text{Score of Treaty}_{kc} = \sum_{i=1}^{n} W_{ci} U_{cij} \qquad (3)$$

Where W_i is the weight of issue i,

U_{ij} is the utility of level of resolution j to issue i,

and n is the number of issues underlying the conflict.

For Constituency I the value of the treaty, consisting of the levels of resolution shown above, is then (values are taken from Table 2):
(.14 x 30) + (.20 x 30) + (.25 x 80) + (.11 x 60) + (.23 x 60) + (.07 x 40) = 53.4

And for Constituency II the value of the same treaty is:
(.07 x 90) + (.04 x 90) + (.48 x 10) + (.14 x 50) + (.16 x 30) + (.11 x 30) = 29.8

How good is this treaty? Can we do better and keep both constituencies happy? These questions are addressed in the following section.

2.4.3 Pareto Optimality Analysis.

The purpose of analyzing treaties is to generate a few which might be acceptable to all of the constituencies involved and to develop treaties that may recast the conflict into a win/win situation. The analysis of treaties may be a time consuming process, requiring calculations, figures, computer programs, etc. and should be performed by the analyst and his team. A group session with the spokespersons from each constituency should then be convened for reviewing the most promising treaties and doing further analysis if necessary (again, it would be wise for the analyst to consult a couple of trusted objective outsiders on the preliminary results before conducting the group sessions.)

The treaty presented above is a middle-ground solution to the conflict because each level of resolution in that treaty is a compromise on each issue. Now let us see what happens if each constituency is allowed to win on what it considers the most important issues. In this example, this would mean that Constituency I is allowed to win on issues A, B, and E, and Constituency II wins on C, D, and F. So the resolution treaty would be (from Table 2): A_4, B_4, C_1, D_1, E_5, and F_1,

The respective scores for the constituencies would be (using equation (3) above):

Constituency I: $(.14 \times 100) + (.20 \times 100) + (.25 \times 0) + (.11 \times 0) + (.23 \times 100) + (.07 \times 0) = 57$

Constituency II: $(.07 \times 0) + (.04 \times 0) + (.48 \times 100) + (.14 \times 100) + (.16 \times 0) + (.11 \times 100) = 73$

Both constituencies improve their position although Constituency II improves much more than Constituency I. So, if the objective of the two constituencies was to improve <u>their</u> respective positions and not to block or beat the other, this treaty would be a better resolution of the conflict for both of them. The concept of mutual improvement is referred to as the Pareto optimality criterion [9]. Pareto optimality is reached when one side cannot improve its position unless the other side's position is damaged.

We started with a treaty that had a value of 53.4 to Constituency I and a value of 29.8 to Constituency II (point A in Figure 1). Any other treaty that improves one of the constituencies without hurting the other is assumed to be an acceptable improvement. The space of acceptable improvements is the cross-hatched area shown in Figure 1. That space includes B (57, 73). Point B represents the treaty made up of levels of resolution chosen on the basis of letting each constituency "win" on the issues they consider most important. There is, however, a set of treaties where neither side can improve their position further without hurting the other's. Those treaties fall on the Pareto Optimal Curve (C). The goal is to find acceptable treaties that come as close to the Pareto Optimal curve as possible.

Figure 1
Pareto-Optimal Analysis of Treaties

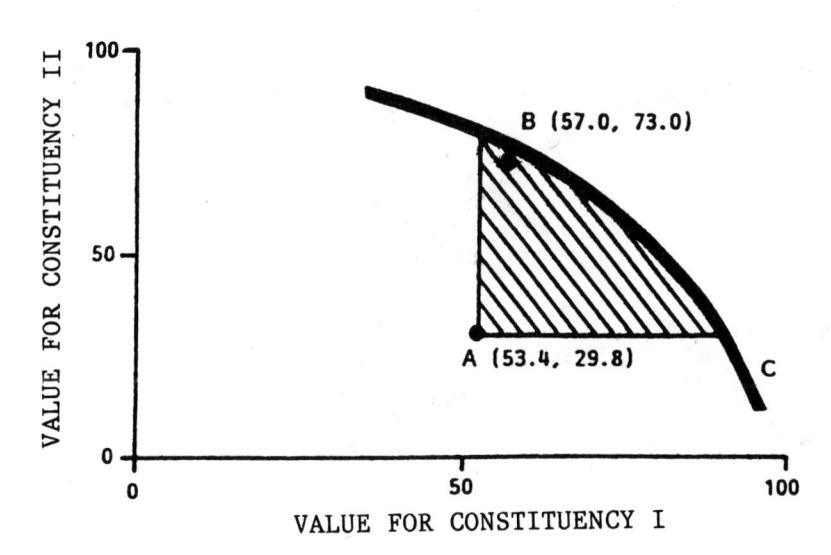

```
VALUE FOR CONSTITUENCY II
100
                    B (57.0, 73.0)
 50
            A (53.4, 29.8)
                                    C
  0
  0            50            100
        VALUE FOR CONSTITUENCY I
```

Often attempts at resolving conflicts follow a process of agreeing on one issue at a time. The problem with this step-by- step approach to conflict resolution is that it divides the conflict into several conflicts. If one side wins on "conflict x", the losing side will try all the harder to win on "conflict y". This phenomenon tends to exacerbate the total conflict. Also, the parties involved in the conflict tend to compromise on each issue rather than search for a better overall solution. Researchers have found that conflict resolution processes that allow logrolling -- when one party trades a concession on one or more issues for reciprocal concessions on other issues by his opponent -- lead to more Pareto-optimal settlements and higher satisfaction than processes purely based on compromise -- when each issue is negotiated separately and in relative isolation from the agreements reached on other issues [3].

Let us look at an example to show that compromising on issues separately, rather than trading-off across issues, can lead to suboptimal solutions. Suppose that we have only a two-issue conflict and that the issues are the amount of funding allocated for family planning services and the age at which adolescents are eligible to use those services without parental consent.

Now, suppose that Figure 2 shows Constituency I's preference toward the amount of funding allocated to provide family planning services: Its preference holds constant up to about $400,000 and then decreases as funding increases. On the other hand, Constituency II's preference increases with increases in funding. If the two constituencies were to compromise on this issue, they might decide that $700,000 (i.e., the intersection point of both preference curves) would be a good amount to select because the two sides would be equally "happy".

Figure 2
Preferences for the Amount of Funding for Family Planning Services

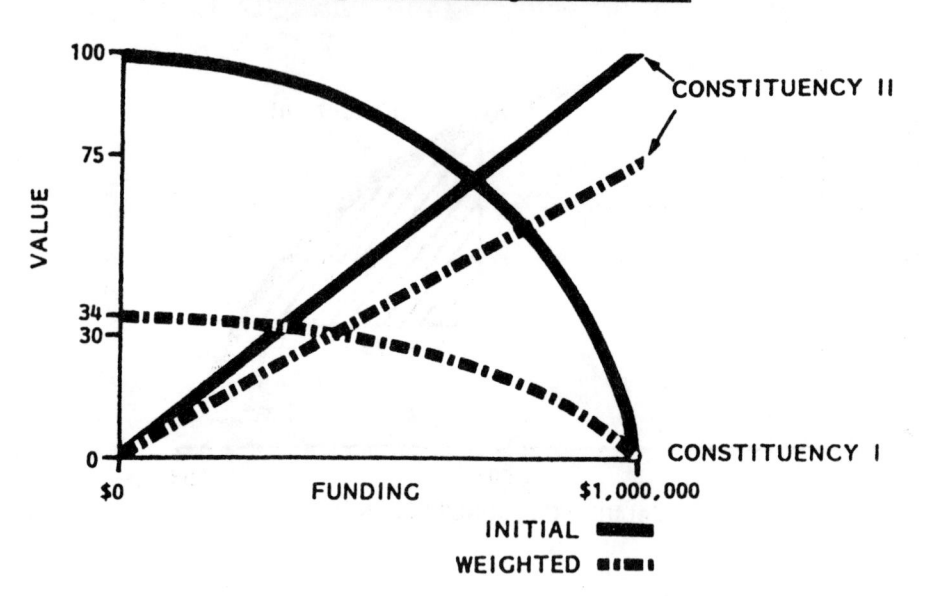

Furthermore, let us assume that Figure 3 reflects the constituencies' preferences for age of eligibility. On the one hand, Constituency I's preference increases markedly after 14 years old. On the other hand, Constituency II's preference curve shows that, after 12 years old, the earlier the adolescent is eligilible, the better. Again, if the constituencies were to compromise they would select 16 (i.e., the intersection point of both preference curves) as the age of eligibility because 16 is the age where both sides have the same preference value.

Figure 3
Preferences for the Age of Eligibility to Have Access to Family Planning Services Without Parental Consent

Moreover, suppose that in this two-issue conflict, Constituency I feels that the issue of age is twice as important as the issue of funding and assume that Constituency II feels that funding is three times more important than age of eligibility as shown in Table 3.

Table 3
Importance Weights for the Issues of
Age of Eligibility and Funding

	Age	Funding
Constituency I	.66	.34
Constituency II	.25	.75

What this says is that the maximum score Constituency I can get on the issue of age is 66 (.66 multiplied by the utility of the best resolution level, i.e., 100) and the maximum score Constituency II can get is 25, while the maximum score for Constituency I on the issue of funding is 34 and Constituency II's score is 75. The initial curves in Figures 2 and 3 were redrawn to reflect these weights.

If a treaty was developed as a compromise on each issue separately (e.g., age = 16 and funding = $700,000), the value of the treaty would be 42.5 (30 + 12.5) for both Constituencies. But there are many treaties that would be superior. One such treaty would be to let Constituency II win completely on the issue of funding because funding is more important to Constituency II than it is to Constituency I, and to let Constituency I win completely on the issue of age because age of eligibility is more important to Constituency I than it is to Constituency II. The values for this treaty would be (66, 75). Thus, this type of behavior, called logrolling, should be encouraged and addressing conflict by compromising on an issue-by-issue basis should be discouraged.

The examination of alternative treaties is an iterative process that can be performed in great detail by using computer programs or intuitively by just looking at the information on Table 2 and getting ideas of how to improve negotiations. The important point is that by understanding the relative importance of issues and levels of resolution it is often possible to find treaties that improve the outcomes for all constituencies by exploring trade-offs across issues.

The purpose of performing this type of analysis is to make sure that all the trade-offs have been explored and understood by the analyst as well as by the different constituencies. The group sessions in which the spokespersons for each constituency discuss the treaties that appear promising for resolving the conflict should emphasize cooperation and compromise.

It is crucial that before the next step in conflict analysis -- when the analyst meets with all the constituencies at once to generate the resolution treaty -- each constituency understands the other side's view and values. This understanding can be increased and clarified through the analysis of treaties presented here.

2.5 The Process of Negotiation

Let us see what we have so far. We have a model of conflict (i.e., goals, issues and levels of resolution) that has been accepted by all parties. We have also a set of weights representing the importance of the issues and the preference for the various levels of resolution for every constituency. Each set of weights represents the value structure of one of the constituencies involved. With the model of conflict and the value structures, we have created, scored and analyzed treaties and arrived, after group discussions with the spokespersons for each constituency, at a few treaties that might be acceptable to all parties.

The next step is to bring the spokespersons representing the different constituencies together to choose a course of action. Note that at this point the conflicting parties have agreed on the issues and the feasible levels of resolution attached to each issue, but they have not agreed on the relative importance of the issues nor on their preferences for the levels of resolution. It is unlikely that an agreement will be obtained on all the issues and for all the levels of resolution because some of the issues are purely ideological, but is is realistic to aim for agreement on certain issues and levels of resolution and to hope for a compromise on the rest.

Coming up with an agreed-upon conflict model is a big achievement in itself. The opposing constituencies have been delineated, the conflict has been specified, the parameters underlying it have been defined, and the value structures of the constituencies have been articulated. Now the analyst is ready for the final phase: bringing the spokespersons from opposing constituencies together to agree on a treaty. The following discussion presents some suggestions and guidelines to increase the probabilities of success in such an enterprise.

Because the issues and level of resolution have been agreed upon previously, the emphasis of the group session is to reduce the differences in perception and judgement of the relative importance of those issues and levels. But where to start? What issue should be addressed first? Should the treaties chosen in the previous step be discussed right away?

Before the group session with all spokespersons, the analyst should try to understand where the differences of judgement come from. The analyst should classify the disagreements on issues on a continuum going from purely _ideological_ to purely _technical_.

Ideological issues are those issues which are based on values and beliefs, which no objective data can prove to be right or wrong, either because there is no data or because the data can be interpreted in widely different ways (e.g., the suggestion that the contraceptive pill is a symbol of male oppression). Technical issues, on the other hand, are issues that can be settled by using objective evidence and are issues that can be addressed with information that does not lend itself to more than one possible interpretation. That is, technical issues can be settled by presenting hard data (e.g., the results of controlled experiments). It is important to differentiate between ideological and technical disputes because the process of negotiation will vary depending on the nature of the disagreement.

For example, the analyst could try to break down the ideological issue into smaller components to localize even further the underlying value difference, or he could try to forego resolving the difference and let one of the constituencies win on this issue and start looking for issues where the other constituencies can win and try to negotiate a trade-off. If, on the other hand, the difference is caused by a lack of information or technical knowledge, an expert in the field of dispute can be brought in to resolve the difference or a comprehensive search for relevant information can be initiated.

Typically, conflicts consists of several issues, and often some of them will be purely ideological in nature. But others will be more technical in nature, and still others might not reflect any ideological difference at all. By working first on these latter issues the rift caused by ideological differences, if not overcome, at least is diminished through a de-emphasis of the ideology separating the parties and a sense of agreement and progress given by resolutions on non-ideological issues. Since disagreements that are ideological in nature are perceived by the concerned parties as zero-sum games, it is important to address them with great care.

A similar problem can arise when assessing the effectiveness of a level of resolution. For example, rejection of abortion as a means of reducing unwanted pregnancies can be due to a difference of opinion on the _effectiveness_ of abortion (e.g., how dangerous or how traumatic is it?); or it can be due to a difference in the ideological _acceptability_ of abortion (e.g., is it murder?). It is important to distinguish among the causes of the disagreement because, as in the case of issues, the negotiation strategy varies.

If the disagreement is based on the acceptability of a level of resolution, the analyst should investigate whether the resolution can be packaged in any other way, whether there are any substitutes for this level of resolution, and under what conditions and for what issue the opposing constituency may be willing to trade it off. On the other hand, if the disagreement is based on differences of perception as to the effectiveness of the resolution being proposed, the analyst should identify sources of expertise and information to prove or disprove its alleged effectiveness.

Once the analyst has classified the sources of disagreement on the issues and the levels of resolution, he has to determine a sequential order in which to present the issues to the constituencies. Here another classification might be useful. Four groups of issues can be identified. A first group of issues is formed by issues where the constituencies agree upon the relative importance of the issue and agree about what level of resolution should be implemented. A second group consists of issues where the constituencies disagree about the relative importance of the issue but agree about what level of resolution should be implemented. A third group of issues is constituted by issues where the constituencies agree about the relative importance of the issue but disagree on the level of resolution to be implemented. And finally, the fourth group is made up of issues where the constituencies disagree both about the relative importance of the issue and the level of resolution to be implemented. The order in which the cluster of issues should be presented to the group of spokespersons from all constituencies is shown in Figure 4.

A further refinement is possible. Within each cluster of issues, the issues can be presented in a sequential order given by the range of the weights on each issue (or variance if more than two set of weights are involved). The more disagreement and polarization there is around an issue, the larger the range (or variance) of the weights on that issue, and the later in the discussion should that issue be presented.

Typically, this ordering will imply dealing with purely technical issues first, and then deal with progressively more ideological issues. This is so because people tend to be much more extreme about ideological differences, while they deal with technical differences in a cooler, more centered and rational way. By discussing the latter type first, a mood of cooperation and constructive problem solving is more likely to be established.

One may ask why spending so much time determining the order of presentation and discussion of issues. The fact is that in conflict situations, bringing the opposing parties together often results in an explosive atmosphere. In these circumstances, it is important that opposing constituencies agree on some issues as early as possible in the meeting. A feeling of accomplishment and understanding must be instilled so that the constituencies put away, or at least suspend, their negative preconceptions of the "other side" and adopt a constructive problem solving attitude.

Starting the group session with issues that can be resolved
quickly, and leaving the more controversial ones for later,
allows for a constructive mood to settle in. Also, in case
that one of the controversial issues cannot be resolved, the
fact that a certain number of issues have already been settled
by that time, diminishes the frustration of a deadlocked
negotiation and assures the constituencies that their efforts
were at least partially successful and that they are not going
to leave the meeting empty-handed.

Figure 4
Classification of Issues to Determine
their Order of Presentation
(Numbers Indicate Sequential Order of Presentation)

Constituencies agree on
level of resolution to be
implemented

```
                    |
    1  ─────────────┼─────────────▶  2
                    |           ╱
                    |         ╱
Constituencies      |       ╱        Constituencies
agree on relative   |     ╱          disagree on
importance of    ───┼───╱─────────   relative impor-
issue               | ╱              tance of issue
                    ╱
                  ╱ |
                ╱   |
    3  ◀─────────────────────────▶  4
                    |
```

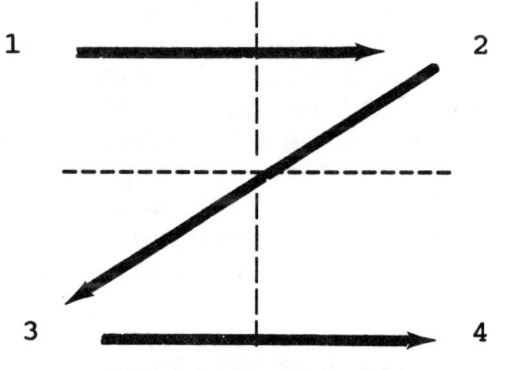

Constituencies disagree on
level of resolution to be
implemented

Throughout the negotiations of differences the analyst must
keep in mind the Pareto-optimal treaties that he developed
with the objective outsiders during the analysis phase. At
the beginning of the meeting, when the issues being discussed
are not controversial, it is better not to bring up these
"fair" treaties. Not bringing up those treaties avoids having
the constituencies focus on final outcomes and shortcutting
the early stages of the process which are critical for setting
a positive problem solving attitude. Later on, if the
negotiation of a controversial issue is deadlocked, the
analyst can use the "fair" treaties to generate a
breakthrough.

Finally, it is important to end the meeting with a concrete
set of future actions. If the analyst was successful in
bringing about an overall resolution and drafting a final

treaty agreeable to all spokespersons, then actions to
implement such a treaty should be agreed upon. On the other
hand, if only a partial treaty was obtained or no treaty at
all, actions that will continue the efforts of conflict
analysis and resolution should be listed. One must remember
that conflict analysis is being done with spokespersons and
that these individuals will have to "sell" whatever agreement
was reached to the constituencies they represent.

2.6 Other Considerations.

An important aspect of doing conflict analysis is timing. An
issue has a life cycle and, at one given point in time,
various policy makers may try to influence it and move it to a
different stage in its life cycle, e.g., try to kill it, or on
the contrary, bring it to the political center stage and
precipitate a crisis.

Because conflict analysis is likely to bring attention to the
problem being considered, the analyst must be aware of whether
the constituencies want to add momentum to the issue, defuse
the possibility of a crisis, or explore the possibility of
creating a crisis. Indeed, depending on the purpose, the
people involved in the conflict analysis may change. For
example, if a policy maker wants to explore how the "other
side" might react to a series of treaties but is not willing
to commit himself to any type of action, conflict analysis
will have to be performed with a group of observers knowledgeable of the opposition. If on the other hand, the purpose
is to raise awareness about a problem, one should perform
conflict analysis by involving as many constituencies as
possible.

Another important aspect of conflict analysis is the necessity
of representing every constituency's value structure without
any distortion. It is often very difficult for an analyst not
to take sides. But if the efforts of conflict analysis are to
succeed, the objectivity of the analyst has to be beyond any
doubt. By objectivity, we do not mean a cold, removed and
aloof objectivity, but an ability to be able to "feel" the
concerns and values of <u>all</u> constituencies. Distorting or not
integrating into the model every constituency's point of view
might lead to lack of participation by the constituency being
excluded, and in later stages that constituency may sabotage
the efforts to resolve conflict.

Also, any distortion of a constituency's values may destroy
the value of the model as a description of the conflict and,
thus, its value as a tool to generate compromise treaties.
The implication for practitioners is the need to develop not
only skills in model building and a familiarity with decision
models but good interviewing techniques, the ability to
assimilate and role-play other people's values, and very fine
interpersonal skills.

Finally, individuals participating in conflict analysis,
and/or the policy makers that might use its results, may ask

why they should use this methodology. One of the payoffs is the clarification of what issues are really conflictive by classifying the differences behind them as disagreements of value or knowledge.

Another payoff of conflict analysis is that, by bringing all the parties to agree to a conflict model and presenting the "other side's" values on the same issues and levels of resolution, there is an increase in understanding, a decrease in the pervasiveness of preconceptions, and thus an increase in the likelihood of implementing trade-offs. Obviously in the best of all cases, conflict analysis not only increases the likelihood of agreement but actually brings a resolution to the conflict by providing a treaty acceptable to all parties.

Time pressures can have a negative effect on the quality of a final settlement. However, once the model of conflict is formed, it allows one to perform sensitivity analyses on the importance weights and the preferences in a very short time, given one has the appropriate computerized support. These sensitivity analyses facilitate the exploration of the acceptability of a variety of treaties by simulating a wide range of constituencies' responses.

3. DE-ESCALATION OF CONFLICT

In introducing the conflict analysis methodology (CAM), we presented it as a strategy to increase the understanding of the underlying sources of conflict. In this section, CAM is proposed, based on previous work in conflict management and resolution, as a step towards de-escalating conflict and increasing the probabilities of a settlement through negotiation.

In a situation where conflict is increasing in intensity, the parties may lose their initial concerns and may concentrate on trying to beat each other, even at the expense of sacrificing some of their payoffs. At this point in the escalation of conflict a party may see itself as "saving face, getting even, teaching the others a lesson, showing to the other it can't get away with it, etc.", like the battered fighter, its satisfaction comes from being able to say, "You ought to see the other fellow". When this mode takes over, it is very likely that the conflict will be expanded to other areas, where conflict might not even have a reason to exist, but is created by one party to make sure that there is ground to get back at the other party in case of losing the present fight.

Conflict escalation involves increasing the number size of the issues disputed, increasing hostility and competitiveness among parties, pursuing increasingly extreme demands or objectives, using increasingly coercive tactics, and decreasing trust. Thomas [11], in a comprehensive review of the literature, identified several causes of escalation, among them were the following: 1) lack of reevaluation, 2) self-fulfillment prophecies, and biases of perception, 3) distortions in communication, 4) increase in distrust and hostility, 5) losing sight of original issue and expanding conflict to other issues, 6) feeling of general incompatibility and 7) lack of a ventilating phase. Let us discuss how CAM addresses these causes of conflict escalation.

The reevaluation process may happen when a party, hearing the other party's arguments, re-evaluates its definition of the issue or its preferred alternative. CAM allows for re-evaluation at several points in the process by facilitating communication, explaining positions and emphasizing problem solving behavior. The methodology insists through out that parties develop an understanding not only of their position but of their opponents' as well.

Self-fulfilling prophecies and biases in the perception of others have a direct effect on the ability to perform trade-offs: An interpretation of anothers' behavior is to a large extent a response to the image people have of each other. CAM's main thrust is to elicit rational, analytical behavior and to clarify, through an iterative process of questioning assumptions, goals and values, the perceptions of the parties involved.

In conflict situations, parties tend to use information to manipulate and coerce the other parties and/or the public at large. Communication becomes distorted, trust is diminished and messages between parties stop being believed or listened to. When this stage is reached, both parties are able to develop their distorted view of each other without any contradiction. CAM tries to dispel any misunderstandings by allowing an explicit presentation of the different parties' positions, and attempts, through the development of treaties, to be a catalyst for discussion on agreed-upon definitions of issues and their potential resolution.

The ultimate stage in an escalation of conflict is reached when the parties get to review their differences and realize that they spread across a large number of issues (keep in mind that in many of these issues, the differences may have been artificially created for the sake of bargaining). A feeling of frustration settles-in, leading to the conclusion that the parties are completely incompatible, that no compromise is possible and a fight for total victory may follow. CAM checks this escalation by limiting the parties to negotiate on the overall treaties and by discussing issues in a specific order that minimizes frustration. Since CAM breaks down the conflict into several issues, it increases the probability of finding a few areas of agreement, thus defeating a feeling of absolute incompatibility.

Researchers have noted that where substantial differences exist, parties must ventilate their feelings to each other and state the issues which divide them before they can begin to seek an integrative solution [11]. That is, a ventilation phase generally needs to preceed an integration phase. CAM encourages, actually demands that, parties state their

Exhibit 4
Summary of the Conflict Analysis Methodology

Step 1   Perform informal interviews with individuals knowledgeable of the conflict at hand. (Purpose: to obtain preliminary list of goals and their importance and an overview of the conflict.)

Step 2   Identify stakeholder groups and their spokespersons. (Purpose: to define the coalitions and different constituencies in the conflict. Identify individuals that will be used later to develop the conflict model and choose "treaties".)

Step 3   Perform assumption analysis. (Purpose: general understanding of the problem, identify ideological versus technical sources of conflict.)

Step 4   Perform in-depth interview with one or several objective outsiders. (Purpose: to refine goals identified in Step 1, check understanding of issues and different set of values involved, start to explore grounds for resolution.)

Step 5   Have spokespersons representing each constituency and a couple of objective outsiders identify goals, issues and level of resolution. Have separate sessions for each constituency. (Purpose: to develop conflict model and identify key levels of resolution that lead to compromise.)

Step 6   Obtain quantitative estimates for issues and levels of resolution from spokespersons. Have separate sessions for each constituency. (Purpose: to quantify the importance and preference of the components of conflict and the levels of resolution.)

Step 7   Form and score treaties. (Purpose: to generate a set of feasible solutions to the conflict.)

Step 8   Perform analysis of treaties with spokespersons. Have separate sessions for each constituency. (Purpose: to generate treaties that are likely to resolve the conflict.)

Step 9   Classify unresolved issues to develop a strategy of negotiation. (Purpose: to increase the likelihood of having a positive outcome.)

Step 10   Present results. Bring together all spokespersons. (Purpose: to generate an acceptable treaty and develop guidelines to implement treaty or agree on further actions to continue the resolution process.)

---

positions, their perception of the sources of conflict and their assumptions. The model building phase usually has a cathartic effect, alleviating hostility and creating an atmosphere conducive to an "integration" phase.

4. CONCLUSION

This article describes a methodology to reduce conflict and build consensus. The Conflict Analysis Methodology (CAM) consists of: identifying the stakeholders, their assumptions, their goals and the appropriate spokespersons to represent their position, identifying the issues underlying the conflict at hand and their possible levels of resolution, developing and analyzing "treaties", and following a structured process of negotiation and consensus building to agree on a final "treaty". A summary of the methodology is shown in Exhibit 4.

The process of negotiation suggested here classifies issues by the nature of the disagreements behind them (ideological vs. technical), and classifies levels of resolution by their acceptability and effectiveness as perceived by the different stakeholders. A specific sequence to negotiate the issues is also proposed.

The main sources of conflict escalation are a lack of understanding among the parties involved, a lack of information as to the other party's position and an emphasis on bargaining behavior. The methodology addresses these sources of escalation by providing a joint definition of the problem, moving the parties toward win/win solutions, and allowing for the underplay of ideological differences by identifying non-ideological areas of agreement.

In general, CAM addresses the dynamics of conflict escalation by increasing communication and emphasizing problem solving. CAM addresses the most critical aspects of consensus building by underscoring the importance of a clear and structured resolution process, by eliciting an understanding of the different positions held by the stakeholders and the potential trade-offs among them.

NOTE

This article is based on an earlier paper titled "Conflict Analysis in Public Policy: A Decision-Theoretic Approach" (University of Vermont, School of Business, WP-03-86, by W.L. Cats-Baril and D.H. Gustafson) and presented at the Second Meeting of the International Task Force on Evaluation of Decision Support Systems, Budapest, March 1986.

REFERENCES

1. Alemi, F., Cats-Baril, W. L, and D. H. Gustafson. (1984) The Integrative Group Process, Center For Health Systems Research and Analysis Working Paper, University of Wisconsin - Madison.

2. Balke, W. M., Hammond, K. R. and G. D. Meyer (1973). An Alternative Approach to Labor Management Relations. *Administrative Science Quarterly*, 18, 311-327.

3. Froman, L. A. and Cohen, M. D. (1970) Compromise and Logroll: Comparing the Efficiency of Two Bargaining Processes. *Behavioral Science*, 15, 180-186.

4. Delbecq, A., Van de Ven, A. and D. H. Gustafson (1975). *Group Techniques for Program Planning*. Glenview, IL: Scott, Foresman.

5. Huber, G. P. (1980). *Managerial Decision Making*. Glenview, IL: Scott, Foresman.

6. Janis, I. L. and L. Mann (1977). Decision Making: A *Psychological Analysis of Conflict, Choice, and Commitment*. New York: Free Press.

7. Keeney, R. L. and H. Raiffa (1976). *Decisions with Multiple Objectives: Preferences and Value Trade-Offs*. New York: John Wiley and Sons.

8. Mitroff, I. I. and T.R. Featheringham (1974). On Systematic Problem Solving and the Error of the Third Kind. *Behavioral Science*, 19, 383-393.

9. Raiffa, H. (1982). *The Art and Science of Negotiation*. Cambridge, MA: Harvard University Press.

10. Rowe, A. J., Mason, R. O. and K. Dickel (1982). *Strategic Management and Business Policy: A Methodological Approach*. Reading, MA: Addison-Wesley.

11. Thomas, K. W. (1975). Conflict and Conflict Management. In M. D. Dunnette (Ed.), *The Handbook of Industrial and Organizational Psychology*, Volume II. Chicago: Rand McNally.

12. Von Neumann, J. and O. Morgenstern (1944). *Theory of Games and Economic Behavior*. New York: John Wiley and Sons.

11 Conferencing to Consensus

Lawrence D. Phillips
Decision Analysis Unit, London School of Economics and Political Science

<u>Generating a common understanding of a problem in a group of people and a commitment to action are the aims of the new group decision support systems.</u>

Better decisions taken in a shorter time can be achieved by using computers in a new way that helps groups of people who are working on major issues of concern to an organisation. This approach helps people to develop fresh insights into a problem, generates a shared understanding of the issues within a group, and creates a sense of common purpose.

Using the new method, one organisation doubled its revenues and profits within 18 months. A new business centre developed a clear mission that was agreed by all department heads and that has guided its increasingly successful operations for three years. an R&D division found that prioritizing projects can be done in a coherent way that takes account of risk. Senior executives of a multi-national discovered that by re-allocating a fixed budget among their operating units, they could substantially increase the corporate benefit.

Each of these results was accomplished by managers who worked intensively for 2 or 3 days in a group, but these groups were markedly different from ordinary management meetings. There were no agendas and no prepared presentations; instead, one or more people from outside the organisation were present to facilitate the group in its work, and a computer was used to provide help in ways undreamed of by information-oriented computer professionals.

What are these new and unfamiliar uses of computers? How can they be of real help to groups of people in organisations? To answer these questions, we must first recognize that, despite all the hype, traditional computer applications are of limited use to senior managers and executives. That's because these people are future-oriented in their thinking, but computers deal mostly with data which are, necessarily, about the past. Although past data might be extrapolated using clever business or statistical models, predictions beyond two years are usually unreliable. Yet the time horizons for general and senior managers typically are well beyond two years, so forecasts are of little use.

Senior executives create the future of an organisation. Because their stance is pro-active rather than re-active, they see data and information as telling them only where the organisation has been and where it might go in the immediate future. The real nub of their jobs is in managing available resources so as to create a more effective future. For this, they need to form preferences about how relatively desirable or undesirable possible futures might be; to make judgements about risk and uncertainty, and about tradeoffs between conflicting objectives such as market share or profit, short-term or long-term; and to choose between different options. In short, to take decisions.

When computers are used to help people form preferences, make judgements and take decisions, we call this preference technology. Contrast this with the more usual use of computers called information technology: helping people to make sense of data, providing modelling and facilitating communication. Information technology is data-oriented and concerned with the past and present; preference technology is judgement-oriented and concerned with the future.

When people working in a group use preference technology, the collection of people, computers and software becomes a Group Decision Support System (GDSS). The computer provides help, but so do the other people, one to another, and it is the addition of a computer to the group that can provide unique forms of assistance.

There are many ways for groups to use computers that don't qualify as GDSSs. In May 1987, a conference on Computer Supported Groups (CSG) at MIT defined CSG as "teams of people working together with computer aids". That includes group decision support, but it also covers several people working together using a local area network, or a group of people collectively exploring a data base.

What about several people sitting at a computer using a spreadsheet program to create a discounted cash flow model and exploring possible futures using the 'what-if' facility? That almost qualifies as a GDSS, but recent developments have progressed well beyond the stage of a few people sitting around a computer.

In these new GDSSs, a group of managers who are sufficiently concerned about some issue to devote 2 or 3 days to it meet away from the company in undisturbed surroundings to work on the problem. They will be helped by one or more facilitators who are not subject-matter specialists, but are experienced in working with groups of people, helping them to structure their discussion, think creatively and imaginatively about the problem, and generate an agreed plan of action. The facilitator helps participants in how to think about the problem, but doesn't tell them what to think. As a result, fruitless discussion is avoided, and the group is encouraged to identify and stick to the key issues.

So far, it sounds like a management meeting facilitated by an outsider. Enter the computer, and the meeting achieves much more than it could have done without electronic assistance. Now it becomes possible to explore differences of opinion in creative ways, develop new and useful insights about a problem, and generate action plans that gain the commitment of all participants.

Why does the computer makes such a difference? Because it enables the group to explore issues of concern in ways that are impossible with verbal arguments alone. Intuition and experience play an important role in decision making, and the computer helps to make these explicit.

For example, groups using the Priority Decision System (PDS), offered by Work Sciences Associates, are encouraged to identify key objectives and to compare them with one another for importance. When these judgements are given to the computer, it works out the priorities of the objectives, and ranks them in order. This is immediately displayed to the group, whose members may be surprised to see that some objectives are given much higher priority than others. If the original comparisons were made by the group as a whole, the computer gives the consistency of the judgements; if members individually gave their assessments to the computer, it provides an indication of the degree of agreement.

The group can then go on to rate identified options, such as programs, policies or budget items, against the objectives, and the computer will develop a list of the options in order of priority. Since all participants are involved in the weighting and scoring, they are usually committed to the resulted prioritization.

Jimmy Algie and Bill Foster, the developers of PDS, have helped a variety of organisations, at all levels, to use the program effectively for problems of decision-making, problem-solving and policy-making. Many organisations use the program without outside facilitation, and individuals can use it by themselves for problems that do not require group attention.

Computers are used in a variety of ways by Wilson Learning Corporation, a subsidiary of the publisher John Wiley, who offer the Innovator, a family of tools that can be used by groups to facilitate creative thinking. One use is as a quick polling facility. Each participant has access to a keypad which registers the user's vote, ranking or evaluation of items. The computer instantly displays the aggregate, and anonymous, responses, allowing the group to assess the degree of consensus, confidence or commitment.

Another use is for producing an Opportunity Map of items that are important in achieving success. The computer display shows the group's judgements about how the organisation is performing on the items, and what the relative value of each item is to the organisation. Four to six categories are usually shown, as in Figure 1. By exploring agreements and disagreements, displayed on the visual picture as upper and lower case letters, the group can begin to develop a consensus.

Finally, Matrix software can be used for action planning. For example, rows in the matrix could be opportunity items, with columns representing departments of the company. The keypads can be used to vote on each cell of the matrix, with discussion leading to identifying the departments thought to be most effective in achieving the desired outcome.

Originally developed by Dr George Ainsworth-Land, the Innovator has been used successfully in many countries, and some companies have trained their own managers to facilitate sessions on a regular basis. Robert Sayre, Senior Vice President of Economics Laboratory, Inc., St Paul, reports that "Wilson Learning Corporation has helped us

MAP INTERPRETATION

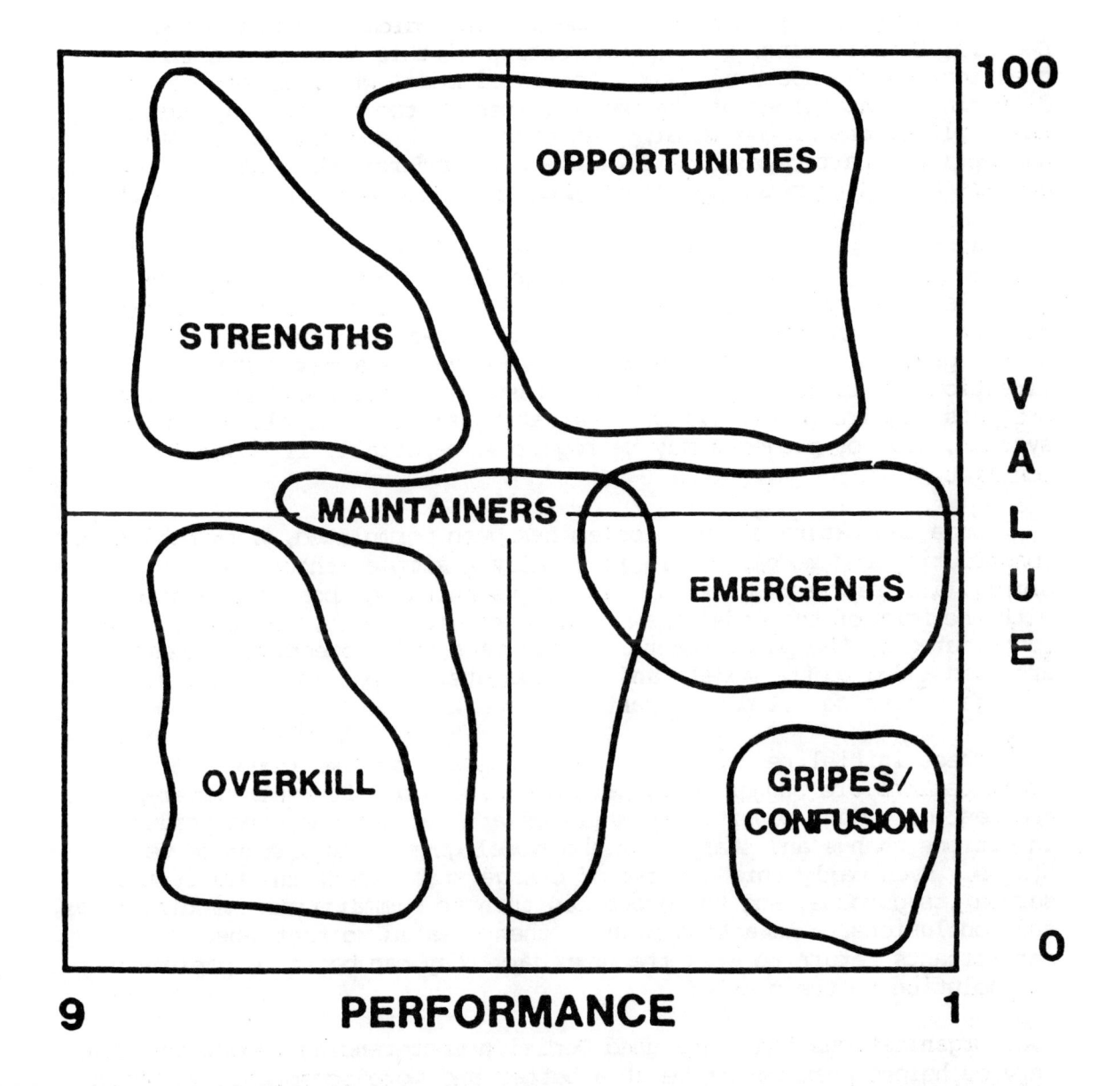

Figure 1: An Opportunity Map. Items rated by participants fall into one of four categories: 1) gripes, which are low in performance and low in value, 2) opportunities, which are low in performance and high in value, 3) overkills, which are high in performance and low in value, and 4) strengths, which are high in performance and high in value.

effectively face difficult decisions honestly with as much effectiveness in Europe and the Far East as within our domestic operations."

Like all GDSSs, the Innovator is a process that requires a trained facilitator to strike the right balance between encouraging creativity, keeping the group task oriented, and using the right computer tools in the right way at the right time. The focus is on the issues of concern and on the problem, not the computer.

This emphasis is evident in one of the oldest forms of GDSS, Decision Conferencing. A unique feature of this approach is the creation, on-the-spot, of a computer-based model which incorporates the differing perspectives of the participants in the group. by examining the implications of the model, then changing it and trying out different assumptions, participants develop a shared understanding of the problem and are helped to reach agreement about what to do.

Although every Decision Conference is different, several stages are common to most. After an initial introduction by the facilitator, the group is asked to discuss the issues and concerns that are to be the subject of the exploration. An attempt is made to formulate the nature of the problem. Does the group need to generate a new strategic direction, or is strategy itself the issue? Perhaps budget items or projects require prioritizing. Evaluating alternative plans, ventures, systems, bids or projects may be required, especially if objectives conflict.

Once the nature of the problem has been formulated, work begins on constructing the model. This is usually a simple, though not simplistic, representation of the group's thinking about the problem, with the form of the model drawn from decision theory, and the content contributed by the participants. Both data and subjective judgements are then added to the model, and the computer output is projected onto a large screen so all participants can see the results.

These initial results are rarely accepted by the group. Modifications are suggested by participants, and different judgements are tested. Many sensitivity analyses are carried out, and gradually intuitions change and sharpen as the model goes through successive stages. Eventually this process of change stabilizes, the model has served its purpose, and the group can turn to summarizing the key issues and conclusions. An action plan is then created so that when participants return to work the next day, they can begin to implement the solution to the problem.

Organizations that have used Decision Conferencing report that the service helped them to arrive at a better and more acceptable solution than they would have achieved using their usual procedures, and agreement was reached much more quickly. Many Decision Conferences have broken through stalemates created previously by lack of consensus, by the complexity of the problem, by vagueness and conflict of goals, and by failure to think creatively and freshly about the problem. Two months after one Decision Conference, a senior manager observed:

"It was the turning point for our group. It changed the mindset of our management team in a very constructive way and we are now following the new strategy very closely".

The model developed in a Decision Conference lends structure to thinking, and allows all perspectives on a problem to be represented and discussed. This helps to take the heat out of arguments that arise from differences in perspective. Thus, the process facilitates communication, providing "a way to talk differently", as one person put it, and it surfaces assumptions that are often different from one person to the next.

Because the model developed by the group shows what the organisation can do, rather than just describing what it does do, creative and lateral thinking is facilitated. Overall, Decision Conferencing helps a shared understanding to emerge from different perspectives, it builds commitment and generates action plans.

Decision Conferencing was introduced in 1981 to Europe by the Decision Analysis Unit, now at the London School of Economics and Political Science. Since 1984, further developments have evolved in collaboration with ICL, initially for their own use and now as a product for their customers. More than 100 Decision Conferences have now been conducted in 12 countries.

An example is provided by the organisation that doubled its profits mentioned at the beginning of this article, the Eastern European Distribution Organisation (EEDO) of ICL, Britain's largest computer company. The manager of EEDO was concerned about the modest performance of his territory, so he decided to use a Decision Conferencing format to review the strategies of his 7 country managers. Each manager was asked to formulate several alternative proposals to the strategy he was currently pursuing, some requiring less resource, others demanding more.

All these proposals were considered simultaneously, with the help of a computer, so that tradeoffs among the countries could be considered in light of corporate objectives. After 14 successive modifications to the model, the group realized that they were incorrectly positioned in every country, that by cutting back in three countries, and re-distributing the freed resource among four of the other countries, a substantial increase in benefit was likely to be obtained at less risk. (See Figure 2.)

Within weeks of the March 1984 Decision Conference, new strategies were implemented as suggested, and by the end of 1985 revenues, orders and profits had all doubled. The improvement in performance was attributed by the EEDO manager to the new strategies formulation at the Decision Conference. Now, sufficient extra resource has been generated to enable the three countries which suffered cutbacks to be re-injected with funds so that they can grow.

Interestingly, this pattern of results has been observed in many Decision Conferences. Dr Cameron Peterson, the original developer of Decision Conferencing who now operates out of Boulder, Colorado, from

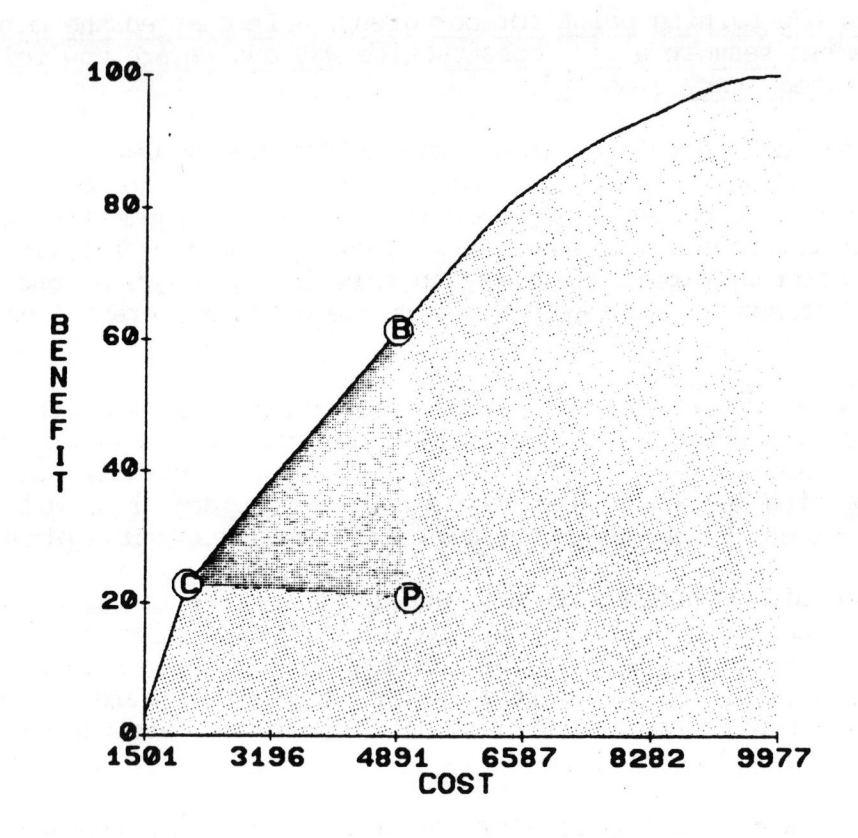

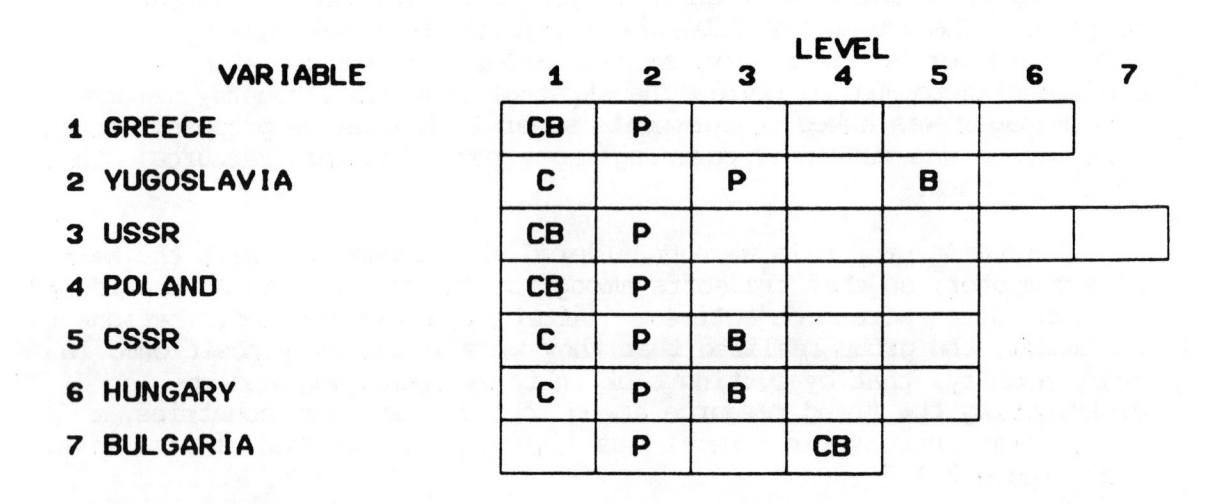

	VARIABLE	LEVEL						
		1	2	3	4	5	6	7
1	GREECE	CB	P					
2	YUGOSLAVIA	C		P		B		
3	USSR	CB	P					
4	POLAND	CB	P					
5	CSSR	C	P	B				
6	HUNGARY	C	P	B				
7	BULGARIA		P		CB			

Figure 2: Evaluation of the 'status quo' strategy. The figure indicates that the status quo, or Planned strategy, can be improved. A Better strategy, at no extra cost, and a Cheaper strategy, at the same benefit, are shown. The table gives changes in strategies that will improve the status quo. Each level is a different strategy, with the higher numbered strategies requiring more resource. Cutbacks from the status quo should be made in Greece, USSR and Poland, and the resource that is released then distributed among the remaining countries.

his company, Decision Conferences, Inc., has found numerous companies who 'trickle-fund' business units that should be closed down so that their resources can be used more effectively elsewhere in the organisation. Dr John Rohrbaugh, from the Decision Techtronics Group of the State University of New York at Albany, has conducted over 40 Decision Conferences in the public sector, and he observes the same failure to 'bite the bullet' there. Mr Peter Hall, from ICL's Decision Conferencing Unit, noted a related difficulty in effecting a change in commitment, but found the Decision Conferencing process effective in establishing a new corporate identity and culture within ICL.

Our experience and research indicate that Decision Conferencing, and perhaps GDSS in general, works best in organisations where
* consultation precedes decision making.
* communication links occur across the organization chart, so that information flows laterally as well as vertically.
* a climate of problem solving exists, in which options can be freely explored rather than manipulated to serve pre-determined solutions.
* authority and accountability are well distributed throughout the organisation.

In choosing a GDSS, an organisation should look for a match of purpose between the needs of the organisation and the aims of the GDSS. In addition, certain features would appear to be desirable. In my view, a good GDSS should
* be problem-centered rather than computer-centered.
* be process-oriented rather than providing subject-matter expertise.
* show some evidence that it can deal with the vagaries of group dynamics.
* be transparent in its operation, so that users will understand and trust the results.
* be based on sound theory, rather than a collection of ad-hoceries so that the system doesn't introduce inconsistencies.
* provide flexible tools that can be adapted to the problem at hand.
* not promise too much; at best they can help a group to perform more effectively, but they can't guarantee good consequences.
* be sufficiently flexible to adapt to the different needs of a variety of management teams.

No doubt the next few years will provide ample opportunities to expand both lists. But by choosing carefully, organisations should be able to benefit in ways that justify the expense of investing in group decision support systems.

Some of the material in this article appeared in Datamation Magazine, a Cahners publication, copyright Reed Publishing USA.